CHRISTIANS IN CAESAR'S HOUSEHOLD

INVENTING CHRISTIANITY

Series Editors

L. Stephanie Cobb

David L. Eastman

In the second and third centuries, insiders
and outsiders alike were grappling with
what it meant to be Christian. In this
period, there were shifting and competing
centers of clerical and textual authority
and disagreements over group boundaries,
interpretive strategies, and ritual practices.
Inventing Christianity examines the
numerous ways in which early Christianity
was "invented"—that is, given definition
and boundaries—by different people in
different times to different ends. The series
contributes to the study of second- and third-
century Christianity by exploring how the
very notion of Christianity developed and
redeveloped in multiple forms and through
cultural interactions.

ADVISORY BOARD

Nicola Denzey Lewis

Kim Haines-Eitzen

Robin M. Jensen

David Konstan

Jeffrey Siker

Jeanne-Nicole Mellon
    Saint-Laurent

CHRISTIANS IN CAESAR'S HOUSEHOLD

The Emperors' Slaves in the Makings of Christianity

MICHAEL FLEXSENHAR III

The Pennsylvania State University Press
University Park, Pennsylvania

Library of Congress Cataloging-in-Publication Data

Names: Flexsenhar, Michael, III, 1984– author.
Title: Christians in Caesar's household : the emper-
    ors' slaves in the makings of Christianity / Mi-
    chael Flexsenhar III.
Other titles: Inventing Christianity.
Description: University Park, Pennsylvania : The
    Pennsylvania State University Press, [2019] |
    Series: Inventing Christianity | Includes bibli-
    ographical references and index.
Summary: "Examines the role of the Roman emper-
    ors' slaves in the rise of Christianity, and how
    imperial slaves were essential to early Christians'
    self-conception as a distinct people in the Medi-
    terranean"—Provided by publisher.
Identifiers: LCCN 2018055873
Subjects: LCSH: Christian slaves—Rome. | Church
    history—Primitive and early church, ca. 30–600.
    | Slavery—Rome.
Classification: LCC HT913.F64 2019 | DDC
    274.45/3201—dc23
LC record available at https://lccn.loc.gov/2018055873

The Pennsylvania State University Press is a
member of the Association of University Presses.

It is the policy of The Pennsylvania State University Press to use acid-free paper. Publications on uncoated stock satisfy the minimum
requirements of American National Standard for
Information Sciences—Permanence of Paper for
Printed Library Material, ANSI Z39.48–1992.

To Juju

CONTENTS

ILLUSTRATIONS

Tables

ACKNOWLEDGMENTS

This book is about the cultural history of early Christianity—from its origins to late antiquity—and the pivotal role that the Roman emperors' slaves played in that history. It is a book that reflects my own history, growing up in the South, where Christianity and slavery were once intertwined, much like in Roman antiquity, and where the effects are still felt today. It is a book that has evolved alongside current debates. I researched and wrote while influential secular and religious institutions publicly questioned their complicated histories and redressed their past ties to slavery. I researched and wrote while groups sometimes violently clashed over monuments of material culture and memories of slavery. I researched and wrote while groups fought over minority cultural representation, marginalization, and persecution. In some ways, then, this book is also entangled in all of these topics. I developed the subject for this book in the intense early years of my studies. A seminar on slavery in Paul's letters showed me how complicated the topic of slavery in early Christianity was and how much was still left unexplored. A seminar on Ostia Antica opened up for me the lives of slaves and freedpersons, especially through the study of their epigraphy. I remember being struck by how complicated those ancient lives were, and surprised at how integrated into Roman society they could be. I thought the topic warranted further investigation. As I began to research the marriage practices of Roman freedmen in Ostia, who in many cases married free women—often women with more money, independence, or social stature—I stumbled upon imperial freedmen. This led me to P. R. C. Weaver's book, *Familia Caesaris* (1972). Weaver's work on imperial slaves and freedmen was utilized in some of the more influential social descriptions of early Christianity. Most notable for me was Wayne Meeks's classic *The First Urban Christians* (1983), which drew attention to the implications of Paul's reference to *familia Caesaris* in Philippians 4:22. I noticed that some other Christian writings after Paul also mentioned—or seemed to mention—Christians in the *familia Caesaris* and that there were even "Christian inscriptions" from some imperial slaves and freedmen. In short, I soon realized that the topic of *familia Caesaris* in early Christianity was really important though largely understudied. Meanwhile, the seminars on slavery in Paul's letters and Ostia Antica were combined with some hot summers of archaeological fieldwork at the ancient Jewish synagogue of Ostia Antica (2009–2016). Studying the Roman world on the ground in the trenches—with Italy's dirt in my face and its sun on my back—helped bring into sharper focus my budding ideas about the relationship between imperial slaves and early Christianity. As part of the University of Texas "OSMAP" field team I often had access both on site at Ostia and in Rome to research materials that would eventually become a book. So as in the case of the seminars, without those summers in Ostia this book would never have happened.

I was lucky to find such an interesting research topic. I was also lucky that others thought the topic interesting as well. A project such as this one would not have been possible without the help of many others. I owe a special thank you to L. Michael White, who taught both seminars and kept me coming back to Rome and Ostia. LM was invariably enthusiastic about my project and continued to be generous with his time and his insights. I will always look back fondly at the many discussions we had in his office over espressos. Thanks also for the input of Steven Friesen, Christine Thomas, Karl Galinsky, and Philip Harland. Even now I see their fingerprints on this book.

Support from the University of Texas at Austin made research and writing much easier. For 2014–15, I was awarded a David Bruton Jr. Named Continuing Fellowship from the University of Texas at Austin, coupled with a Summer Research Fellowship from the Institute for the Study of Antiquity and Christian Origins from the University of Texas at Austin. Both of these awards funded on-site research in Rome and archival research at the American Academy in Rome. An invitation to participate in an international, interdisciplinary conference (Philippi, From *colonia Augusta* to *communitas Christiana*) at the site of ancient Philippi in July 2015 also provided avenues to integrate new research into the book. Again, the University of Texas and the Institute for the study of Antiquity and Christian Origins funded my travel and research. I am grateful to the organizers of the conference—Steve Friesen, Dan Schowalter, Chris Thomas, James Walters, and Michalis Lychounas—for the opportunity to present. Traveling in Greece during the "crisis" was quite an adventure, but our Hellenic hosts could not have been more hospitable. While staying in the Balkans for the conference I was able to meet and discuss my ideas with several people who had overlapping interests in the northern Aegean. And on multiple occasions since then I have benefited from conversations with Angela Standhartinger and Cédric Brélaz. Other conferences made for lively settings to present my work. The Pauline Epistles unit of the Society of Biblical Literature was an important venue for what has become chapter 1. The Christian Apocrypha unit of SBL offered another setting to preview what has become chapter 2. I thank Brent Landau for inviting me to present and for the encouraging response of Tony Burke. My friend Douglas Boin deserves a special thank-you here, and not just for reading portions of the manuscript. Throughout the process Doug became a kind of mentor. I am grateful for all his advice.

Numerous other people, in many and sundry ways, helped bring this book to fruition. The University of Texas Interlibrary Loan Office deftly managed my constant requests. Shiela Wincester had a knack for tracking down my obscure bibliographic references. My colleagues at Rhodes College also fostered a supportive environment. Conversations with Rhiannon Graybill and Patrick Gray pushed me onward. Dan Ullucci and Sarah Rollens also read and provided helpful comments on sections of the manuscript. Kenan Padgett and the staff of the Interlibrary Loan Service at Rhodes worked hard to get me the sources that I needed to finish the book. The students in the Digital Media Lab—Ashley Bruneau and Jamarr McCain—were kind enough to help me edit the images.

The archaeological and epigraphic material presented in this book was often hard-won. Locating an artifact in Rome can sometimes be a Sisyphean task. It took me multiple summers to find the sarcophagus monument of Marcus Aurelius Prosenes, and I risked life and limb to photograph it. The ability to acquire permissions for images was a concern, especially for those of monuments that are now inaccessible. But several library and archival staffs in Rome were exceptionally helpful. Working at the American Academy in Rome was an absolute delight. Daria Lanzuolo of the German Archaeological Institute in Rome, Piero Crescenzi of the Pontificia Commissione di Archeologia Sacra, Carlo dell'Osso of the Pontificio Istituto di Archeologia Cristiana, and Laura Forgione from the Accademia Nazionale dei Lincei all have my gratitude. Also, Pascale Kahn of the Bibliothèque Nationale de France obligingly fielded a flurry of emails to help me.

In 2016 Geoffrey Smith first told me about the Inventing Christianity series at Penn State University Press. He then kindly brought my project to the attention of one of the series editors. I am thankful that Geoff took this initiative. David Eastman and Stephanie Cobb, coeditors of the series, were both receptive to my project. I am very appreciative that they saw what it could be. At the 2016 North American Patristics Society meeting I sat down with David Eastman and Kathryn Yahner, acquisitions editor at Penn State University Press, who spoke with me for over an hour about my project and about the series. It was a generous conversation. I could sense our mutual interest and I am lucky to have had such personalized attention. From that very first meeting at NAPS Kathryn was great to work with and carefully led this book to maturity. Thanks also to the anonymous reviewers who not only read the manuscript closely but engaged with all aspects of my argument to give very helpful feedback. Katie Van Heest of Tweed Editing worked wonders with the deep structures of the manuscript and showed me a bigger vision for the book. The staff at Penn State University Press were excellent. Hannah Herbert helped me greatly with the final preparation of the manuscript, especially the minutiae of images and documentation. Jennifer Norton and Stephanie Scott ushered the book smoothly through the copyediting stage to the production stage. Thanks to my copyeditor, Marian Rogers, whose diligent work sniffed out my many mistakes.

Writing a book can be grueling. There are ups and downs. There are late nights and early mornings, long periods of silence and of solitude. I am fortunate to have had a network of friends and family to support me. In the course of writing this book I tried to help raise a toddler and an infant. Both of these creatures became the most wonderful interruptions that any writer could hope for. They were my inspiration. My parents also graciously let us live with them. Their arms were always open, their hands always free. Their house often felt like a hostel-day care center, but because of them I was able to work more. Yet absolutely nothing relating to this book would have been remotely possible without my wife. From absentee years of graduate school to research trips abroad to interminable writing sessions, from listening to my ideas and complaints to doing extra house-work to watching the boys—she has supported me (and us) throughout this whole journey. To say "thank you" seems silly. I cannot express the depth of my gratitude. This book is a testament of her dedication to me. For that, I dedicate it to her with love.

ABBREVIATIONS

AE   *Année Epigraphique*

ANF   *Ante-Nicene Fathers*

AvP   *Altertümer von Pergamon*

BCAR   *Bullettino della Commissione Archeologica Comunale di Roma*

CIG   *Corpus Inscriptionum Graecarum*

CIL   *Corpus Inscriptionum Latinarum*

GRIA   R. Kearsley, *Greeks and Romans in Imperial Asia*

ICorinth   *Corinth: Results of Excavations Conducted by the American School of Classical Studies at Athens*

ICUR   *Inscriptiones Christianae Urbis Romae*

IG   *Inscriptiones Graecae*

IGR   R. Cagnat, *Inscriptiones Graecae ad Res Romanas Pertinentes*

IK   *Inschriften griechischer Städte aus Kleinasien*

ILCV   *Inscriptiones Latinae Christianae Veteres*

ILS   H. Dessau, *Inscriptiones Latinae Selectae*

IPOstie   *Inscriptions du Port d'Ostie*

ISIS   *Le iscrizioni sepolcrali latine nell'Isola sacra*

IvE   *Die Inschriften von Ephesos*

LSJ   H. G. Liddell, R. Scott, and H. S. Jones, *A Greek-English Lexicon*

LTUR   *Lexicon Topographicum Urbis Romae*

LTURS   *Lexicon Topographicum Urbis Romae Suburbium*

Malta   *Report on the Phoenician and Roman Antiquities in the Group of Islands of Malta*

MAMA   *Monumenta Asiae Minoris Antiqua*

NSA   *Notizie degli Scavi di Antichità*

PG   Patrologia Graeca

Philippi   P. Pilhofer, *Philippi: Katalog der Inschriften von Philippi*

PL Patrologia Latina

POxy Oxyrhynchus Papyri

SEG Supplementum Epigraphicum Graecum

TLL Thesaurus Linguae Latinae

INTRODUCTION

> Caesar said, "Who made you alive?" Empowered by the
> strength of his faith, Patroclus said, "Jesus Christ, the king
> of the whole world and the ages."
>
> —*MARTYRDOM OF PAUL*

On a miniature in the *Miroir Historial,* a fifteenth-century encyclopedia in French, the apostle Paul stands in a pulpit. With a white beard and halo, dressed in a brilliant blue mantle and scarlet cloak, he preaches to a seated audience of superbly dressed men and women. Their eyes are all trained on him. But in the back a man in a mustard tunic with a crimson belt and green cap is upside down. He is falling, flailing helplessly from above. In the miniature's lower register this thin-bearded figure now lies on the floor. His face is pallid and plastic. His eyes are closed in death. Paul stands over him. The first two fingers of the apostle's right hand offer a sign of invocation. From his left hand a banderole flows: "I pray for you, in the name of Christ, that you breathe and that you say whom you saw." Then in the final sequence Paul stands directly before the Roman emperor himself. The crowned ruler, resplendent in his garments, sits on his throne. A sword rests on his shoulder; his feet are perched on a pillow. The index finger of his left hand extends toward the young man in the mustard tunic who is now standing, alive, to the emperor's left. The young man is wide-eyed and distressed. He shows the emperor the palms of his hands. An armored guard nudges behind him and behind Paul. More guards file in.

This masterpiece of mid-fifteenth-century manuscript illumination, executed in stunning detail by the workshop of the Parisian illuminator Maître François, captures a defining moment in early Christianity.[1] The man in the mustard tunic is Nero's cupbearer, a slave boy named Patroclus. But as he is about to confess to Nero he has been made alive by "Our Lord Jesus Christ, King of all Existence." It is the decisive scene from the late second-century text known as the *Martyrdom of Paul.* With his declaration,

FIG. 1 Illuminated scene from the *Martyrdom of Paul* showing the imperial slave
Patroclus before the emperor Nero. Mid-fifteenth-century miniature from the *Miroir
Historial*, X:xvi (BnF fr. 50, fol. 314v).

Patroclus's defiant act will precipitate Paul's own confession before the
emperor, and then the apostle's famed martyrdom in Rome (fig. 1).

Here context is important. Far from being tucked away in some
obscure manuscript the setting of the miniature is quite dramatic. The
Miroir Historial was an encyclopedia of world history from creation to present. The illuminated text was part of Vincent de Beauvais's (ca. 1194–1264)
three-volume encyclopedia (*Speculum Maius*) on nature, doctrine, and
history. The encyclopedia's volume on history, called the "Great Mirror"
(*Speculum Historiale*), was especially popular at the time. It expounded on
such major topics as Alexander the Great, the emperor Constantine, the
Prophet Muhammad, and King Charlemagne. The history volume was in
enough demand that a century later, working in Bruges, Jean de Vignay (ca.
1285–1348) undertook the enormous task of translating Vincent's text from
Latin into French. A number of luxurious, illuminated manuscripts of the
new French version, which was now called the *Miroir Historial*, were then

produced during the Middle Ages, including the beautiful manuscript from the Parisian illuminator Maître François. Copied and dispersed to audiences in various forms, the encyclopedia of history also seems to have found a welcome home among Europe's royalty. Vincent's original *Speculum Maius* had been sponsored by none other than King Louis IX of France (1214–1270), and later one of the more luxurious manuscripts of the French *Miroir Historial* was housed in a collection of King Edward IV of England (1442–1483). That an encyclopedia standard in Europe for over two centuries records a scene with a Christian imperial slave as an event of world history, worthy of illumination, and sharing pages with Alexander, Constantine, the Prophet Muhammad, and Charlemagne, speaks volumes about how compelling the idea of Christians in Caesar's household could be.

More than a millennium before Jean de Vignay published the translation of Beauvais's *Speculum Maius* as the *Miroir Historial* and before the illuminator Maître François produced that stunning miniature, Christian writers in the second and third centuries were also calling attention to Christian slaves of the Roman emperors. This book explains why. By analyzing textual and material evidence from the first to the sixth century, spanning Roman Asia and the Aegean rim to Gaul and the coast of North Africa to the imperial capital itself, this book investigates Caesar's household as a focal point for the invention of early Christianity. It argues that the Roman emperors' slaves and freedpersons were essential to early Christians' self-conception as a distinct people in the Mediterranean. From generating origin myths in Rome, to establishing a shared history and geography there (chapter 2), to differentiating and negotiating assimilation with other groups, both inside and out (chapters 3–4), to expressing commemorative language, ritual acts, and a material culture (chapters 2, 4–6)—members of Rome's imperial household were integral to each of these cultural developments in early Christianity.

This book also subverts the conventional narrative. For nearly a century New Testament and early Christian scholarship has been prone to emphasize the social, economic, and political impact that Christian imperial slaves and freedmen had on early Christianity whether in the first, second, or third century. In the reigning paradigm, Christian slaves in Caesar's household are interpreted as Christianity's social pioneers. As they advanced socially these slaves and freedmen also helped Christianity to develop steadily, and more or less smoothly, to positions of power in the Roman Empire.[2] According to this pioneer narrative, Christianity's social ascent began with the apostle Paul's mention of "Caesar's household" (Phil 4:22). While he was imprisoned in Rome Paul converted several influential slaves and freedmen from Caesar's household—the so-called *familia Caesaris*—and sent on greetings from these "saints" in his letter to the Philippians (Phil 4:22). This was Christianity's Trojan Horse. Over the next two centuries Christian imperial slaves and freedmen continued serving Caesar in Rome. They multiplied especially under the emperors Marcus Aurelius (161–80 CE) and Commodus (180–92 CE), and continued to flourish during the Severan period (193–235 CE), transforming the social profile of Christianity in the process, and inching the new religion ever closer to the seat of power. By the mid-third century, the story goes, there were enough prominent Christians in the imperial household that the emperors Decius and then Valerian initiated an empire-wide persecution of Christians, including a purge of their own households. The emperors failed, marking the beginning of the end of Greco-Roman paganism. The emperors' slaves had laid the groundwork, and the process would soon culminate in the triumph of Christianity under Constantine.

Historical work over the last generation of scholarship has challenged various aspects of this narrative. And yet the lion's share has remained intact. Although it was set in motion in nineteenth-century scholarship the narrative is not a relic from a bygone era.[3] In various forms, from the overt to the subtle, it continues to cast a shadow over the evidence. The narrative has allowed a body of ancient literary and epigraphic references— from Paul's first mention of "Caesar's household" in Philippians 4:22 to catacomb epitaphs of imperial slaves—to be routinely cited as historical evidence for Christians in Rome's imperial household and thus as a sign of Christianity's rise to power.

The pioneer narrative starts with interpretations of Paul's letter to the Philippians. From the nineteenth to the twenty-first century, it was taken for granted that when Paul sent greetings from the "saints from Caesar's household" (Phil 4:22) he was imprisoned in Rome, as per Acts 28. But because Rome was the presumed provenance of Philippians it was also thought that Paul wrote Philippians later than the letter to the Romans, which clearly indicates that Paul had not yet been to Rome (Rom 15:22–29). Ordering Paul's letters like this not only influenced reconstructions of Paul's life but altered the historical reconstructions of early Christianity's social trajectory.[4] On the one hand, placing Philippians after Romans allowed scholars to canvass the Roman letter, especially the extended greetings in chapter 16, in order to attach names to Paul's greetings from "Caesar's household." The thinking is that the list of names or households in Romans 16 must have included some of the "saints" that Paul would later mention in Philippians 4:22. On the other hand, fresh archaeological discoveries in nineteenth-century Rome also yielded material that scholars could then use to elucidate the imperial household and Paul's reference to it. A new monumental corpus of Latin inscriptions from the Roman world—the *Corpus Inscriptionum Latinarum*, founded by the German savant Theodor Mommsen in 1853—made epigraphic evidence widely accessible. The corpus of inscriptions was mined for additional names to illuminate those names listed in Romans 16, and by extension, the "saints from Caesar's household" in Philippians 4:22. The tenuous method of combining the textual and material evidence was repeated over and again.[5]

The British scholar J. B. Lightfoot led the way. By the second half of the nineteenth century Lightfoot had connected Philippians 4:22 to several names from Romans 16 to names that also occurred in Roman inscriptions. When the same names recorded in inscriptions also appeared in Paul's letter to the Romans it suggested to Lightfoot at least a "very faint probability about the identity of people." Some of those "saints from Caesar's household" (Phil 4:22), according to Lightfoot, were also slaves in the household of Narcissus (Rom 16:11). Lightfoot identified this Narcissus mentioned in Romans 16:11 as the emperor Claudius's freedman Tiberius Claudius Narcissus.[6] The identification was quite a stretch. The imperial freedman Narcissus was "the Croesus of the Romans," the Roman Rockefeller.[7] As Lightfoot readily understood, Narcissus was (in)famous in Roman historiographic sources for his power. He was reportedly worth a whopping 400 million sesterces, making him—according to one modern estimation—the richest person in the history of the Roman Empire outside of the emperors themselves. Narcissus was in charge of imperial correspondence (*praepositus ab epistulis*), effectively determining the flow of communication with the emperor, and would receive the decoration of a Roman magistrate (*quaestor*). Narcissus's influence (*gratia*) was so great that he was apparently responsible for the future emperor Vespasian's appointment as legionary legate. Vitellius, who became one of the short-lived emperors of 69 CE, reportedly even revered Narcissus—in the form of a golden image—as a guardian deity among his own household gods (*lares*).[8] To say the least, by identifying Narcissus from Romans 16:11 as the famous imperial freedman and by connecting him to the "Caesar's household" Paul mentions (Phil 4:22), Lightfoot projected a steep social trajectory for the new Christian movement.

The same projection of Christianity's ascent continued when Lightfoot linked the "saints from Caesar's household" (Phil 4:22) to the ensuing generation of Roman Christians attested in the Apostolic Fathers literary corpus. In his tortuous explanation Lightfoot claimed that "Clement," commonly known as the late first-century bishop of Rome and the author of *1 Clement*, was a freedman of Flavia Domitilla and Titus Flavius Clemens, cousins of the emperors Vespasian and Domitian.[9] Comparisons with other Roman bishops who had been of "servile origin" such as Callistus (future Pope Calixtus I), a slave of Carpophorus who was "an officer in the imperial palace," made the identity of Clement as a freedman of the imperial household more likely according to Lightfoot. Besides that, the reports from the "Cemetery of Domitilla at Rome" published in 1865 by the illustrious Italian archaeologist Giovanni Battista de Rossi also pushed Lightfoot to categorize "Clement" as a dependent in the emperor Domitian's wider household. The burial grounds of the Domitilla cemetery, it was thought, belonged to Flavia Domitilla, who was a convert to Christianity. She had granted burial space to the Christians in her household, an area later known as the hypogeum of the Flavi Cristiani. And when Lightfoot combed through Mommsen's *CIL* volumes, especially volume 6 (Rome), and found many inscriptions dated to around the time of Clement that recorded imperial freedmen with the name Clemens his suggestion about the identity of the esteemed Clement was solidified.[10]

Lightfoot's method of connecting inscriptions to early Christian letters turned up still more Christians in the imperial household during the Flavian period. Lightfoot proposed that Claudius Ephebus and Valerius Bito, the couriers of *1 Clement* (*1 Clem.* 65), were also imperial freedmen. The basis for this identification was that Ephebus's name matched the emperor Claudius's gens (*Claudii*) while Bito's matched the empress Messalina's (*Valeria*). Several inscriptions from Rome also included imperial slaves and freedmen with the names Claudius and Valerius appearing together. The correlation of the nomenclature signified that Ephebus and Bito were brought up in the imperial household, would have been included in Paul's salutation to the Philippians, and could hardly have been unknown to Paul, who wrote from Rome to the Philippians around 62 CE. These Christians in the late first century—Clement, Ephebus, and Bito—ensured that, henceforward, the imperial household was a chief center of Christianity in the metropolis.[11]

By identifying Christians in the imperial household from the mid-first to the second century, Lightfoot could then explain how Christianity accrued power in the empire. "In the palace of the Caesars, when [Paul] arrived in Rome he found among the members of the imperial household, whether slaves or freedmen, some who had already embraced the new faith and eagerly welcomed his coming." This "progress of Christianity," stated Lightfoot, "*raised* the church in Rome to a position of prominence," initiated the "long struggle, which raged for several centuries, and ended in establishing the Gospel on the ruins of the Roman Empire." It was through the emperor's slaves and dependents that "[Christianity] advanced silently step by step, till at length it laid its hands on the princes of the imperial house."[12]

Lightfoot had laid the foundation for a triumphalist narrative. Remarkably, Lightfoot's claims about the identities of Narcisuss (Rom. 16:11), Clement, Claudius Ephebus, and Valerius Bito remained secure in scholarship for generations, even to the cusp of the twenty-first century. To this day, Lightfoot's description of Ephebus and Bito as influential Christian imperial freedmen continues to be accepted by some as evidence for early Christianity's social development (appendix 1). The longevity of these dubious identifications attests to the explanatory power of the narrative, which intensified with time. A generation later Adolf von Harnack's magisterial *Die Mission und Ausbreitung des Christentums in den ersten drei Jahrhunderten* (1902) bolstered and expanded Lightfoot's ideas. When in the last part of the second volume (book 4) Harnack shifted from a focus on mission to the historical courses of expansion in either geographical, institutional, or social terms he unveiled "an astonishingly learned" compendium of all the passages that mention the numerical growth of the early Christians. The compendium included Christianity's spread among the "upper classes" followed immediately by a survey of its spread "at court."[13]

Harnack's explanation for the expansion of Christianity at court amounted to a primary-source tour of all known literary and epigraphic references to Christian imperial slaves or freedmen beginning with Paul's first-century reference to the "saints" in Philippians 4:22, which he also presumed was written from Rome. Harnack followed Lightfoot, connecting "Caesar's household" (Phil 4:22) to Narcissus of Romans 16:11 as the famous imperial freedman, and then to Clement, Claudius Ephebus, and Valerius Bito from *1 Clement*.[14] Harnack also listed additional references from the second century that have by and large gone unquestioned: Euelpistus from the *Martyrdom of Justin and Companions;* Hippolytus's reference to Callistus and Carpophorus; Irenaeus of Lyon's reference to the "faithful ones" in the royal court; Tertullian's remark about Christians filling "the palace" and the example of Proculus Torpacion. And to make his case for Christians at court in the early third century, Harnack also included the inscription for Caracalla's "Christian high chamberlain (Marcus Aurelius) Prosenes," which De Rossi had first interpreted as a Christian inscription. Harnack ended by reiterating Eusebius of Caesarea's declaration that the emperor Valerian's (253–60 CE) "court was full of pious people; it was a veritable church of God." For Harnack these citations showed that Christianity's inward "spread" in the imperial court, even at an early period, became a factor that was occasionally quite important in the long-term expansion of Christianity in the empire.[15]

But even when Lightfoot and Harnack's methods were later altered and their triumphalism was more restrained the tentacles of the narrative remained stuck. During the 1970s, when a new "social description" of early Christianity began to emerge, the pioneer narrative was still operative.[16] In the "social organization" approach that investigated both the social forces that led to the rise of Christianity and the social institutions of early Christianity the narrative is most pronounced.[17] In his tome *The Rise of Christianity* (1984), for example, W. H. C. Frend pays homage to the validity of Harnack's conclusions. Though without devoting a section to Christians at court, in Frend's diachronic analysis of Christianity's sociopolitical growth in the empire the fingerprints of the old narrative are evident. The examples cited—Paul's "converts" among imperial freedmen in Rome, the "influential" Christian freedmen Clement, Claudius Ephebus, and Valerius Bito (*1 Clement*), and the powerful chamberlain Marcus Aurelius Prosenes—are benchmarks in Frend's chronological approach. The references link the "success" of the Pauline mission in Rome to "its full harvest" during the third century and then to the "triumph" of Christianity a century later.[18] Only a decade ago, in article in an international peer-reviewed journal, Dimitris Kyrtatas repeated more of the same. From the very beginning, says Kyrtatas, the Christian community of Rome included members of the imperial household—people who "often held positions of power or could appeal to other members of the imperial household who held such positions of power." Kyrtatas cites Paul's letter to the Philippians, the imperial freedman Clement of Rome, Irenaeus's reference to the "royal court," and Hippolytus's details about Callistus as a "member of the *familia Caesaris*." For Kyrtatas, these citations help to show how the church of Rome was powerful, influential, and wealthy within the broader catholic church of the Roman world.[19] When the same references can be cited over and over again as evidence for Christianity's growing power, but without any explanation for how the process of advancement actually occurred, the narrative is driving the historiography.

In a similar way, looking at shorter time periods and integrating knowledge of the *realia* with social and political history in an informed theoretical framework, the "social history" approach to early Christianity has at times sustained the narrative as well.[20] Here the most prominent example is Peter Lampe's wildly popular *From Paul to Valentinus* (revised in 2003)—a work that Robert Jewett hailed as the "most important historical and sociological study ever written on Roman Christianity."[21] Like Harnack's work a century before, Lampe's book presents a list of Roman Christians in the *familia Caesaris*, though with some correctives and a few additions. Besides the usual suspects—Claudius Ephebus, Valerius Bito, and Marcus Aurelius Prosenes—the list includes a eunuch named Hyacinth, a freedman named Florinus whom Irenaeus mentions, the emperor

Caracalla's Christian "wet nurse," and from the material record, Aurelius Primus and Alexander.[22] The compendium is crucial for Lampe's book. As the capstone, the collection of Christians in the *familia Caesaris* is part of a diachronic analysis that ostensibly "confirms" previous generalizations about the social development of Christian communities in Rome, especially from the time of Commodus on. Lampe measured the "social ascent" of Roman Christianity by documenting the social status of individual Christians in different social strata of Roman society. In this method, the individual Christians in the *familia Caesaris* are taken as Christianity's social "representatives."[23] With the conventional literary and epigraphic references as a blueprint, Lampe's treatment of Christians in the imperial household bespeaks the same pioneer narrative of the nineteenth century.

Apart from the method of compiling literary and epigraphic references as historical evidence, what allowed key appendages of the narrative to survive for so long are particular assumptions about Christianity. At the broadest level the pioneer narrative of social ascent is largely the result of a teleological view of history. The view takes Christianity's "success" for granted and works backward to seek causal explanations and contributing factors. In this "simplified appropriation of evolutionary logic," even a synchronic approach to Christians in Rome's imperial household, one focused on a single example—the "saints" from Caesar's household, Clement, or Claudius Ephebus—often predicts how the example bodes well for Christianity in the longer term.[24] Phrases like "already in the first century" and "at so early a date," with reference to Christians in Caesar's household, imply that the end is known, the outcome a forgone conclusion, and the example more formative than perhaps it really was.[25]

Equally deleterious, in historiographic narratives about Christianity other assumptions often appear in biologized form.[26] One such assumption is genealogical. Previous work on Christians in the imperial household has consistently arrayed the literary and epigraphic references in a historical chain. In so doing, the configuration constructs a kind of genealogical relationship. Not only does such an arrangement assume that, essentially, all references to Christians in the imperial household—from different time periods and theological projects—are diachronically related. The configuration also imagines that the Christians in the imperial household referenced in the sources from one period were somehow related to the Christians in the imperial household referenced in another. The saints in Caesar's household whom Paul mentions were historical ancestors to, say, Carpophorus and his slave Callistus whom Hippolytus of Rome mentions. Carpophorus and Callistus, the "faithful ones" in the royal court whom Irenaeus mentions, and the Christians whom Tertullian says fill the "palace" are portrayed as part of the same "Christian community," even the same as those imperial slaves recorded in inscriptions. With the genealogical assumption, "Caesar's household" appears to be an "enclave" for an ever-increasing number of Christians, especially from the late second century onward.[27] The only explanation offered for the intergenerational presence of Christians in the imperial household—to quote Kyrtatas's 2006 articulation—is that the Christians "survived and multiplied."[28]

Yet the concept of survive and multiply also rests on another unspoken premise, an assumption that Christianity was like a contagion. It has been a truism of scholarship that Christianity was a religion that gained converts because a message was continually proclaimed and that message was met with exclusive belief.[29] Once an initial core of Christians appeared in the imperial household, therefore, it was "entirely natural" that they proselytized and other imperial slaves and freedpersons converted.[30] The process was repeated, one must suppose, until Rome's imperial household was later a "veritable church of God."[31] The idea that Christianity spread from imperial slaves is actually derivative of traditional approaches to ancient Mediterranean religions more broadly. The spread of mystery cults of the Roman world, once termed "Oriental religions," and commonly characterized as Christianity's longtime but ultimately doomed competitors, was routinely explained by citing the movement and influence of slaves who, taken to Italy, would "import something of their beliefs."[32] Nowhere is such a view more potent than in Franz Cumont's authoritative *Les religions orientales dans le paganisme romain* (1906), in which Cumont explains how Mithraism passed from Asia into the Latin world by pointing to the activity of imperial slaves and freedmen: "[Mithraism] possessed missionaries in the Oriental slaves who were to be found everywhere, engaging in every pursuit, employed in the public service as well as in domestic work, in the cultivation of land as well as in financial and mining enterprises, and above all in the imperial service [i.e., imperial slaves and freedmen] where they filled the offices. Soon this foreign god gained the favor of high functionaries and of the sovereign himself."[33] Nearly a century later Cumont's rendition of Mithraism's ascent to the "favor of high functionaries," above all through imperial slaves and freedmen, was cited in Dimitris Kyrtatas's *The Social Structure of the Early Christian Communities* (1987) as a direct corollary for Christianity's rise to the sovereign himself through the influence of Christian imperial freedmen.[34] Still left unexplained is how exactly the "foreign god" of the Christians, because of imperial slaves and freedmen, actually gained favor with the higher-ups in Rome.

To give the semblance of an explanation, many have simply fallen back on phallogocentric metaphors of penetration. To quote just one, the presence of Christians in Caesar's household, says Gerd Theissen, meant that Christianity had in some cases "penetrated the elite."[35] Yet the metaphor of penetration then gives a tacit nod to an ontological assumption that Christianity was a self-evident entity, that there was an essence to the religion, that somehow "Christianity" had a distinct and independent existence in the world apart from the sociopolitical and cultural context. Christianity was an ideological system of exclusivity, homogeneity, and totalization according to the conventional narrative. The result is that Christianity is assumed to be, as James Rives once claimed, "genuinely novel, if not absolutely *sui generis*."[36] And so we arrive at the heart of the pioneer narrative—Christianity's uniqueness.

Many of the underlying assumptions about Christianity in the Roman Empire have been challenged in recent scholarship. From genealogical questions and historiography to belief as an applicable criterion for understanding early Christianity to the nature of conversion to the concept of Christianity as totalizing to the meaning of religion in the ancient world to Christian identity itself—all have proven to be much more complex than previously thought.[37] Equally important, historians of late antiquity have emphasized that rather than coming to a grinding halt in the fourth century, the old Roman ways, including worship of Rome's gods, continued on even through the sixth century.[38] In all, recent scholarship has pushed for more nuanced, and descriptive, categories of analysis when telling the story of early Christianity. This book does the same. It places the evidence in the cultural context of the ancient Mediterranean and in the ancient epistemological categories of self-definition. Here the phrase *familia Caesaris* is paramount. The long-standing impression that the emperors' slaves and freedpersons, collectively and conventionally known as the *familia Caesaris*, were socially and politically powerful has been essential to the more recent articulations of the pioneer narrative. For that reason assumptions about the *familia Caesaris* also need to be challenged.

The *Familia Caesaris*

Since P. R. C. Weaver's work on imperial slaves and freedmen was first published in 1972 and was subsequently adopted by New Testament and early Christian scholarship the *familia Caesaris* has been understood as a broad category in ancient Roman society. *Familia Caesaris* has been the umbrella phrase for all the emperors' slaves and freedmen en masse, describing a kind of imperial civil service, an official bureaucracy of occupations, or posts, with a routinized career structure, which provided its members regular opportunities of upward social mobility, economic capital, and

sociopolitical influence; and a semi-elite status group in the social stratification of Roman society—the so-called *ordo libertorum et servorum principis*.[39]

The *familia Caesaris* as an elite, empire-wide bureaucracy would serve as
an ancillary model for social descriptions of early Christianity in the 1970s
and 1980s.[40] Two tenuous associations between imperial slaves or freedmen
and Christian communities have resulted. In a kind of mental synecdoche,
the supposed social level of individual Christians in the imperial household (e.g., Marcus Aurelius Prosenes) has become representative of the
social level of the whole Christian community at that time. The association
between the individual and the whole is made even when secure knowledge of the experience of the imperial slave or freedperson is unknown.
Likewise the supposed nature of the *familia Caesaris* as a whole has also
come to personify the experiences of individual Christians thought to be
members of the *familia Caesaris*, again, even when details about those individuals (e.g., Valerius Bito) are entirely lacking. The reconstructions of
the social lives of those Christians in the *familia Caesaris* have then been
articulated ever more precisely with details added about when the imperial
slave would have been manumitted, what training he would have received
at what imperial school, and what post he might have held in the imperial
bureaucracy.[41] Because of the way that the *familia Caesaris* is understood
it has continued to allow some to project individual Christians, or even
Christianity collectively, as moving into the elite strata of Roman society.[42]
In short, the *familia Caesaris* has often functioned, even if unintentionally,
as a social mechanism for the pioneer narrative. But whether explaining the
forces that led to Christianity's rise in the Roman Empire (social organization model) or assessing the social, political, or economic levels of early
Christian communities in Roman society (social history model), those who
have discussed Christian imperial slaves and freedpersons as members of
the *familia Caesaris* have overestimated their number, power, and influence.

With that in mind let me briefly outline some of the problems with
the conventional understanding of the *familia Caesaris*, several of which
Roman historians have already noted. The initial reasons for characterizing imperial slaves and freedmen as a semi-elite, political-administrative
body are complex but may be summed up like this. When the first and
still only detailed studies of imperial slaves and freedmen were appearing
in the 1960s and early 1970s prosopography was the primary method of
analysis. Prosopography focused on the careers, connections, and social
interactions of the elite, aristocratic families and their political groupings
especially in the political, governmental, or administrative spheres. The
prosopographic method looked at imperial slaves and freedmen in this
vein.[43] The collectivity of all the emperors' slaves and freedmen was more

readily compared to the equestrians than other groups of slaves and freed-persons. Weaver's *Familia Caesaris* (1972), still the most definitive study of imperial slaves in the Anglophone world, is the exemplar. The work combined prosopography with schematized data collected from inscriptions. And with the equestrians as a ready model it incorporated then new sociological models that were based on "elite social mobility" and status dissonance. While innovative at the time the models of social mobility that Weaver used presupposed an incredibly high ceiling for imperial slaves and freedmen. Weaver's work made it seem that rising from "humble" slave status in a junior post to "senior" freedman posts exercising great power was somehow ordinary, if not expected.

At the time, the bulk of all investigation of imperial slaves and freed-men, which comes almost exclusively from epigraphy (mostly epitaphs), also focused on collecting social and demographic data from inscriptions. Detailed analysis of epigraphic nomenclature, status indicators, and chronology was the basis for any social survey of imperial slaves. But investigations like Weaver's occurred prior to studies of the "epigraphic habit," which, among other things, first questioned how inscriptions were invested in a cultural practice and communicated impressions to audiences rather than assuming that they simply recorded demographic or social data.[44] Still more revealing, the foundational studies of imperial slaves and freedmen that were published in the 1960s and 1970s occurred mostly prior to the establishment of Roman social history as a subfield and thus prior to the first detailed studies of Roman slavery as a social, rather than a just legal or economic, phenomenon.[45]

In light of recent studies on Roman slavery, it is now clear that the emperors' slaves really were slaves. Imperial freedmen really were former slaves. They experienced violent domination, natal alienation, and dis-honor—three elements that, combined, are now standard in the definition of Roman slavery. The emperors' slaves and freedmen were also subjected to "involuntary labor." They exemplified the definition of slavery that Moses I. Finley explored in his masterful *Ancient Slavery and Modern Ideology* (1980)—a work that unfortunately did not alter the picture of imperial slaves.[46] Even those "positive" aspects that have prompted claims that the emperor's slaves and freedmen "did not typify life in servitude"—mone-tary rewards, marriage patterns, social mobility, manumission—were still mechanisms of "carcerality," or symbolic imprisonment.[47]

While hierarchical and bureaucratic functions developed over time for imperial slaves and freedpersons at no point are we dealing with admin-istrative departments in the modern sense, or with formalized career structures. A bureaucracy proper occurred first in late antiquity and then only with free personnel. But even as bureaucratic changes occurred over two and a half centuries imperial slaves and freedpersons never lost the basic character of being slaves and freedpersons. They were part of the emperor's personal property (*privatus*) while still being public workers of the *res publica*.[48] However removed from his person, slaves and freedpersons were dependent on the emperor as their master or patron. They were still under his kyriarchal power.[49] To be sure, there was a natural hierarchy for imperial slaves and freedpersons pertaining to their labor type, whether administrative or domestic. Yet a hierarchy was expected for any large slave group, whether in Rome's aristocratic households or on an American antebellum planation. The point is that a variety of hierarchies—social, ethnic, and occupational—developed over time from a combination of both internal and external forces acting upon social relations within the slave community. The hierarchies evolved above all from experiences of and varying accommodations to *slavery*.[50]

The experience of imperial slavery was diverse just as other forms of slavery were. There was social mobility for some imperial personnel. It could be dazzling. Certain individual imperial slaves and freedmen, to the utter indignation of elite Roman authors, were so filthy rich and so influential over and above their legal status that they might affect the imperial power structures themselves. Claudius's freedman Narcissus is a prime example. And some ancient poets and philosophers appear to have offered specific imperial slaves and freedmen a degree of deference, even if performed out of necessity, because of whom these imperial slaves or freedmen represented—the emperor himself. Early Christians did the same, as we shall see. However, social mobility among imperial slaves always had limits, and it was never equitable. The preponderance of the epigraphic evidence for imperial slaves and freedmen is for those who were in positions still near the bottom or entry level of the so-called bureaucracy. Because many of these persons were the slave system's more-skilled laborers—couriers (*tabellarius*/ταβελλάριος), assistants (*adiutor*/βοηθός), bookkeepers (*tabularius*/ταβλάριος), recordkeepers (*commentarius*), and tax collectors (*exactor*)—they were deemed worthy of an occupational designation and epitaph in the first place. Other slaves, especially less-skilled laborers (e.g., couriers), seem to have had no expectation for further advancement, as Weaver himself notes. The slave system's inbuilt limitations meant that the recorded occupation on a stone, often made by imperial slaves or freedpersons themselves, is typically "the highest post actually reached by the *end* of a career."[51] An inscription might record a slave's upward mobility, but that mobility had already occurred. The sheer quantity of imperial slaves and freedpersons was also morbid. With numbers soaring easily into the tens of thousands for a single emperor, a finite number of posts (*officia*/ὀπίκια) and a rather short average life expectancy for slaves—forty years is an aggressive estimate—upward mobility was a veritable rat race. Meanwhile, at the upper level, imperial freedmen bureaucrats and wealthy power brokers were only a "tiny privileged minority" among the thousands of imperial slaves and freedmen who worked clerical tasks in cities, served in the imperial palaces and villas, or were attached to estates and properties for agricultural work or resource exploitation.[52]

Besides that, the implication that some imperial slaves or freedmen married freeborn women, usually thought to be crucial evidence for upward social mobility in the *familia Caesaris*, has rightly been questioned based on the methodology and sample size.[53] The prospect or expectation of manumission for imperial slaves has likewise been effectively overstated by the extrapolation of surprisingly little evidence.[54] Not much is known about manumission in imperial slavery, but the bleak reality of the data that has been charted is that imperial slaves were manumitted toward the end of their short lives—a few years on either side of thirty.[55] By comparison, according to a study of manumission among the aristocratic Statilii and Volusii families of Rome a quarter to a third of the household was manumitted. This is a "strikingly high" rate. All the same, it still leaves the vast majority of the household enslaved.[56] Analogously, we can say that a large proportion of the emperors' slaves were manumitted while at the same time recognizing that a large proportion never gained their freedom. Although manumission did presuppose some social mobility, the residue of dishonor and the extension of the slave's "moral education" were then enacted in the patron-client relationship. It is thus an unfair exaggeration to suggest that after manumission the emperors' slaves "vaulted to monied prominence among the freeborn."[57] Actually, manumission sustained the very system of slaveholding. It was an incentive of domination, and, paradoxically, it spurred slaves to hard work and obedience.[58]

In addition to the methodological problems underlying common conceptions of the *familia Caesaris*, there are two patent anachronisms that have persisted. The description of imperial slaves and freedmen as a second-order aristocracy like the equestrians—the *ordo libertorum et servorum principis*—is a gross distortion. No such description existed in the ancient world. Still the most damning blow to the conventional understanding of the *familia Caesaris* comes from the principal architect himself. After describing the social status and mobility, the hierarchies and bureaucracy, of the massive organization called the *familia Caesaris*, Weaver dropped a stunning confession: in antiquity there was no such thing as "the" *familia Caesaris* in the general collective sense.[59] To say this another way, placing all the emperor's slaves and freedmen together in a single unit called the *familia Caesaris* is entirely artificial. What we know as "the" *familia Caesaris* is a modern construct that became a commonplace only after the publication of Weaver's book with the eponymous title.[60] According to Weaver's own explanation, the ancient usage of the phrase *familia Caesaris* (or Καίσαρος οἰκία in Greek) referred to a specific group of imperial slaves in a certain locale of the empire (chapter 1).

Instead of a social or administrative *ordo* such as the equestrians, and instead of a "ramifying secretariat" with hierarchical bureaus, the emperors' slaves and freedpersons were by and large more like other groups of slaves and freedmen in the Roman world. The experience of most imperial slaves or freedpersons can hardly be called socially ascendant, at least not to the heights often presumed in New Testament and early Christian scholarship. The collectivity of the emperors' slaves and freedmen must be understood within a sprawling system of imperial slavery, though still basically one of the "bloated servile households" of Rome's aristocracy.[61] Ancient Christians certainly understood imperial slaves and freedpersons in this way. Christian writers even relied on a discourse of imperial slavery to define themselves within the Roman Empire. As a constitution of knowledge, a language, and a social practice, imperial slavery was used to produce and reproduce meanings and behaviors in various contexts. The discourse of slavery, or "doulology" as Chris de Wet calls it, was a complex system of statements, signs, ideas, and practices associated with labor and human property but shaped the very essence of ancient subjectivities and relationships. Slavery was a power discourse, and it was a fundamental one in early Christianity.[62]

The Discourse of Imperial Slavery

It is probably impossible to overstate the extent to which imperial slavery affected ancient life. Visible in essentially every setting were manifestations of the emperors' human chattel. This is not to say that there was a constant show of coercive force. In the Roman world, rather, the social framing of such coercive power was manifest in what Orlando Patterson calls a personalistic idiom. Power was primarily direct and transparent.[63] People living in the Roman Empire perceived the status of individual persons along a single dimension of power: that of claims and powers in other persons. To put the concept more in the language of the central Roman value of "authority" (*auctoritas*), everyone was under the dominion of someone else.

Slavery was also defined not just in a legal sense but more palpably in a corporeal one. All bodies were heteronomous in ancient Christian thought. The body was made to be ruled by another.[64] Domination in its complex displays was the baseline. What mattered was one's positionality, the number and kind of bodies one was controlled by, and the number under one's control. With such a system in place people did not seek to become free in the more modern sense of isolation from the influence of others, but rather to become further embedded in networks of protective power. Isolation was the surest way to become enslaved.[65]

The ultimate network of power in the Roman imperial world was quite clear, just as its source was unmistakable. Everyone was under the dominion (*auctoritas*) of the emperor. Imperial slavery was the supreme example. The emperor's slaves and freedpersons, scattered about the Mediterranean, were constant reminders of the capillaries of power and the emperor's long reach. Imperial personnel were at once victims of slavery and, in another sense, harbingers of slavery. Roman elites conceived of their imperial project in the provinces in terms of the master-slave, patron-client relationship.[66] As the material record bears out, the articulation of the emperor's power through his surrogate personalities—his slaves and freedmen—was also accomplished in sundry ways, both monumental and minute. So much so that it is safe to say that over three centuries, in virtually any part of the Mediterranean in which there was a known Christian community, those Christians likely had some contact—whether personal or indirect—with an imperial slave or freedperson. The breadth of imperial slavery in the Roman world was that profound.[67]

As pervasive as the bodies of imperial slaves were in the Roman Empire, no less ubiquitous were the insidious metaphorical and symbolic aspects of slavery. The symbolic features of slavery were connected to the complex of norms, values, ideas, and patterned behavior that we call culture.[68] Power relations between master and slave, in other words, depended not only on the threat of violence (social) or the capacity to persuade another person (psychological) but on the cultural facet of authority (*auctoritas*). That authority rests on control by the master of a culture's "symbolic instruments" or "whips." These symbolic whips are the counterparts to the physical instruments and are also used to control the slave's body. They include naming, clothing, language, body marks, and so on. And for Patterson, at least, no instrument of culture was more significant in defining the power relations of master-slave than natal alienation. Whether by forced migration or birth, a slave was stripped of ethnic ties and became a genealogical isolate, a socially dead person.[69] The slave was then totally dependent on the master. There was a "perverse intimacy." The slave's only life was through and for his master.[70] David Brion Davis has echoed Patterson's view of the slave's condition: "At least in theory and in law, the slave has no legitimate, independent being, no place in the cosmos except as an instrument of her or his master's will."[71] Roman slavery was thus a highly symbolic domain of human experience, as Patterson says. A slave was symbolic of the defeated enemy, the power of the local gods, and the superior honor of the community.[72] The view of a slave's condition as natal alienation and as an instrument of the master's will also could and did "symbolize an ideal of religious allegiance to and total dependency on god."[73]

Of course, natal alienation or social death was not necessarily the lived experience of slaves, as John Bodel and Walter Scheidel emphasize. The point is equally true for imperial slaves. But natal alienation and social death do epitomize the hegemonic norms and ideals of Roman culture.[74] They therefore contribute to the ideological framework in which early Christians operated when they called attention to Christians in Caesar's household.

Within Roman slave society the symbolic utility and flexibility of slaves were well known. The topic of slavery, in all its insidious shades, was not only prevalent in the rhetoric of early Christian writings—for example, in discussions of the passions and self-control. At nearly every level the theology of early Christians was permeated by slavery. Even the very conception of God and how Christians understood their relationship to their god was informed by slavery. Because the body was thought of as heteronomous, the discourse of slavery (doulology) also bridged the institutional and metaphorical/symbolic forms of enslavement. Both human bodies, which were meant to be ruled, and cosmic bodies were understood through the lens of slavery. Paul regularly calls himself a "slave of Christ," describes spiritual freedom as slavery to God and righteousness, and relates that Christ even took on the form of a slave (μορφὴ δούλου). Others reinscribed this discourse. The self-descriptors of slave to God or slave of Christ continued to be used in later Christian writings to mark authority (Col 4:7, 12; 2 Tim 2:24; Tit 1:1; James 1:1; 2 Pet 1:1; Jude 1). The underlying issue of this slavery discourse, as de Wet incisively recognizes, is that the divine figure whom Christians worshipped—God the father or his son Jesus Christ—functioned as a slaveholder.[75] Consequently, the line between secular, human slavery ("horizontal") and slavery to nonhuman, personal beings or spiritual entities ("vertical") was blurred. The line between horizontal and vertical slavery, or real and symbolic slavery, could be so blurry, de Wet argues, that early Christians may *not* have understood slavery to God only in a metaphorical sense. In antiquity the status of being a slave of God was part of a much broader cosmological, "doulological" framework of reality, a reality much more expansive than the modern understanding of slavery.[76]

It is the symbolic aspect of the imperial slavery discourse that allowed early Christians to appropriate Caesar's household as a prism for their self-presentation. Early Christians participated in the discourse of imperial slavery by making members of Caesar's household into representative symbols. The emperors' slaves were made into symbols of piety, heresy, tranquility, or hegemony in order to serve the needs of Christian communities as they sought to define themselves. And because of the emperor's unique power and imperial slaves' unique position in relation to the power source—worldwide yet centralized—Rome's imperial household offered a unique template for early Christians. The Christian notion of slavery to God mirrored a slave *familia* of the emperor. In that sense, imperial slavery was a model of slavery to God par excellence. In the long run the significance of the imperial household was its utility as a symbol of Christian cultural power. Perhaps more than any other feature, that cultural symbolism helps account for the popularity and persistence of the narrative about Christians in the imperial household—a narrative that was crystallized in the *Martyrdom of Paul* and exalted a millennium later in that miniature from the *Miroir Historial.*

The modern narrative of Christianity's rise to power through the imperial household does in fact have some deep, ancient roots. But these ancient roots are grounded in a discourse of slavery. Being conscious of the discourse thus reveals a more complex relationship between the modern and ancient narrative. Early Christian authors knew full well that some imperial slaves and freedpersons could be powerful. Yet when Christian authors referenced Christian members of the imperial household they were not stating the case that Christians were advancing socially. Christian authors are almost entirely silent on the social, political, or economic power of those Christians in the imperial household whom they cite.[77] Early Christian writers such as Tertullian or the author(s) of the *Martyrdom of Paul* spotlighted Rome's imperial household not so much to show that Christians had moved *up* in Roman society as that they had moved *in*. As in the case of other groups in the Roman world—such as the Batavians in the early imperial period, who essentially invented themselves as the emperor's ethnic soldiers—the second- and third-century Christian references to the imperial household were collective self-images. They were strategies of inventing "Christian" as a distinct ethnic identity (*genos, ethnos, laos*) in the midst of a mosaic of peoples.[78]

Eventually, though, the imperial household was utilized to tout the rise of Christianity. The fourth-century Christian apologist Eusebius of Caesarea was the first Christian writer to include the imperial household in a full-fledged narrative about Christianity's ascent. His sweeping account of the church from Christ to Constantine, which is unmistakably triumphalist, twice emphasizes that Christians "filled" the imperial household—once during his discussion of the reign of Severus Alexander (235 CE) and then again during his discussion of the reign of Valerian (253–60 CE; Eusebius, *Hist. eccl.* 6.28 and 7.10.3). The portrayal of the third century as a hotbed for conversions, especially among Rome's elite and those in the households of the emperors, would hold sway for the next sixteen centuries.[79] Be that as it may, Eusebius says nothing about those pivotal Christians who filled that regal space during the reigns of Severus Alexander and Valerian. Eusebius gives no names and no particulars. Apart from the larger arc of his narrative he attaches no story to their faceless existence. Nor, it seems, does Eusebius need to. In each of his claims about Christians filling the imperial household Eusebius framed those Christians in the imperial household symbolically. Eusebius's entire account of the church was a Christian cultural narrative, a grand story that Christians wished to tell about themselves as a people. From the perspective of a recent "victor" working backward to predict the destiny of the church, Christians filling up an emperor's house was the hallmark of a people who had reached the pinnacle of the empire. Though on its face Eusebius's narrative assigned structure and meaning to the history of Christians as a collective people among other peoples, for Eusebius this "new people" was superior to all others.[80] Eusebius calls attention to Christians "filling" the emperor's house like a reservoir in order to anticipate an ensuing persecution from the current powers and, through Christian martyrdom, an eventual breakthrough of the church.[81] Eusebius narrativized those Christians in a persecution-martyrdom model of historiography. In so doing, Eusebius utilized a discourse of imperial slavery that transformed the imperial household into a symbol of Christian cultural supremacy. Here is the root of the modern pioneer narrative.

Plan of the Book

By undercutting the historical reconstructions and methods that underlie the pioneer narrative, this book reveals a disjunction between the way that modern scholarship has utilized the imperial household to invent early Christianity and the way that early Christians utilized the imperial household to invent themselves. Not only was the sociopolitical impact of Christians in Caesar's household much more modest than typically assumed, but the history of Christians in the imperial household was far more checkered. The same literary and epigraphic references to Christian imperial slaves and freedmen have been repeated in scholarship because almost always these references are taken at face value. In the absence of an alternative interpretation the references lead to a confirmation bias of the old pioneer narrative. But the history of Christians in Caesar's household cannot be written by simply summoning and arraying the time-honored literary and epigraphic references. There were some individuals serving the emperors in Rome who would have called themselves Christians, or been deemed by others to be so, by the end of the second and the beginning of the third century. The interesting problem is that despite the commonly cited references there is no evidence for Christians in the imperial household in Rome before that time (appendix 1). Even then the long-term effect on the sociopolitical rise of Christians in the Roman Empire was inconsequential compared to what those Christians were made to represent for the wider Christian movement.

So the starting point for my investigation is to question why, in the first place, the writings of the second and third centuries were mentioning Christians serving the emperors in Rome and in what forms they were doing so. I propose to interpret the allusions that second- and third-century authors made as forms of community memory. The main reason for this approach is that apart from Paul's greetings in Philippians 4:22, which were contemporaneous with the "saints from Caesar's household," all later references to Christians in the imperial household were composed decades—and in one instance (*Acts of Justin and Companions*, Rec. B) over a century—after the individual imperial slave had apparently lived. While it is still possible to recover some of the historical situation the implication is that when Christian authors and their communities were citing Christians in the imperial household they were not conveying bona fide historical descriptions that can be plucked and replanted in historiographic narratives. The historical accuracy of the references must be questioned and their function must be assessed if for no other reason than that when Christian authors made claims about Christians serving the emperors they left to curious modern historians far more questions than answers.

Indeed, it is striking just how little the ancient Christian writers say about the imperial slaves whom they reference. One wonders, in what way was that person serving the emperor considered to be a Christian? When, where, and under what circumstances did the imperial slave begin to participate in a Christian group? What type of Christian group was it? What forms and frequency did the participation take? What was the social status or power of the individual(s)? What other piety and worship practices did the individual(s) maintain when their owner/patron was also a divine being? And *how*, to begin with, did the authors actually know that the person serving the emperor was a Christian?

A close look at the actual lives of imperial slaves and freedpersons
helps to answer some of these questions. One distinguishing feature of this
book is its persistent use of the vast corpus of inscriptions that imperial
slaves and freedpersons left behind. At several points the stones cry out and
challenge the conventional narrative. Other times the epigraphic evidence
qualifies or renders more intelligible the claims of Christian literature.
Ultimately, though, the reason why early Christian authors were largely
silent about the imperial slaves referenced in their writings is that they
were crafting representatives for their communities. They were claiming the
emperors' slaves and freedpersons as Christians and doing so for practical
and theological purposes.

The idea of Christians in Caesar's household was powerful and sus-
tainable because almost without fail it was anchored in the apostle Paul's
first salutations from the "saints from Caesar's household" (Phil 4:22). The
book begins here with Paul's famous greetings. Chapter 1 first explains
what Paul meant by "Caesar's household" (*familia Caesaris*). Drawing from
epigraphic evidence, recent work on Roman slavery, and information from
Paul's other letters, chapter 1 reclaims the ancient usage of the phrase
familia Caesaris to sketch a new profile for "Caesar's household." Paul's
familia Caesaris was a group of imperial slaves working together in financial
administration in Asia, most likely at Ephesus, though other locations in
Asia are possible. The social profile of "Caesar's household" then helps
explain who the "saints" were. They were not Paul's new converts but older
acquaintances of the Philippians who also practiced some piety toward the
Jewish god. The Philippians already knew the "saints" when Paul passed
on their greetings. The two groups most likely shared networks through
common kinship and labor and the migratory patterns in the Aegean help
account for these interconnections.

But the trail of those "saints" whom Paul mentions goes cold in the
Aegean. To that end, chapter 1 not only gives a first look into the lives of
imperial slaves, but also separates Paul's "Caesar's household" (*familia Caesaris*) from any later Christian references to Christians in Rome's imperial
household. Not every imperial slave, much less a freedperson, was part
of a *familia Caesaris*. And not every reference to a Christian imperial slave
or freedperson meant that they were part of the same group, "the" *familia
Caesaris*. Deducing from later literary and epigraphic references a list of
Christians in "the" *familia Caesaris* is thus a nonstarter.

The detailed social history of chapter 1 contains the essential historical
background against which the next three chapters unfold. The geographic
and historical chasm that separates Paul's *familia Caesaris* from later references to Christian imperial slaves in Rome is the backdrop for chapter 2.

As the memory of Paul faded farther into the past, a new story about the apostle-making disciples of Nero's slaves became integral to inventing a Christian cultural history and geography in the imperial capital. The *Martyrdom of Paul* creates a martyrdom tradition about Paul in Rome by reworking the apostle's earlier reference to "saints from Caesar's household" (Phil 4:22). The cultic and topographical features of late second-century Rome, especially the *horrea*, facilitated the new stories about Paul and those imperial slaves. The *Martyrdom of Paul* also utilizes the converted imperial slaves to open up the imperial palace to Christian geographic imagination and to contest symbolically for Christian cultural space in the Roman Empire. Later the story of Paul and Caesar's household was intertwined with apostolic narratives that glorified the apostle Peter. The *Acts of Peter* build on the Pauline traditions to claim that Peter had followers from Nero's household as well. Within the *Acts of Peter*, more specifically the *Actus Vercellenses* version, the editorial focus on imperial slaves provided a way to tie together the martyrdom stories of Paul and Peter in Rome under Nero. Chapter 2 then concludes by charting out some of the related stories about Rome's founding apostles converting the imperial household. The stories of Peter, Paul, and converted imperial slaves were told and retold in apostolic narratives that simultaneously generated a unique artistic motif in late antiquity.

Just as memorializing "Caesar's household" was crucial for establishing a cultural history and a geography in Rome, so recalling certain individuals who had served the emperors in Rome became important for defining group relations in the present. Chapter 3 offers two contemporaneous examples from the early third century. Rome's imperial household was utilized by Hippolytus of Rome and Tertullian of Carthage to police community boundaries against perceived internal and external threats. In disputes about heretics and persecution both Hippolytus and Tertullian (re)constructed certain individuals who had served the emperors in Rome. In his theological polemic the *Refutation of All Heresies*, Hippolytus tells a satirical, fictionalized story about Callistus, the domestic slave of Carpophorus, a "faithful man from Caesar's household." Hippolytus characterizes Callistus as a domestic slave in order to ostracize him as a heretic and to elevate his own position in a Christian community. In his apology *To Scapula* Tertullian of Carthage also cites a certain Christian named Proculus Torpacion as a trustworthy physiotherapist who had served the Severan emperors in Rome's imperial palace. Tertullian does so in order to plead for tolerance toward Christians in North Africa in the wake of recent violence. Some historical information about how Christian groups in Rome and North Africa interacted with the emperors' slaves and freedpersons during this period can be recovered from the texts. But a Christian cultural history centered on "Caesar's household" in Rome (chapter 2) was also behind what both Hippolytus and Tertullian were doing with their references to individuals in the imperial household. To regulate their respective communities the authors had reworked the tradition about Paul and Caesar's household in Rome.

Chapter 4 demonstrates that the same kind of creative work with the imperial household continues in the second half of the third century, when Christians attempt to circumscribe their worship practices. In the aftermath of the Edict of Decius (250 CE) an editor (or editors) composed a new account of the *Acts of Justin and Companions*—the purported martyrdom account of Justin Martyr (ca. 165 CE). From the earlier version of the *Acts of Justin* the editor(s) recreated the Euelpistus character as a martyred "slave of Caesar" who had refused an imperial edict requiring worship of the Roman gods. The editor(s) did so to redefine Christian piety as an exclusive activity—it was a piety not to be shared with other gods. In the process the editors refashioned Euelpistus to be like the Patroclus character from Caesar's household in the *Martyrdom of Paul*. Here one of Caesar's slaves, in becoming a "slave of Christ," once again becomes exemplary for all Christians. The chapter also explains that editorial work continued to refine Euelpistus the slave of Caesar even in the fifth century. By drawing from studies of Roman slavery, Roman household rituals, and inscriptions that imperial personnel left behind the chapter then illustrates how imperial slaves like Euelpistus were expected to, and did, worship other gods including the emperors themselves. The piety expected of imperial slaves is exactly the historical reality against which the new version of the *Acts of Justin* (Rec. B) idealized and distorted Euelpistus—a slave of Caesar turned martyr for Christ. For many imperial slaves the exclusive worship of Christ was not so clear-cut.

The introduction of material culture and household rituals elicits questions about the potential problems with identifying Christians in Rome's imperial household from the material record. Chapter 5 applies this insight to a monument that has long been cited as the premier evidence for Christians in the imperial household—the sarcophagus for the third-century imperial freedman Marcus Aurelius Prosenes (*ICUR* 6.17246). But reconstructing the archaeological context of the monument and utilizing other, similar inscriptions from imperial freedpersons show that the Prosenes monument defies the religious categories of Christian/pagan that have been used to classify it. The monument reflects instead the burial customs, commemorative practices, and ritualized spaces typical of other imperial slaves and freedpersons who were conveying piety toward their deceased patron, Prosenes, and toward the divine emperor. These standard Roman characteristics also apply to other inscriptions from imperial slaves or freedpersons that have been highlighted as additional evidence for Christians in Caesar's household (appendix 2). The case study of the Prosenes monument offers a chance to rethink the implications of Christians in Caesar's household and the effect that both ancient and modern memory have had on historical reconstructions. The sarcophagus also helps illustrate how the meaning of "Christian" was not creedal and exclusive, but always manifold and situated for the emperors' slaves and freedpersons.

Chapter 6 takes the case study of the Prosenes monument underground, into Rome's catacombs. Inscriptions of imperial slaves and freedpersons that were found there and that subsequently have been categorized as Christian epigraphy do reflect a Christian material culture. However, the commonly cited inscriptions are not additional evidence for Christians in Rome's imperial household during the third century. Articulating the archaeological development of select catacombs (San Sebastiano ad Catacumbas, Praetextatus, Callistus, and Priscilla), and the evolution of epigraphic content on the stones themselves, reveals that the commonly cited inscriptions were actually reused. The epitaphs of imperial slaves and freedmen were strategically recut, and their symbols, especially the fish and anchor, were harvested in order to create new Christian funerary monuments only at a later date, in the fourth century. This insight not only challenges some of the early third-century dating of catacomb areas, particularly in the *piazzola* of San Sebastiano ad Catacumbas. It also shows the ways in which the initial epigraphic activity of imperial slaves and freedpersons was later vital for the invention of a distinct Christian material culture in late antiquity.

Overall, the investigation of Christians in Caesar's household has serious ramifications for how the rise of Christianity has traditionally been conceived. But just doing a historical investigation of this sort is incomplete without acknowledging the difference that it makes. For that reason the conclusion of the book considers more closely how the discourse of imperial slavery was related to early Christian claims on members of Caesar's household. Memory was essential. It reformulated members of Caesar's household into symbols that would shape the cultural contours of early Christianity.

In sum, this book recounts how, over several centuries, the Roman emperors' slaves and freedpersons were vital for the processes of early Christian culture-making. The book also sheds some much-needed light on the complicated lives of imperial slaves and freedpersons, the ways their lives may have intersected with Christian groups in Rome, and the

modes in which they fleshed out the diverse meanings of Christian in antiquity. The result is a more nuanced perspective on some of the defining
characteristics of early Christianity, and indeed, a more nuanced view of
Christianity's development in the Roman Empire. The Roman emperors'
slaves and former slaves did help usher Christianity onto a world stage.
Only they were not social pioneers in Christianity's inevitable march to
power. They were custom-made features of its cultural evolution.

Note on Terminology

One of the problems facing any investigation of this kind is that in antiquity there was no single, standard term or phrase to designate all of the
Roman emperors' slaves and freedpersons as a collective mass. Within an
imperial dynasty the succeeding emperor would accrue the "possessions"
of his predecessors, including all the slaves. A change in dynasty would
generally follow the same practice. Throughout this book, therefore, I use
"imperial personnel" as my own re-descriptive umbrella phrase for any or
all imperial slaves and/or freedpersons anywhere in the empire. I also use
the phrase "imperial household," with an eye toward the broadest ancient
meaning of "household," to designate any person serving the Roman
emperors as either slaves or freedpersons specifically in Rome. The phrase
"Caesar's household" is a direct English translation of the Latin *familia
Caesaris* and of Paul's Greek phrase Καίσαρος οἰκία in Philippians 4:22.
When I use the double quotation "Caesar's household" it refers either to
Paul's expression in Philippians 4:22 or to a quotation of Paul's expression
in other ancient texts. When I use the term *serve,* as in those "serving the
emperor(s)," it indicates those persons who were working for the emperors
as slaves or freedpersons, whether in the palace or elsewhere, including
in the larger imperial administrative system. The term *slave* indicates a
person—male or female—whom the emperor legally owned as property.
The term *freedperson* is a gender-inclusive expression for any imperial
slave who has been manumitted. When I use the term *freedman,* it is either
because I am talking about a former slave of the emperor who was male,
or because I am channeling the traditional ways of describing members
of "the" *familia Caesaris.*

CHAPTER 1

PAUL, THE PHILIPPIANS, AND CAESAR'S HOUSEHOLD (PHIL 4:22)

> Paul had no connexions with the court; the salutations he once sends from them "that are of Caesar's household" are not from princesses and ministers, but from simple Imperial slaves, petty clerks, employed perhaps at Ephesus in the departments of finance or of crown lands.
>
> —ADOLF DEISSMANN, *LIGHT FROM THE ANCIENT EAST*

When Adolf Deissmann wrote this in 1910, he must have known how radical it was. The idea that Paul and "Caesar's household" were not in Rome, and that those from Caesar's household whom Paul mentions were simply slaves of finance, went against nearly every previous interpretation. In fact, only a few years earlier—in a work that would become the definitive social history of early Christianity for the next century—another Adolf had taken the exact opposite view. Adolf von Harnack opened volume 2 of his monumental *Die Mission und Ausbreitung des Christentums in den ersten drei Jahrhunderten* (1902) by surveying the inward spread of Christianity among the aristocracy and Rome's imperial court. For Harnack, the greetings Paul conveyed from the "saints from Caesar's household" in Philippians 4:22 were evidence precisely for "connections of Christians and the court" and signaled the initial point of Christianity's inward spread. Harnack had largely reiterated tradition. Deissmann, however, had conducted extensive fieldwork. In 1906 and again in 1909 he spent significant time at Ephesus during the initial excavations of the city by the Austrian Archaeological Institute, which hosted him and his eminent colleague, the archaeologist Friedrich von Duhn. Besides the material evidence Deissmann collected from the site on his own, the newly compiled epigraphic catalogues of

Theodor Mommsen and Rudolf Herzog were also crucial factors in Deissmann's radical departure from tradition.[1]

Today, many of Deissmann's initial observations have proved to be prescient. Hardly anyone thinks that Paul's expression "Caesar's household" (ἡ Καίσαρος οἰκία; Phil 4:22) meant the palace of the Roman emperor in Rome or his biological family.[2] Now most would suggest that what Paul was talking about were saints in the *familia Caesaris*—an entity commonly defined as the collectivity of the emperor's slaves and freedmen in the imperial bureaucracy spread throughout the Roman world. There is also a growing consensus that Paul did not write Philippians from Rome, but from the province of Asia, likely from Ephesus.[3]

Despite the shift in understanding following more recent sociological work on Philippians, an explanation that accounts for the saints from "Caesar's household" (*familia Caesaris*) within the distinct environment of the first-century Aegean region is still largely absent.[4] Questions remain about who was in the *familia Caesaris* Paul mentions and how the "saints" were connected to Paul and the Philippians in the first place. Because the traditional location of Rome is still preferred in some circles of scholarship, the traditional explanation that Paul made Christians among Caesar's household in Rome—the bedrock of the pioneer narrative—has continued to be credible.[5]

Yet an Asian provenance for Philippians offers the best answer as to why Paul sent greetings from "saints" in a *familia Caesaris* to the Philippians and how there was an especially close connection between the two groups. The *familia Caesaris* of Philippians 4:22 was a particular, local group of imperial slaves. It was a *familia* of Caesar in Roman Asia, not a reference to a group in Rome or even an empire-wide organization of slaves and freedmen. By delving into the available details about imperial personnel in the Aegean region, and by paralleling those details with information from Paul's other Aegean contacts, a fresh profile of Paul's *familia Caesaris* emerges. In turn, that sketch helps explain how Paul passed on greetings from individual "saints" in that particular *familia Caesaris* to the Philippian community because the two groups already knew each other. Indeed, the "saints" and individuals in Philippi shared a common cult because they were most likely already connected by kinship and labor networks in the northern Aegean.

The backstory to Philippians 4:22 that I offer here is in many ways more ordinary than the pioneer narrative would imagine. The first known connection between a group of Christ devotees and members of Caesar's household in the first century also stands in sharp contrast to later Christian stories about Paul and Caesar's household in second- and third-century Rome.

Disambiguating the *Familia Caesaris*

When the first Roman emperor, Augustus, made Ephesus the new capital of Asia and the residence of the proconsul (ca. 30/29 BCE), a plethora of administrative and commercial demands—great and small—opened up in service of the "imperial economy." The census, land and/or resource allocation, natural resource exploitation, supply systems, complex taxation and tribute levying, collection, and documentation all required a vast network of nonelite, working people.[6] The paperwork alone must have been incredible. Much of the activity, though certainly not all, would have centered in the local *praetorium*—a common provincial, civic building that Paul also mentions (Phil 1:13).

For the many tasks involved in such an enterprise, the emperors would put up their personal property and former property in the form of their slaves and freedpersons. The majority of imperial personnel who worked in Ephesus would have been "sub-clerical" imperial slaves—a footman (*pedisequi*), an attendant or guard (*custodes*), a herald or monitor (*nomenclatores*), a secretary or clerk (*notarius*/νοτάριος), or a courier (*tabellarius*/ταβελλάριος). Besides these were the "clerical" imperial slaves or freedmen—an assistant (*adiutor*/βοηθός), bookkeeper (*tabularius*/ταβλάριος), recordkeeper (*commentarius*), tax collector (*exactor*), underslave (*vicarius*/ού(ε)ικάριος), cashier (*arcarius*/ἀρκάριος), or account manager or steward (*dispensator*/ οἰκονόμος/ταμίας).[7] During the first century, western Asia also experienced regional and interregional developments—a demographic and urban boom both in the population of existing cities or poleis (e.g., Ephesus) and in the total number of poleis. As the "Customs Law of Asia" (62 CE) affirms, Ephesus was "the biggest emporium of Western Asia Minor," the regional center of a provincial and extraprovincial economy, which the imperial economy intersected.[8]

The tectonic movements of Roman imperialism ensured a steady stream of the emperor's slaves and freedpersons into Asia and especially Ephesus, Asia's "First and Greatest Metropolis." Indeed, contrary to some who argue for a Roman provenance for Philippians based on the enormous amount of imperial slave and freedman inscriptions from Rome, the epigraphic record bears witness that Ephesus was a major center for imperial personnel.[9] Overall, the epigraphic footprint of imperial personnel in Ephesus, whether in the first, second, or third century, is bigger than in any other city of Roman Asia (tables 1–2).

Typical of the epigraphic habit, imperial freedmen are the most visible. They had a monumental presence in the capital from the very beginning of the principate as the triple gate of Mazeus and Mithridates

TABLE 1 Imperial slaves and freedpersons in Ephesus, first century BCE to first century CE

Name	Descriptor(s)	Date	Source(s)
Gaius Julius Nicephorus	• imperial freedman • prytanis • conventus civium Romanorum member	1st c. BCE	IvE 6.859 (Greek)
Gaius Julius [. . .]	• imperial freedman • patron for synod (conventus civium Romanorum?) • donations for Roma and Artemis	1st c. BCE (50–27 BCE)	IvE 6.859a (Greek)
Gaius Julius [. . .]	• imperial freedman • tomb for family (son and wife)	1st c. BCE–1st c. CE	IvE 6.2272 (bilingual)
Mazeus	• imperial freedman • monumental benefactor	4–3 BCE	IvE 7,1.3006 (bilingual)
Mithridates	• imperial freedman • monumental benefactor	4-3 BCE early 1st c. CE	IvE 7,1.3006 IvE 3.851 (bilingual)
Successus	• imperial freedman	1st c. CE	IvE 6.2210 (bilingual)
Ampliatus	• house-born slave of Successus, imperial freedman • died nineteen years old	1st c. CE	IvE 6.2210 (Latin)
Eutychus	• imperial slave dispensator	1st c. BCE–1st c. CE (ostotheke)	IvE 6.2255a (Latin)
Zmaragdus	• dispensator (imperial slave)	1st c. BCE–1st c. CE	IvE 6.2270 (Latin)
Ikarus	• slave (vicarius) of unnamed dispensator	1st c. BCE–1st c. CE (ostotheke)	IvE 6.2270 (Latin)
Eutactus	• imperial freedman • procurator (inheritance tax) of Asia and Lycia	80 CE	IvE 2.262 (bilingual)

in the commercial agora of Ephesus unmistakably attests. The emperor's freedmen were foundational in other ways as well. Like the tip of an iceberg, they were the upper level of a network beneath which flowed many more imperial slaves who are less visible in the material record.[10] It is within, around, and through this bustling provincial context, I suggest, that Paul's "Caesar's household" developed. But, first, what was "Caesar's household"?

To begin in broad strokes, the Greek phrase that Paul uses for "Caesar's household" (Καίσαρος οἰκία) is the direct equivalent of the Latin phrase *familia Caesaris*. In antiquity, when the Latin phrase *familia Caesaris* is used, whether in literary or epigraphic sources, it does not designate

TABLE 2 Geo-chronological distribution of imperial slaves and freedpersons in Roman Asia

Location	Name	Descriptor(s)	Date	Source
Pergamum, Mysia	Latinus	• imperial freedman	1st c. CE (Flavian)	SEG 59, 1497
Pergamum, Mysia	Carpophorus	• imperial freedman • *tabularius* of the province of Asia Minor	2nd c. CE	AvP 8,3.107
Nacolea, Phrygia	Unknown	• slave of Germanicus (Καίσαρος Γερμανικοῦ... δοῦλος) • epitaph for son Philo	18 CE or soon after	MAMA 5.201 (Greek)
Nacolea, Phrygia	Craterus	• slave (*Caesaris nostri servus*) • tax collector (*exactor*) of the *res publica* of Nacolea • *pro salute* inscription for Commodus and Craterus by citizens of Nacolea	180–92 CE (Antonine)	MAMA 5.197 (Latin)
Nacolea, Phrygia	Publius Aelius Onesimus	• freedman (*Augusti libertus*) • will (*ex testamento*) • distributions for homeland of Nacolea (*patria mea amantissima*) on birthday of Hadrian	117–38 CE (Hadrianic)	MAMA 5.202
Synnada, Phrygia	Hyacinthus	• slave • *tabularius* • imperial quarries • wife from Arruntii family	54–68 CE (Neronian)	MAMA 4.53 (bilingual)
Lysias, Phrygia	Amion (woman) Diadoumenos (man)	• slave (Καίσαρος δούλη) sets up tomb (τὸ ἡρῶον) for her partner (ἀνήρ) • slave (Καίσαρος δοῦλος)	Unknown	MAMA 4.114 (Greek)
Synnada, Phrygia	Amiantus	• freedman (*Augusti libertus*) • notetaker/recordkeeper (*a commentaris*) • epitaph for Flavia Eutychia (mother)	1st–2nd c. CE (Flavian)	MAMA 4.62 (Latin)
Synnada, Phrygia	Titus Aelius [. . .]	• freedman (*Augusti libertus*) • house-born slave (*verna*) • procurator • honorary inscription for Antoninus Pius	138–60 CE (Antonine)	MAMA 4.55 (Latin)
Laodikeia Combusta, Pisidia	Thalamos (man) Chreste (woman)	• slaves (κυρίων Καισάρων δοῦλοι) • epitaph/tomb while living (ζῶντες)	Unknown	MAMA 1.29
Dionysopolis, Phrygia	Dokimos	• slave of Domitia Augusta (Δομιτίας Σεβαστῆς δοῦλος) • donates materials for building	90 CE or later	MAMA 4.293 (Greek)

Location	Name	Descriptor(s)	Date	Source
Hadrianopolis, Phrygia	Kosimos	• house-born slave (κυρίου Καίσαρος ούέρνα) • peacekeeper, guard (εἰρηνάρχη) • votive for the Greatest God (Διὶ Μεγίστῳ)	2nd c. CE or later	MAMA 7.135 (Greek)
Tyriaion, Phrygia	Marcus Aurelius Eukleides	• freedman ([ἀπελεύθερος Καίσα]ρος) • votive for the Greatest God (Διὶ Μεγίστῳ)	2nd c. CE or later	MAMA 7.107 (Greek)
Galatia (mod. Insuyu)	Aur(elius) Epagathus	• freedman (Σεββαστῶν ἀπελεύθερος) • supplier of the records office/registrar (ἰνστρουμεντάριος ταβουλαρίων) • epitaph/tomb for himself and free wife while living (ζῶν)	2nd c. CE or later (late Antonine)	MAMA 7.524 (Greek)
Galatia (mod. Kuyulu Zebir)	Julianus	• house-born slave (ούέρνα τῶν Σεββ(αστῶν) • epitaph (?)	Unknown (prob. 2nd c. CE or later)	MAMA 7.544 (Greek)
Pisidia, Galatia	Theophilus	• freedman (Σεβαστοῦ ἀπελεύθερος) • procurator (ἐπίτροπος) • epitaph for Kalligenos, house-born slave/foundling (θρεπτός)	Unknown (prob. 2nd c. CE or later)	MAMA 8.341
Tabai, Caria	Publius Aelius Parthenokleos	• freedman (Καίσαρος ἀπελεύθερος) • epitaph on sarcophagus	120–35 CE or later (Hadrianic)	MAMA 6.170 (Greek)
Laodikeia	Tiberius Claudius Trypho	• freedman • triple gateway donation	84–85 CE (Domitianic)	MAMA 6.2 (bilingual)
Smyrna, Ionia	Telesphoros Julianus	• imperial slave (δοῦλος Καίσαρος) • tomb for wife (?) Claudia Olympia	Flavian	IK 23.225
Alexander Troas, Troad	[. . .]	• imperial freedman • honorary inscription for Septimius Severus	193–211 CE	IK 53.25

imperial slaves and freedmen, much less all imperial slaves and freedmen in the bureaucracy. It designates a specific, local group of imperial slaves. In the only detailed ancient description of the *familia Caesaris*, the late first-century curator of Rome's aqueducts, Julius Sextus Frontinus (ca. 40–104 CE), portrays the groups of imperial slave workers (*familiae Caesaris*) who maintained the city's water ducts as the direct counterparts of the groups of public slave workers (*familiae publicae*).[11]

The key to understanding "Caesar's household" in Philippians 4:22 is ancient slavery terminology. The identity marker *Caesaris*/Καίσαρος was the preferred term for individual imperial slaves, whether in the Latin West or Greek East (figs. 2 and 3). *Familia* was the preferred term for a particular group of slaves. The terminology reflects the general tendency to specify slave groups with local or functional aspects: *familia urbana*, *familia rustica*, *familia publica* or *liberti et familia publica*, *familia castrensis*, *familia monetalis*, *familia XX libertatis*, *familia gladiatorial Caesaris*, *familia ludi magni*. Within this semantic range, *familia* was also readily used to designate a group of slaves as distinct from a group of freedmen, designated as *liberti*. When the terms *Caesaris* and *familia* were joined, therefore, the phrase *familia Caesaris* stressed the slave origin of the individuals under discussion.[12] To give one succinct example, an inscription from Rome put up by some of the emperor's freedpersons and slaves to honor the eternal imperial house and sacred Silvanus distinguishes the two groups as *liberti et familia Caesaris*.[13]

FIG. 2 Inscription of an imperial slave named Antiochus, self-designated in Latin as Caes(aris) N(ostri) S(ervus) in line 3. Late first century CE. Stoa of Attalus. Athens, Greece.

FIG. 3 Inscription of an imperial slave named Antiochus, self-designated in Greek as Καισ(αρος) Δουλ(ος) in line 7. Late first century CE. Stoa of Attalus. Athens, Greece.

MAP 1 Map of the Aegean region, showing Roman provinces, cities of Paul's mission, and known places of imperial personnel.

Here is one *familia Caesaris*. There were many such individual *families* of Caesar's slaves in the empire.

But the exact Latin phrase *familia Caesaris* is actually quite rare. The exact Greek phrase Καίσαρος οἰκία is even rarer. Most often the use of *familia* appears in conjunction with the specific work that slaves did for the emperor (*Caesaris*), sometimes even giving the exact geographical location of the *familia*. One *familia Caesaris* describe themselves first as a *collegium*, and then as a "family of our Caesar's couriers" (*familia tabellariorum Caesaris*) who reside in Narbo (the present-day port city of Narbonne, France).[14]

Another example, from the opposite side of the Mediterranean, that does use the exact Latin *familia Caesaris* comes, interestingly enough, from Paul's immediate context in the Aegean. The inscription is from Coela, a city in the province of Thrace (*Thracia Chersonesos*), near present-day Eceabat, Turkey. Located on the Hellespont—the strait separating Asia and Europe—Coela was a vital crossing point between Roman Asia and Macedonia, with the Aegean to the west and the Dardanelles, as the Hellespont is known today, to the east (map 1). The inscription even dates to the early Neronian period, 55 CE to be precise. It is dedicated first to the "divinity (*numini*) of the imperial house." It then records that two patrons, with their own money "made the bath for the people (*populo*) and the family of our Caesar" (literally, the *familia Caesaris nostri*).[15] This *familia Caesaris* at Coela was a discrete, local group—a counterpart to the local people (*populo*)— who either worked the imperial lands of the Thracian Chersonese and/or helped administer that area.

The slavery terminology employed in the literary and epigraphic comparanda throw much more light on the "Caesar's household" (*familia Caesaris*) that Paul mentions. The dimensions of a *familia Caesaris* were both bureaucratic and domestic. Although as a naming practice the descriptor *familia*/ἡ οἰκία was an idiom of power—part of a slavery discourse in antiquity—that defined the power relations of master-slave (conclusion), the descriptor *familia*/ἡ οἰκία was also self-designated. Groups of slaves chose to call themselves *familiae*. This self-definition implied a complex social texture, even kinship structures. Such *familiae* were made through connections of substance, eating, living together, procreation, and emotion.[16] Like the groups from Narbo and Coela, the individuals in Paul's *familia Caesaris* were associated as a slave *familia* not just by compulsion, but because they lived and worked together in the same area, had ethnic ties, and shared labor, cults, or family connections.

What this means is that the *familia Caesaris* that Paul knew was, on the one hand, a local group of imperial slaves. Paul's expression Καίσαρος οἰκία does not "naturally" refer to members of Nero's family, dependent kin of any degree of relationship as well as to household slaves and various retainers, all of which would make up a very large group. Nor does the expression indicate "the imperial service" or the "imperial bureaucracy" as a collectivity. It refers to slaves who worked in a particular part of the broader imperial bureaucracy. And in no way does the reference in Philippians 4:22 favor a Roman provenance for Paul's letter because the majority of the members of the *familia Caesaris* would have been stationed in Rome.[17]

On the other hand, that *familia Caesaris* that Paul references may have chosen to designate others besides adult male functionaries as part of its group, particularly imperially owned women. The women may have been wives or daughters of imperial slaves, but they also could have been managers of other imperial slaves in that *familia*.[18] Despite legal restrictions, imperial slaves regularly took slave and free women as their partners (*contubernalis*/συμβίος) in their assigned work areas. Because of this practice, young enslaved persons (girls and boys) could also have been part of "Caesar's household." House-born slaves (*vernae*/οἰκογενής) are well attested in the ancient sources, and the material record has left glimpses of this rich social fabric among imperial personnel in first-century Ephesus.[19]

While the possibility of such complex social dynamics for "Caesar's household" (Phil 4:22) should remain in view, the available evidence is largely restricted to the bureaucratic dimension. Here the epigraphic evidence for imperial slaves in the Aegean, along with information about two other people whom Paul references in his letters, allows a more detailed sketch of "Caesar's household" to emerge.

Sketching a Profile of Paul's "Caesar's Household"

Because the *familia Caesaris* that Paul references lived and worked in the eastern Mediterranean, at least some of them would have already possessed the professional skills and the social networks that the urban, provincial settings of the Greek East demanded. As part of the imperial bureaucracy these workers' skills would include particularly those related to financial administration—taxes and expenditures—but also to public services such as aqueducts, libraries, correspondences, roads, public works and buildings, as well as imperial projects such as mines and marble quarries. Based on these trends, those in Paul's "Caesar's household" who worked in the imperial bureaucracy would generally be mid- to lower-level imperial slaves who had already achieved some upward mobility in the system, though had probably reached their limit.[20]

The evidence that exists from first-century Ephesus, and certainly from Ephesus in the following century, indicates that imperial slaves were indeed engaged largely in finance related to the imperial treasury (*fiscus*/φίσκος). Under these imperial slaves also existed an extensive, though largely epigraphically inconspicuous, retinue of other slaves in similar tasks (*vicarii*).

So Deissmann was right. In all likelihood, the labor that those from "Caesar's household" performed, whether in Ephesus or elsewhere in Asia, was in the area of imperial finance. What makes this even more likely for those from "Caesar's household" is that financial work also fits well with other individuals known to be in Paul's larger social field.

An important clue for deciphering more specifically what kind of work those from "Caesar's household" did is Erastus from Corinth. Paul mentions the name once (Rom 16:23). Of all the individuals named in Paul's letters Erastus is the only one to whom Paul attaches any occupational information. He calls Erastus a οἰκονόμος τῆς πόλεως. This occupational phrase indicates that though not an imperial slave, Erastus was a public slave. And public slaves worked alongside imperial slaves not only in Rome but in provincial centers and colonies, even sharing group designations—*familia publica* and *familia Caesaris*, respectively—and similar remuneration for their work. In fact, at the political and administrative level, the system

of imperial slavery developed through the preexisting public slave system.[21] The two slave groups functioned very much in parallel.

Within the wide range of duties that public slaves had to perform, and
in terms of skill and responsibilities within the slave system, an οἰκονόμος
was somewhere in the middle area. Erastus probably had a low- to mid-level
financial position in Corinth's bureaucracy. Likewise, Tertius ("Number
Three"), who was Paul's scribe for his letter to the Romans (Rom 16:22),
and Quartus ("Number Four," Rom 16:23) are also analogues for those in
"Caesar's household." Both seem to have been either slaves or freedmen in
the household of Erastus, or slaves who worked under (*vicarius*) Erastus
in Corinth's financial administration—hence their ordinal names.[22]

To translate these parallels, a counterpart in the imperial slave system
for Erastus's position as public slave is a *dispensator*, as an inscription from
an imperial slave on the island of Chios shows.[23] A *dispensator* was typically a slave, and the work performed, usually in the provinces, could
entail a range of duties—almost always unspecified in the inscriptions.
But in essence the tasks required financial stewardship or management of
imperial funds (*fiscus*) for one or more accounts (*rationes*). The work could
include signing off on expenses and allowing disbursements of money (as
"cashier par excellence"); receiving funds owed to the *fiscus*, such as the
provincial tax (*tributum*); or entering into contracts using the *fiscus*. Some
dispensatores appear to have been important persons whose activities were
quite profitable in the imperial economy. Such is the case for an imperial
dispensator from first-century Ephesus who is identified as Eutychus Caesaris. His exact financial responsibilities are unknown, but based on the
fine workmanship of his cinerary urn (*ostotheke*) he became quite wealthy.[24]

Dispensatores did not work alone. They normally had underslaves (*vicarii*) as their future replacements, and this position may be the imperial
slave parallel for Quartus (Rom 16:23). Notably, the majority of inscriptions that *vicarii* produced come not from Rome, where the majority of
imperial slave and freed inscriptions survive, but from the provincial centers of administration and "customs posts," like Ephesus.[25] In first-century
Ephesus, for example, a certain Ikarus is recorded as the *vicarius* of an
imperial *dispensator* named Zmaragdus.[26] Once enslaved, both Ikarus and
his *ordinarius* Zmaragdus worked in finance as cashiers or collectors, and
spent at least part of the time in the provincial capital, though they likely
traveled as well.

One other parallel for Erastus among imperial personnel is a manager (*vilicus*). The term is most commonly associated with a slave bailiff
who oversaw other slaves in an agricultural setting (*villa*), but *vilici* had
broader applications as well. Imperial *vilici* could manage other slaves at

customs stations (*stationes portorium*), or imperial mines and workshops where they also could collect for the *fiscus*.[27] Or, as in Nemausus, Gallia Narbonensis (present-day Nîmes), an imperial slave (*vilicus*) could be one of several managers of the inheritance tax in a city.[28] In still another case from Rutaeni in Gallia Aquitania (present-day Villefranche-de-Rouergue), one slave manager named Zmaragdus is honored by the *familia Caesaris* of Tiberius (*familia Tiberii Caesaris*) who worked at the mines under Zmaragdus.[29]

Based on the above comparisons, the "Caesar's household" that Paul references was likely engaged in financial labor and was probably headed by a *dispensator* or a *vilicus*, like Erastus in the public slave system at Corinth. And if Quartus or Tertius, not necessarily Erastus, was singled out as a believer in Paul's letter to the Romans, as has been suggested by Steven Friesen, then I would also suggest a similar identification for "Caesar's household." The "saints" from "Caesar's household" were those imperial slaves working under a *dispensator* or *vilicus*, like Erastus.[30] They were clerks, couriers, assistants, bookkeepers, and so on, and as he does with Quartus and Tertius in Romans, Paul calls attention to these "saints" in his letter to the Philippians.

The parallels between Erastus, Quartus, Tertius, and imperial slaves mentioned in Philippians 4:22 thus go beyond social status or labor function. To recognize other connections between the "saints" in that *familia Caesaris* and the Philippians and how all three—Paul, the "saints," and the Philippians—were connected requires us to first look at the nature of ancient letter-writing. To that topic I now turn.

Connecting the "Saints" and the Philippians

When Paul passed on greetings to the Philippians in Macedonia "especially" from the "saints," he was not introducing the two groups. They already knew one another.[31] It is for that reason that Paul merely forwards the saints' hello at the end of the letter. This kind of greeting is highly conventional, virtually a cliché of ancient letter-writing. The friendship motifs and sharing language (συγκοινωνεῖν, κοινωνεῖν) throughout this portion of the letter also presume previous familiarity and/or fellowship (Phil 4:14–14).[32] Indeed, the term μάλιστα, which Paul uses in his forwarded greetings (Phil 4:22), intimates an "especially" close connection between the saints and some of the Philippians. By comparison, the only other time that Paul uses "especially" in reference to a person is with the slave Onesimus, whom Paul calls his child (Phlm 10), his heart (Phlm 12), and then "a beloved brother, especially to me" (μάλιστα ἐμοί; Phlm 16).

Sharing a common cult would certainly be one way that the "saints" and the Philippians were especially close. But what exactly that common cult meant is more open to question than previous approaches have let on. The conventional declaration is that the saints were "Christian" members of Caesar's household. Others have also suggested that "Caesar's household" referred to another house church or house churches. In these interpretations, the "saints" were a group of Christians who sent greetings to their counterparts in Philippi. In a bold stroke, one scholar even translated Philippians 4:22 as "all the saints who belong to the church of Ephesus also greet you, especially the imperial slaves."[33] All of this goes too far beyond the evidence.

The term "saints" was not necessarily a synonym for "church," much less for "Christians." And the saints' piety, devotion, or loyalty to Paul's god certainly meant something other than simply "churchgoing." While the term "church" could encompass "saints," the two were distinct. Paul writes to "all the saints in Philippi" (Phil 1:1), for example, but later singles out the Philippians (Φιλιππήσιοι) as a very particular assembly (ἐκκλησία; Phil 4:15).

In fact, the term "saints" had a range of meaning in Paul's writings. Paul uses it for people he knew well (Rom 16:26–27), but also for people he did not know so well, did not work with as closely (e.g., Rom 1:7), or who even represented a wider geography in his apostolic vision.[34] The range of meaning is further illustrated in Philippians 4:21–22 where Paul distinguishes between "brothers/sisters with me" (οἱ σὺν ἐμοὶ ἀδελφοί) and "all the saints" (πάντες οἱ ἅγιοι).[35] The appellation "brothers and sisters" intimates Paul's closest ties—his "dears" (ἀγαπητοὶ; Phil 4:1)—as does the title "coworkers" (συνεργοί), which he uses for select persons like Clement (Phil 4:3). Paul was certainly not equally intimate with all saints everywhere.

In this case, I would argue that "saints from Caesar's household" was a broader reference to those who, like Paul and the Philippians, practiced some form of piety (εὐσέβεια) toward the Jewish god. At some important time or in a significant way, some imperial slaves from a *familia Caesaris* in Roman Asia had shared (κοινωνία) in the business of giving and receiving, as Paul puts it (Phil 4:15), either with Paul himself or with other saints, such as those at Philippi. The act of sharing—in whatever form—was the basis for Paul designating them "saints."

But being pious for the Jewish god, even for that god's son, was not necessarily uniform. For any group there were interactional dynamics. Practitioners had links to cults based on several factors such as geography or interpersonal relations, each of which was contingent and often circumstantial.[36] One example from Roman Corinth helps to illustrate the point. In Corinth, there was a certain Sagaris who was a slave (*vicarius*) of Alcimus, a house-born slave (*verna*) of the emperor and a cashier (*arcarius*). When Sagaris was in Corinth he offered a votive to Sacred Venus and the *gens* of the Corinthian *collegium* of the Augustales or the Augusti, depending on the interpretation. Sagaris participated in a cult devoted to particular deities, and he had some connection to an association of that cult in Corinth. But how often or how devoted Sagaris was likely depended on his circumstances. For another inscription recording this same Sagaris reveals that he spent time in Athens as well, where he also had established relationships (*consilium*). Sagaris was probably all over the province of Achaea, in fact, since this second inscription specifies that his superior slave Alcimus was a cashier "of the *province* of Achaea."[37] Knowing at least some of Sagaris's life path as a slave, it may be presumptuous to think that Sagaris always gave the same level of attention to his gods and his *collegium* in Corinth.

By the same measure, it would also be presumptuous to think that whatever devotion the saints from Caesar's household had toward the Jewish god was always fixed. More likely, their piety was contingent, simultaneous, supplementary, or even secondary to other relationships.[38] In addition to their connection with the Philippians, the imperial slaves whom Paul met probably did have some connection to a similar group of devotees in Ephesus or broader Asia. But they could have been on the periphery, not in a core; regular participants in cultic activities, or irregular participants. Given the position of slaves as imperial property and their relationships with other imperial slaves in a *familia Caesaris*, it was likely difficult to maintain exclusive loyalty to the Jewish god and/or his son. Among other duties there were certain cultic practices that imperial slaves and freedpersons were expected to perform to show piety to their imperial master (see chapter 4).

Whatever "saints" might mean in this case, the relationship between the saints, Paul, and the Philippians was based on previously shared social networks between the saints and the Philippians across the northern Aegean. By networks I mean the webs of family, friends, neighbors, coworkers, and so on that could provide material, financial, or informational assistance to individuals or groups. The webs were formed through commonalities such as ethnicity, geography, kinship, work, and cult, all of which could overlap and interpenetrate one another.[39] Paul himself, along with his friends and coworkers, operated in such webs as they moved from place to place in the eastern Mediterranean. These networks were the means by which Paul's different acquaintances, friends, and constituencies could share in giving and receiving.

While others have rightly noted that there must have been a backstory to the saints and the Philippians and have offered some explanation, the layers of social relationships in which imperial slaves operated have rarely been considered.[40] A brief case study from the eastern side of Roman Asia offers an instructive example of why such interconnections are important for considering the situation of Paul's letter.

At Synnada, in Phrygia, there was a certain Hyacinthus who identified himself as a *tabularius*/ταβλάριος of the emperor Nero. On a plaque, he honored his partner (*contubernalis*), Arruntia Attice, and his son, Arruntius Iustus.[41] Given his position and the conspicuous lack of the free-status epithet (*lib. Aug.*), Hyacinthus was most likely a slave who worked at some type of bookkeeping for the famous, imperially-owned marble quarries at nearby Dokimeion. But the web of relationships in which Hyacinthus lived was extremely dense. Hyacinthus's partner, Arruntia Attice, was the daughter of a Lucius Arruntius, and was therefore a freeborn woman of the important L. Arruntii. Members of that family appear in western Asia at Sardis, Temenouthyrai, and Eumeneia, as well as in the Synnada area where, by the late first century BCE, some of the Arruntii had settled. There in Phrygia the family also forged connections to associations such as the "Roman settlers" and the "Romans doing business."[42]

In other words, because of his partner, Attice, Hyacinthus was connected to a prominent immigrant Italian family whose members stretched across the entire province. He was also connected to a family that had occupational ties to other Roman associations made up of Italian émigrés in the so-called Roman diaspora. The Arruntii families even had direct ties to the provincial financial administration of Asia in Ephesus itself.[43] Because imperial personnel in the provinces often married or partnered with locals, Hyacinthus's integration was not so uncommon.[44]

The example of Hyacinthus demonstrates that the connection between certain imperial slave "saints" and the Philippians was likely far more intricate than Paul's fleeting salutations might suggest. Their commonality of cult would also have been one of several relationships that bound the two groups together. Indeed, the shared devotion that the saints and the Philippians had toward the Jewish god would have been an outgrowth of their other, older, social formations such as family, kinship, friendship, business, and so on, whether in Ephesus, Roman Asia, or even Philippi. After all, family and occupational networks typically had some kind of cultic elements as well.[45]

The formation of such family and occupational networks was due in large part to the migratory flows of people in the northern Aegean. In the big picture, there was a greater degree of migration in the Roman Empire than previously assumed by both archaeologists and ancient historians, as recent work has indicated. And imperial slaves were a key part of the migratory patterns in the Roman world. They worked all over the Mediterranean,

FIG. 4 Fragment of a Latin honorary inscription for the emperor Tiberius, set up in Philippi by the imperial freedmen Cadmus, Atimetus, and Martialis (lines 5–6).

sometimes crisscrossing it while making acquaintances, friends, and families as they went.[46] Imperial slaves also moved within particular provinces on official duties, and the local population was, in certain cases, expected to help transport them to their next stop with wagons, pack animals, mules, or donkeys.[47]

At the same time, there was a circuit of imperial personnel on the Aegean rim. Evidence for imperial slaves and freedpersons has survived in each of Paul's major stops in the Aegean—at Thessalonica, Corinth, Ephesus, and Philippi (fig. 4).[48] The nature of official business suggests a functioning system of communication and travel between cities, with imperial personnel relying on networks of people, including people at Philippi, a strategic spot on the Via Egnatia.

The urban economy and labor market of Ephesus, a major entrepôt of the region, also pushed and pulled a diverse population from all over Asia and the Aegean basin. Interregional migration among neighboring provinces, from Macedonia to Asia, was particularly pronounced, since people often moved to a geographically contiguous market in labor or land.[49] The most recent studies of the Roman colony of Philippi underscore that from the earliest days, through family networks and economic exchange, the colonists and foreign residents there had connections with neighboring cities, specifically with northwestern Asia Minor.[50]

Given these realities on the ground, I see two probable scenarios. Certain members of the Philippian Christ group knew the "saints" because they were part of a kinship network that had been dispersed across the Aegean. Slavery often divided families, especially if imperial personnel were moved. Such division was the case for the family of a certain Marcus Ulpius Chariton who was born on the island of Sardinia, then worked at Tarsus, in Cilicia, only later to die in Rome as an imperial freedman at the age of thirty-five. When or where he was an imperial slave, his epitaph does not say. But he was commemorated in Rome on a bilingual Latin-Greek inscription by his sister Ulpia Charitine, and by his kinsman (*cognatus*) Publius Aelius Africanus. He, too, was an imperial freedman. The Africanus cognomen indicates that he served the emperor in one place, perhaps Africa, while his relative Chariton did the same in another place.[51] The family eventually reunited at a key hub.

Others families had similar stories.[52] There is even evidence from a fragmentary letter from Oxyrhynchus, Egypt, that in an effort to better themselves and their families, some might move away from their families and attempt to "become an imperial freedman," evidently by voluntarily running the gauntlet of the imperial slave system.[53] The expectation of the family would, in any case, be crucial for migration decisions, since often the long-term preservation of the household was at stake.[54]

In addition to a kinship network, common occupation or labor, including related industries, services, and trade networks, would also have ensured that the saints whom Paul mentions were closely associated with the Philippians.[55] Imperial slaves and freedpersons often engaged in "private" or independent commercial and industrial enterprises not connected with their service to the emperor. Textiles was one such industry.

A funerary altar from Miletus on the coast of Asia, for example, records in Greek that one of Nero's slaves—name lost—was an attendant or official for purple dyers, probably a purple-dyeing association (ἐπάνω τῶν πορφυρῶν).[56] Though the inscription is fragmentary and so not clear on whether the other purple dyers were imperial slaves as well, the group had geographical and occupational affiliates. Purple dyeing was practiced all along the Ionian and Carian coasts, while related groups who worked in cloth or weaving are also attested in numerous cities of Asia.[57] Trade in textiles circulated people and material throughout Asia, but also back and forth from the province's western littorals to numerous markets around the empire. The textile business stretched between interrelated cities and relied on an intricate network of people in related services (producers, merchants, shippers, etc.). Much of this activity passed through Ephesus.[58]

There is also evidence for a centuries-long trading network of purple textiles between Asia and Macedonia. Two Macedonian cities in particular, Philippi and Thessalonica, were in the textile circuit with Asia during the imperial period, and both places had purple-dyeing associations (πορφυροβάφοι).[59] This industry is the setting for how the author of canonical Acts conceived of the apostle Paul's first connection to Philippi. It has even been suggested that the purple-dealer Lydia of Thyatira, introduced in Acts 16:14, was a member of the *familia Caesaris*, and that the greetings in Philippians 4:22 were from Lydia and her associates.[60] The problem, of course, is that Paul never mentions a Lydia in any of his letters, nor does Acts specify that Lydia was an imperial slave or freedwoman. Only the broader historical reality is that a related industry—such as textiles—in a geographically contiguous market would facilitate opportunities for the saints and some of the Philippians to connect regularly.

The upshot of delineating these networks is that the saints' primary connection to Paul and the Philippians need not have been based on "conversion," especially not of the traditional type—an internal, spiritual, psychological turn. The activities of imperial slaves in the Aegean region were conducive to several kinds of interrelationships with the Philippians and would have produced various levels of interaction with Paul's patron deity. Though not the only explanations, to be sure, the shared networks I have described above are the two most likely social formations that account for the cultic connections between the saints and the Philippians.

To push this even further, if the "saints" and some of the Philippians were already connected in some way via social networks, then Paul's greetings from the "saints" probably has more to do with his connection to the Philippians than with a new missionary endeavor among Caesar's household. It was the Philippians, after all, who were having to send Epaphroditus to support a troublesome apostle.[61]

In the end, whatever happened to those "saints from Caesar's household" is lost to history. Despite some attempts to decipher in the late first- or early second-century letter *1 Clement* a connection between the "saints" and later Roman Christians, the "saints from Caesar's household" belong in the Aegean where Paul left them (see appendix 1). As far as the evidence goes, in all his other extant letters, Paul never speaks of them again. The historical impact of the "saints" is not in the *longue durée* of early Christianity, but in the immediate context of Paul's Aegean mission.

However, the ancient tradition that Paul wrote Philippians from, and was eventually martyred in, Rome ensured that the saints would live on in the collective memory of early Christianity. A century and a half after the historical Paul had ceased writing, a new story developed. Christians seized on the idea that Paul had made converts from among Caesar's household in Rome. The idea became a foundational narrative that not only shaped early Christianity through the second and third centuries but helped launch a tradition that would endure for millennia.

CHAPTER 2

PAUL, PETER, AND NERO'S SLAVES

Martyrdoms and Apostolic Acts

> And a great crowd came out to him from Caesar's house-
> hold and immediately believed in the word so that there
> was a great joy for Paul and those hearing.
>
> —*MARTYRDOM OF PAUL*

How and where Paul died is a bit of a mystery. From the time that Paul penned his letter to the Philippians the phrase "Caesar's household" has carried the potential to be interpreted in a Roman setting with Paul on the cusp of death (Phil 1:20–26; 2:17). Combined with this, the account in canonical Acts tells how Paul had appealed to Caesar and had remained in Rome for two years awaiting his trial, while 2 Timothy, ostensibly written by Paul, also claimed that the apostle was in Rome "being poured out like a libation" (2 Tim 1:17; 4:6). When taken together, these texts appear to have Paul's story end in Rome. Despite these canonical hints, however, it seems that no one knew—or no one had articulated, at least—exactly what happened at the end of the apostle Paul's life. The text of *1 Clement*, which attests to Roman Christians at the end of the first and the beginning of the second century CE commemorating Paul and Peter's deaths as "noble examples" of martyrdom, does not actually report when or where either apostle had died.[1] Even Irenaeus of Lyons, who was writing around 180 CE and was quite intent on establishing apostolic succession in Rome, does not mention that the apostle Paul actually died in Rome either. In fact, the entire early Christian literature to the middle or even late second century CE knows nothing about Paul's martyrdom in Rome.[2]

But as the apostles faded farther into the past and Christians in the 130s began shedding ties to an original Judean homeland, to Jerusalem the apostolic hub, and to Israel and its traditions, Christians were facing a problem. There was a growing need to place the "heroic 'founders' of the movement" in a new homeland.[3] So Christian communities did what any similar group in the Roman Empire would have done to "counteract the danger of rupture, the possibility of a fatal disconnect between a community and its past, the loss of memory that spells unraveling of identity in the present and future."[4] Christians constructed a new past about Paul and Peter's martyrdom in the imperial capital—Rome.

The shift to Rome was a multifactorial process. At the broadest level, Rome was the hegemonic center. It carried an ideological weight that served current interests in manufacturing political capital or cultural cachet, even if it lacked the apostolic heritage of cities like Jerusalem, Antioch, Corinth, and Ephesus.[5] The development of apostolic martyrdom stories attempted to establish a Christian cultural history through spatial connections with Rome and its martyred apostles. The collective process, which construed the past so that present communities could sustain themselves, involved mythmaking, historiography, and ritual commemoration. The process also involved stories (*memoria*) that were tied to the Roman urban landscape. While Christians crafted the martyrdom stories, they built cult sites to commemorate where in Rome the apostles Paul and Peter had died.[6] By the end of the second century, Christian tradition had produced the details and had securely fixed Paul and Peter's martyrdoms in Rome.

Yet the stories about Paul and Peter's martyrdoms in Rome—stories that were vital for the self-conception of Christians in antiquity, not to mention claims to apostolic succession—were intimately tied to Christians in Caesar's household. Indeed, the renowned martyrdoms of Paul and Peter, known from the *Martyrdom of Paul* and *Acts of Peter*, revolved around stories about the apostles making disciples of Nero's slaves. Both texts, through their use of imperial slaves, created a Christian cultural history and geography in Rome.

The stories about Caesar's household and the apostle Paul were particularly powerful especially since a ready story line was already offered by the apostle Paul himself (Phil 4:22). Accordingly, the *Martyrdom of Paul* reworked "Caesar's household" from Philippians 4:22 as etiological source material to establish Paul's Roman martyrdom. Certain topographical features of Rome mentioned in the *Martyrdom of Paul* were then associated with Caesar's household and bolstered the cultic veneration of Paul's martyrdom in Rome. Beyond that, it was the imperial slave characters in the martyrdom story who ultimately opened up the imperial palace to the Christian geographic imagination. By focusing on Christian imperial slaves the *Martyrdom of Paul* contested symbolically for Christian cultural space in the Roman Empire. Like the portrait of Patroclus captured in the *Miroir Historial*, the image of Christians in Caesar's household would continue to shape Christians' worldview throughout late antiquity and into the medieval period.

Along the way, the story of Paul and Caesar's household was also inter-twined with apostolic narratives that glorified the apostle Peter. The *Acts of Peter* build on the story of Paul and Caesar's household to describe how *both* Paul and Peter had made followers from Nero's slaves. The two refer-ences to Christians in Caesar's household within the same apostolic acts provided a way to tie together the martyrdom stories of Paul and Peter in Rome under Nero, harmonizing disparate and competing traditions about the two famous apostles. The imperial household, as a locus of creativity, was essential for creating Paul and Peter's apostolic traditions in Rome and for fashioning a Christian cultural history that both apostles were martyred under Nero in Rome. These budding traditions about Christians in the imperial household then inspired later apostolic narratives as well as distinct artistic representations in late antiquity. Let us begin with the story of Paul's death.

Stories of Paul and Caesar's Household

The *Martyrdom of Paul* provided a foundational story upon which early Chris-tians would build a larger narrative of their past in service of their present and future. Some of the most memorable details about the apostle to the gentiles—details that would forever be associated with Paul—were spelled out in this text. The story makes it crystal clear that Paul was martyred in Rome, that he died specifically by beheading (τραχηλοκοπηθῆναι), that upon decapitation milk spurted from his headless body, and that his execution was directly ordered by the emperor Nero, with whom Paul had met face-to-face.

But what is often overlooked is that within the text all of these events occurred for a specific reason—Paul's connection to Caesar's household. The text opens by recounting how Paul arrived in Rome, rented a "store-house" (ὅρριον; Lat. *horreum*) outside the city, and became famous for his teaching. His fame spread throughout Rome so that "a great crowd (πλῆθος πολύ) from Caesar's household" came out to him and immedi-ately believed in the "Word." Among them was Patroclus, a cupbearer of the emperor Nero. Once while seated in a high window listening to Paul preach, Patroclus nods off and falls to his death. This was quickly reported to Nero by his domestic slaves (οἰκέται) who were also there. But Paul raised Patroclus from the dead and sent him away with "the others from Caesar's household." Meanwhile, Nero learns of Patroclus's death and is

grieved. But after he returns from the bath he is informed by his servants
that Patroclus is not dead. He is alive. Perplexed, Nero orders Patroclus
to come to him, and there before his imperial master Patroclus confesses
Christ as king of the whole world and the ages. Enraged, the emperor then
issues an edict that hunts down and kills those found to be Christians. Paul
is among those arrested. And so it is that Patroclus, an imperial slave from
Caesar's household, sets off the main events that lead to Paul's martyrdom.

The Patroclus scene drives the plot of the story. If that were not
enough, the story calls attention to the imperial household three other
times in the opening. A "great crowd from Caesar's household" comes
out to hear Paul; Nero's domestic slaves (οἰκέται) were also at the *horreum*
and reported Patroclus's death to Nero; and "the others from Caesar's
household" who were at the *horreum* took the restored Patroclus back to
the palace (*Mart. Paul* 1). The repetition emphasizes the importance of
Caesar's household.

But the *Martyrdom of Paul* was not working from a tabula rasa. The
Caesar's household underscored in the text has been recycled. The phrase
"from Caesar's household" (ἐκ τῆς Καίσαρος οἰκίας), which the *Martyrdom of
Paul* repeats several times, was extracted verbatim from Paul's own words
in Philippians 4:22. The phrase from Paul's letter is reused to explain not
only how Paul was martyred in the imperial capital but also how, in the
first place, the apostle would have had direct access to the emperor himself.
By continually weaving the phrase that originated from the apostle's stylus
into a live narrative about the apostle's death, the author(s) had a powerful
tool to rework their community's past.

Ancient Rome's cultic and topographical environment was also essential to this reworking. The *Martyrdom of Paul* presupposed a context in
which prayer and/or cultic veneration at Paul's tomb in Rome was already
established. Before Paul is beheaded he instructs his guards, "Go quickly
[at dawn] to my tomb and you will find two men praying—Titus and Luke"
(*Mart. Paul* 5). The word used for tomb (τάφος) is the equivalent of the
Latin *sepulchrum*. It indicates a definable burial space for Paul in Rome's
urban topography, rather than just a potter's field.

Apparently by the early third century, at least, a commemorative
monument had been built for Paul within easy reach of the Roman Christians. During this same period, according to the fourth-century church
historian Eusebius, the Roman presbyter Gaius, a contemporary of Zephyrinus, boasted about the "trophies of the apostles Peter and Paul," telling
his opponent Proculus to "go to the Vatican or the Ostian Way" to find
the "trophies (τρόπαιον) of those who founded this church."[7] The latter
"trophy" appears to have been a monumental tomb of Paul that sat within

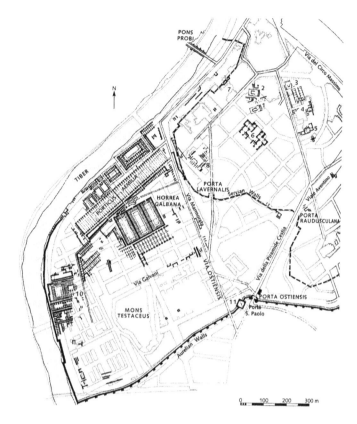

MAP 2 Map of southern Rome / Aventine Hill outside the Servian Walls, showing the *horrea* district and Porta Ostiensis (Ostian Way).

the large Roman burial grounds on the Ostian road (the present-day Via Ostiense), just south of the ancient city. The physical memorial—whatever it was—allowed enhanced stories about Paul's martyrdom to develop, and the martyrdom traditions, in turn, worked to buttress the practice of tomb veneration.[8]

By comparison, the *Martyrdom of Paul* opens with Paul in a *horreum*. The detail about a *horreum* provided an additional topographic link to Rome, of course. But more than that, the *horreum* also becomes part of the cultic landscape of Paul's martyrdom in Rome because of Caesar's household. On the ground, the *horrea* of ancient Rome were especially noticeable south of the city, near Rome's great emporium on the east bank of the Tiber (map 2).[9] This is the location of the critical Horrea Galbana, for instance. This is also the area, outside of Rome's Servian Walls, that the author(s) of the text most likely had in mind when they stated that Paul rented a *horreum* "outside Rome" (ἔξω Ῥώμης). The district south of the city with its several *horrea* stretched east from the southern tip of the Aventine Hill toward Porta Ostiensis (present-day Porta San Paolo), less than a thousand meters away. And it is at Porta Ostiensis that the "Ostian Way" began, the road on which, according to Gaius, Paul's "trophy" was located.

The connection between the cultic environment surrounding Paul's martyrdom and the *horreum* south of Rome is made even stronger because imperial slaves were regulars in Rome's *horrea*. The imperially owned *horrea*, such as the Horrea Galbana, were in fact managed by imperial slaves and freedmen who were conveniently called *horrearii*. An inscription from the Hadrianic period records that two imperial slaves, Major and Diadumenus, along with Crescens, an imperial freedman, were all *horrearii* who donated a plaque for the god Silvanus. Major, Diadumenus, and Crescens are also recorded in another inscription from Rome. In 128 CE, they donated a much larger plaque in honor of Hercules and the Sacred Imperial House, but they did so in collaboration with a particular division of workers (*cohors II*) and laborers (*operari*) of the Horrea Galbana.[10] These groups of workers and laborers appear to be imperial slaves who were also housed in one of three large colonnaded courtyards of the *horrea*, which were equipped with rooms for accommodation on each side (fig. 5).

Imperial slave managers then oversaw the cohorts who worked at the *horrea*. In other cases, the jobs that imperial slaves and freedpersons did around the *horrea* are known. They were wool-cape makers (*sagarius*) or bookkeepers for the marble (*tabularius a marmoribus*).[11] And the plaques dedicated by imperial slaves and freedmen, such as those of Major and Diadumenus, would originally have been fastened to the *horrea* themselves, making the connection between the building and its personnel quite visible.

The author(s) of the *Martyrdom of Paul*, if not also the audience, must have understood that the *horrea* were exactly where members of the emperor's household could be found in Rome. The allusion to the *horreum* in the text acted as an initial authenticating feature that affixed the new memory of Paul and "Caesar's household" to a material space in Rome that was real, imaginary, and symbolic.[12] The cumulative effect is that the *horreum* was a topographical feature that generated a "spatial trail" by which to remember the story's primary actors—Nero's slaves—and further animated the cultic landscape surrounding the veneration of Paul as a martyr.[13]

If Rome's *horrea* were the backdrop for "Caesar's household" in the *Martyrdom of Paul*, then the palace on Rome's Palatine Hill (παλάτιον) was center stage. The palace is where the driving action of the plot unfolds. It is in this imperial space that Patroclus confesses Christ; where other of Nero's ministers and bodyguards declare that they, too, are "soldiers of

FIG. 5 The Horrea Epagathiana, from ancient Rome's port city, Ostia Antica, showing a high window.

that eternal king"; where Paul is twice summoned in chains (δεδεμένος) and preaches to the emperor Nero; where the Romans clamored on behalf of the persecuted Christians, "Enough is enough, Caesar, for these people are ours. You are destroying the power of the Romans" (*Mart. Paul* 3); and finally, where Paul reappears to Nero "when many philosophers and leaders, both rich and distinguished, were standing with Caesar" (*Mart. Paul* 6).

As the centerpiece in Rome's imperial topography the palace again underscored the role of Caesar's household in Paul's martyrdom story. More than anyone else, *the* decisive character who precipitated the action was Caesar's slave boy Patroclus. He was the reason for Paul's martyrdom in Rome. It was Patroclus's death, resurrection (ἀνέστη), and confession of Christ before the supreme ruler Nero inside the palace itself that paved the way for Paul's own confession before Nero inside the palace, Paul's death, and later Paul's resurrection (ἐγερθῆναι). The Patroclus sequence is integral to the whole martyrdom story. It was most likely, as Glenn Snyder has suggested, an oral and/or written source included in the original, written form of the martyrdom, which was separable from the larger *Acts of Paul* (ca. 170–80 CE).[14]

To make Paul's martyrdom story work the author(s) rescripted the scene from Acts 20:7–12 when a certain Eutychus fell from a window and died while listening to Paul preach.[15] The author(s) must have had no materials besides Acts 20:7–12 to help them find a cause for Paul's imprisonment, trial, and execution. The author(s) probably did not know anything else but the claim of the Roman church (e.g., the third-century presbyter Gaius) that Rome was the place where the great apostle was martyred.[16]

The rescripted Eutychus story from Acts 20 is a crucial pretext for launching the Patroclus sequence, to be sure. Yet it was still secondary to the reuse of "Caesar's household" from Philippians 4:22. This pericope from the apostle himself was the *tableau vivant* from which Patroclus emerged. It was the primary material from which the author(s) could create a cause for Paul's imprisonment, trial, and execution in Rome specifically. And even at the conclusion of the story, after Paul has been martyred, has reappeared before Nero, and just before the executioners visit Paul's tomb, the story once again recalls Patroclus. Nero, terrified from his encounter with the resurrected Paul, orders that "all the [Christian] prisoners be set free, including Patroclus" (*Mart. Paul* 6).

From beginning to end, therefore, a member of "Caesar's household" frames Paul's martyrdom in Rome. And because the *Martyrdom of Paul*, as Snyder has argued, would certainly have been used—or was even composed—specifically for the commemoration of Paul's feast day, and was also likely used for catechetical instruction and baptismal practices in its penultimate form, the Patroclus sequence is all the more important. The commemorative, catechetical, and ritual text featured in its earliest extant form, and as an integral part of Paul's martyrdom story, an imperial slave.[17]

Opening Christian Cultural Space

As decisive as "Caesar's household" and the Patroclus character in the *Martyrdom of Paul* was for positioning a founding apostle's martyrdom in Rome, and for justifying and bolstering Paul's apostolic cult there, the idea of Christian imperial slaves did something else as well. The text also used imperial slaves from Caesar's household to contest for and claim cultural space in the Roman Empire. The focus on Caesar's household worked to resist the spatialities and the power of contemporary society. By homing in on members of Caesar's household and the palace the martyrdom narrative attempted to break domestic and political boundaries and to institute a new site for power.[18] The "great crowd" from Caesar's household that believed in the Word took the risen Patroclus back to the imperial palace—to the symbolic heart of Roman hegemony. An enslaved cupbearer like Patroclus was regularly close to the emperor, just as several of the domestic slaves in the story would have been. Within the story world, therefore, Patroclus's position provided the necessary space for him to make a direct challenge to the emperor's authority by confessing Christ as "king of the whole world" (*Mart. Paul* 2).[19]

In placing a Christian imperial slave in the palace space, the *Martyrdom of Paul* opened the imperial palace henceforth as a "spatial imaginary" and a "coordinate" in the Christian geographic imagination. As a new site, the imperial palace became a symbolic meeting space for Christian audiences to negotiate power and meaning in their social and geographic landscape. More than that, the imperial palace was also the symbolic platform upon which the text could claim a global footprint for Christians.[20] Once in the palace Nero asks Paul why he secretly entered into the Roman Empire (εἰς τὴν Ῥωμαίων ἡγεμονίαν) and enlisted soldiers (στρατολογεῖν) from his kingdom. Paul responds, "We levy soldiers not only from your kingdom but also from the entire world" (ἐκ τῆς οἰκουμένης ὅλης; *Mart. Paul* 3). The claim to universality is a common one in early Christian writings, but it is not a "self-deluding assumption of numerical superiority," as Judith Lieu says. "In an imagined geography the world belongs to the Christians."[21]

Christians in the household (οἰκία) of Caesar were emblematic of Christians throughout the world (οἰκουμένη). Just as an army that conquers the capital of its enemy also commands de facto all the enemy territory, so here "enlisting soldiers" in the imperial capital—among Caesar's household no less—attempted to reorder, in a symbolic sense, the place of Christians in the empire's territory.[22] Apart from the military metaphors for Christian expansion—Paul tells Nero "we serve in an army" (στρατεύειν)—and the eschatological warnings—Paul tells Nero that "fire is coming upon the whole Roman world" (οἰκουμένη; *Mart. Paul* 4)—the text participates in an imperialist discourse in order to challenge the power of the emperor. To claim Patroclus and other members of Caesar's household as Christians was to assert that Christians had infiltrated the emperor's network and replaced him with Christ as supreme king. This discourse allows the text to argue that Christians are now everywhere in the world, and that in the earliest days of their movement they had overtaken a commanding symbolic space—the hegemonic center. Consequently, the martyrdom story contends, Christians should not—and cannot—be marginalized in the world.[23]

As the *Martyrdom of Paul* made claims on cultural space through its emphasis on Caesar's household and the palace, it simultaneously moved the audience back and forth through time. On the one hand, the story ensured that members of the imperial house would be remembered in a landmark event of the community's cultural history.[24] The *Martyrdom of Paul* created a tradition that Christians had been in Caesar's household in Rome from the very beginning. On the other hand, despite the story's legendary and fantastical nature, there probably were some imperial slaves or freedpersons in Rome who were crossing paths with, or participating in, Christian groups during this period. As the text construed the past, modulating Philippians 4:22 and Paul's death for its current purposes, it allowed audience(s) to reconstitute present possibilities of Christians serving in Caesar's household. The present milieu actually influenced the imagination as it worked to reproduce the past. The construal of the past meant that in late second-century Rome the idea of Christians serving the emperors would now have a certain historical, even apostolic, pedigree.

In sum, the spatial and temporal aspects of Caesar's household, weaving through one another, were integral to sustaining the story of Paul's martyrdom in Rome. The reading, hearing, or ritualizing of Paul's martyrdom story, in turn, transformed Caesar's household into a veritable trademark of Christian cultural history and remade the imperial palace into a toponym in Christian geography. The tradition of Paul and "Caesar's household" then allowed future communities—even those giving precedence to another apostle—to reconstitute themselves in the empire's cultural landscape.[25]

Stories of Peter and Caesar's Household

While the use of "Caesar's household" was crucial for establishing Paul's apostolic tradition in Rome, Paul was not the only apostle whom early Christians linked with Rome's imperial slaves. For some Christians, their cultural history and apostolic pedigree were generated by memories about Peter and the imperial household in Rome. In the *Acts of Peter* the imperial household also frames Peter's martyrdom in Rome under Nero. But these acts do so paradoxically by first working with memories about Paul and Caesar's household in Rome. In the opening scene of the *Acts of Peter*, Paul prepares to depart for Spain when

> a great crowd of women knelt down and fervently entreated the blessed Paul, and they kissed his feet and escorted him to the harbor (*in portum*), and with them Dionysius and Balbus from Asia, who were Roman knights (*equites Romani*) and illustrious men (*splendidi viri*). And a senator named Demetrius kept close to Paul on his right hand and said, "Paul, I could wish to leave the city, if I were not a magistrate, so as not to leave you." And so said some from Caesar's household (*de domo Caesaris*), Cleobius and Iphitus and Lysimachus and Aristaeus and two matrons, Berenice and Philostrate, with the presbyter Narcissus, after they had conducted him to the harbor. (*Acts Pet.* 3)[26]

After this departure scene, the narrative immediately shifts to Peter, who arrives in Rome and battles the hapless magician Simon Magus in scenes reminiscent of *Harry Potter*. At the end of the acts comes Peter's famous martyrdom in which he is crucified upside down, under the authority of the urban prefect Agrippa. Peter then appears to his patron and esteemed convert the senator Marcellus, who relates the vision of the apostle to the other brethren. Marcellus and the brethren strengthened one another "until the coming of Paul to Rome," the text reads. With that, the story ends, it would seem.

Oddly, though, the text jumps to Nero who "later discovered" that Peter had died. Nero censured the prefect Agrippa because Nero had wanted to give Peter a much crueler death. For Peter, the text relates, "had made disciples of some of his [Nero's] 'servants' (lit. 'hands'; πρὸς χεῖρα αὐτοῦ/*ad manum*) and caused them to leave him" (*Acts Pet.* 41). Like Paul in the *Martyrdom of Paul*, the apostle Peter had apparently also made converts among Nero's slaves.

Within the same apostolic acts there were two memories about the imperial household, each concerned with establishing Christian history in Rome: one for Paul and one for Peter. But this is strange. Typically, apostolic acts focus on only one apostle, and in a narrative about Peter the initial Pauline material seems quite out of place. Even more bizarre is the mention of Peter and Nero's servants when the plotline had reached its end with Peter's death. A closer look at the textual forms of the *Acts of Peter* indicates a deliberate, editorial focus on Caesar's household.

The earliest surviving Greek witnesses of the *Acts of Peter* do not include the opening scene with Paul leaving Rome en route to the harbor with members of Caesar's household.[27] That scene is preserved only in the later *Actus Vercellenses* and is the text from which I quote at the opening of this section. Preserved in the sixth- or seventh-century Vercelli codex, the *Actus Vercellenses* are considered to be an "independent new version" of the *Acts of Peter* that came into existence in the late fourth century when the text was translated from Greek into Latin in North Africa or Spain.[28] The few parts of the *Acts of Peter* story that reference Paul—including the opening with Caesar's household—are also the most suspect in the *Actus Vercellenses*. The references are crowded into the first three chapters of the work, are not well integrated into the text, and cause a number of discontinuities. Added to this are stylistic considerations. The Latin in the opening differs from the Latin in other chapters. All this suggests that the opening scene with Paul and Caesar's household was a later interpolation into a Greek *Acts of Peter*, even as late as the mid-third century.[29]

However, the stylistic considerations of the *Actus Vercellenses* indicate that the awkward ending about Peter and Nero's servants was a later addition as well. The ending bears more relation to Paul than to Peter. The appearance of Nero, Christine Thomas observes, also destroys the temporal framework of the *Actus Vercellenses*, which places Peter in Rome only twelve years after Christ's death, thus making Peter's martyrdom under Nero (54–68 CE) impossible. Not to mention, nowhere else in the *Actus Vercellenses* is Nero the perpetrator of Peter's death. The conversions in the imperial household play the same role in the *Actus Vercellenses* as they do in the *Martyrdom of Paul*, Thomas further notes. The conversion of imperial slaves angers Nero, becomes the indirect cause of the first persecution of Christians, and frames an apostle's martyrdom account. Despite the fact that inserting Nero into the story ruptures the chronology, it seems that this additional ending in the *Actus Vercellenses* was trying to set the ecclesiastical record straight by ousting the lesser-known Agrippa in favor of the emperor Nero.[30]

At the same time, the additional reference to Peter and Nero's slaves associated the story of Peter's martyrdom with Paul's martyrdom. The *Actus Vercellenses* formulated Paul's return to Rome from Spain a year later, providing Peter ample narrative space to do his work in Rome. The story gives every impression that those clinging to Paul as he departed—namely, some from Caesar's household—would still be there when he returned. The *Actus Vercellenses* then gesture toward Paul's martyrdom at the hands of Nero, which in the story world, would occur in the following year. As Paul prepares to depart a sound from heaven breaks in to say: "Paul the servant of God is chosen for this service for the time of this life, but at the hands of Nero, that godless and wicked man, he shall be perfected before your eyes" (*Acts Pet.* 1).[31]

The double reference to Paul and Peter making Christians among the emperor's household changed the mood of the codex itself. In the Vercelli codex, the *Actus Vercellenses* follow the so-called Pseudo-Clementine *Recognitions*. Composed in Syria, this fourth-century novel, likely based on a lost Greek original from the first decades of the third century, relates the adventures of one Clement of Rome—later called Pope Clement I—with the apostle Peter.[32] The *Recognitions* is also anti-Paul in several respects, not least of which is the role of Clement as Peter's protégé. In the first century, the apostle Paul had stated that a Clement was *his* coworker (Phil 4:3).[33] At the level of the codex the allusions to the imperial household in the *Actus Vercellenses* could temper the anti-Pauline attitude of the preceding *Recognitions*. For the readers of this codex the two apostles would now "share" the glory of disciple making in Nero's household.

So by concentrating on imperial slaves at the beginning with Paul and at the end with Peter, the redactor(s) could tie together stories of Peter and Paul and fashion the tradition that Christianity's two greatest apostles were both martyred under Nero in Rome. Overall, the goal of the editorial activity surrounding Nero's slaves was to create a martyrdom harmony between Peter and Paul, counterbalancing memories of apostolic conflict that began in the first century and continued well after in the competing traditions.[34]

And yet considering how the *Actus Vercellenses* lionize Peter and commemorate his martyrdom, the reference to Paul and Caesar's household is all the more striking. Among other things the reference shows just how attached Paul and Caesar's household had become in Christian tradition by the third century. While the relationships between the *Acts of Peter* and the *Acts of Paul* may continue to be debated, the opening portions of the *Actus Vercellenses*, at least, were certainly reimagining the story of Paul and Caesar's household in Rome that is found in the *Martyrdom of Paul*.[35] By adopting and adapting the story of Paul and Caesar's household, the *Actus Vercellenses* created analogous traditions about Peter in Rome as well as a parallel cultural history in the apostolic narratives that followed.

Caesar's Household in Christian Apostolic Narratives and Art

In the following centuries references to Christians in Caesar's household would continue to appear in commemorative narratives about the apostles Paul and Peter in Rome. For its part, the tradition about Peter and the palace staff remains in certain Petrine trajectories. The sixth- or seventh-century Syriac text called the *History of Shimeon Kepha Chief of the Apostles* relates that Shimeon Kepha (i.e., Peter) "multiplied the teaching in the region of Rome, and many from the household of Caesar also believed in the teaching of our Lord" (*Shimeon Kepha* 29). This text shows a dependence on the Pseudo-Clementine literature (e.g., the *Recognitions*) and on the lost Syrian translation of the *Acts of Peter*.[36] For the audience of this text it was Peter who would be remembered as the sole apostle to Caesar's household in Rome.

On balance, however, the Petrine connection to Rome's imperial household never took root in Christian commemorative narrative as strongly as the Pauline connections did. The author of the *History of Shimeon Kepha Chief of the Apostles*, for instance, also seems to have produced a text called the *History of the Holy Apostle My Lord Paul*. The story picks up just after Peter's martyrdom in Rome. It was then that Paul returned from Spain to Rome and made disciples in the city, "including a great multitude from the household of Caesar" (*My Lord Paul* 9).[37] Here again, this text associates Caesar's household primarily with Paul's martyrdom in Rome under Nero. Likewise, Pseudo-Linus's parallel accounts of the martyrdoms of the apostles Peter and Paul in Rome, which date from the late fourth to the fifth or sixth century, respectively, link only Paul to Caesar's household, not Peter.[38]

The tradition about Paul and Caesar's household is even more clear-cut in Pseudo-Marcellus's *Passion of the Holy Apostles Peter and Paul*. Preserved as two related works in Greek and Latin from the fifth or sixth century, the story has Peter and Paul working in Rome together and collegially, no less. Both texts were produced in Rome with an emphasis on apostolic harmony, but Peter is ultimately presented as superior to Paul.[39] Nonetheless, as both of Rome's founding apostles overtake the city with preaching so successful that it ultimately brings them before Nero, the divergent traditions are evident. The text relates that Peter's preaching converts innumerable people, including specifically the empress Livia, Nero's wife, and Agrippina, the wife of the prefect Agrippa. Paul's preaching, by contrast, makes converts specifically from the military (*militia*) and from the palace (*palatium*), so that even the royal chamberlain (*ex cubiculo regis*) comes to Paul (*Passion* 10). This Pauline tradition, which harkens back to Patroclus in the *Martyrdom of Paul* and to the earliest interpretations of "Caesar's household" in Philippians 4:22, seems to have been widely transmitted through the Pseudo-Marcellus line. The text was translated into Coptic, Arabic, Old Irish, Armenian, Georgian, and Old Slavonic, propagating the association between Paul and Caesar's household.[40] So whether identified with Peter in Rome, or more commonly with Paul, the tradition about Christians in Caesar's household would have a persistent place in Christian narratives throughout late antiquity.

At the same time that such apostolic acts were being produced in late antiquity, there was also a proliferation of images portraying Peter and Paul together, sometimes embracing one another.[41] The media were diverse, but the most striking in this artistic repertoire are those images that depict Peter and Paul standing together specifically before Nero. The motif seems to have been especially popular in the Western Empire, with two prominent examples: on the twelfth-century window panels known as the "Life of St. Paul" at the Gothic Chartres Cathedral in France, and on the twelfth-century mosaics at the Cathedral of the Nativity of the Most Holy Mother of God in Monreale, Sicily. The motif depends on the tradition that both apostles had converted the emperors' slaves, were ushered before the emperor to account for it, and were then martyred together under Nero.

In the end, both the *Martyrdom of Paul* and the *Acts of Peter* used and created stories about Christians in the imperial household to commemorate Paul's and Peter's martyrdoms in Rome. By doing so, both texts constructed a Christian cultural history and a geography centered in the imperial capital. In this sense, the focus on Christians in the imperial household was apologetic; it was meant to make claims about Christians' past and place as a people in the world. And over time the telling and retelling of these apostolic narratives that highlighted the imperial household would exalt the origins of Christianity as one of world-historical importance. More immediately, though, at the beginning of the third century, the link between Caesar's household and Paul's apostolic heritage in Rome was appropriated in new apologetic projects.

CHAPTER 3

ROME'S IMPERIAL HOUSEHOLD IN

CHRISTIAN POLEMIC AND APOLOGETIC

Caesar is more ours than yours.

—TERTULLIAN

The story of Paul's martyrdom in Rome, tied as it was to Caesar's household, was in many ways ground zero. It signaled a new phase in Christian culture-making. The foundational origin story of Paul's martyrdom would also help to define relations with inside and outside groups throughout the third century.[1] As Christian writers at the outset of the third century took up the stylus to fight with one another and with the "nations," they began to call up individual Christians in Rome's imperial household.[2] They did so for various reasons. In a polemical treatise called the *Refutation of All Heresies*, one writer commonly known as "Hippolytus of Rome" recounts a story about a certain Carpophorus, a "faithful man from Caesar's household," and his domestic slave Callistus—later known in Christian annals as Pope Calixtus I. Meanwhile, Hippolytus's younger contemporary Tertullian of Carthage, in his apology to the proconsul Scapula, calls attention to one Proculus Torpacion. Tertullian says this man was a Christian, that he had served the emperors Severus and Caracalla "in the palace," and that the emperors had known that Proculus was a Christian.

Although previous investigations have accepted these references as prima facie evidence for Christians in the imperial household during the Severan period, the references are much more rhetorical than usually recognized. Both references to individuals in the imperial household appear at pivotal moments in the respective projects, and only by disentangling the rhetoric is it possible to recover some of the historical situation.

To advance their own theological and social viewpoints, Hippolytus and Tertullian were in reality carefully crafting images about those individuals from the imperial household. It was the persona of those individuals, and what those individuals were made to represent to their respective audiences, that allowed the two authors to police their communities against perceived threats. To ostracize his polemical opponent Callistus as a heretic and carve out his own place within the community, Hippolytus produces a slave satire about Callistus that parallels the slave satires of Lucian of Samosata. Tertullian, on the other hand, puts Torpacion on display as a prototypical Christian in order to forestall violence and plead for tolerance toward his North African community. The references to Christians in Rome's imperial household can thus vary. The variability and flexibility of such references reflect the discrete rhetorical purposes of each author, his relationship to the individual referenced, and the manifold connection between the Christian communities and the individuals from the imperial household.

However, behind the presentation of these individuals there was an older story. When Hippolytus and Tertullian referenced people from "Caesar's household" and "the palace" respectively, they drew on a tradition about Paul and Caesar's household in Rome that is manifest in the *Martyrdom of Paul*. Each author tapped into the tradition to different depths and to different ends. Yet both authors demonstrate to modern readers how useful—and potent—the stories about Paul and Caesar's household were during this period. And nowhere was the story more useful than in a Roman setting amid a bitter dispute over claims to apostolic authority.

Caesar's Household and a Local Dispute in Rome

In the waning years of the Severan dynasty (ca. 218–35 CE) the author conventionally known as Hippolytus of Rome was writing a ten-volume polemical treatise that attempted to refute every form of what he deemed to be heresy.[3] The ninth book, an "account and refutation of those heresies that have sprung up in our day," introduces the author's main opponent—a certain heretic named Callistus (*Haer.* 9.1.1). According to the author, Callistus was a domestic slave (οἰκέτης) of a certain Carpophorus, "a faithful man from Caesar's household" (ἀνδρὸς πιστοῦ ὄντος ἐκ τῆς Καίσαρος οἰκίας). What follows is an exhaustive story about Callistus, which purportedly occurred during the reign of the emperor Commodus (180–92 CE).

The story goes like this. One day Carpophorus entrusted his slave Callistus with no small sum of money (χρῆμα), ordering him to bring in a profit (κέρδος) through the banking business (πραγματείας τραπεζιτικῆς). So Callistus tried his hand at a bank—literally, a money table (τράπεζαν)—at Rome's public pool (Piscina Publica). Under the pretext of investing with Carpophorus, certain Christians ("widows and brothers") entrusted Callistus with their money. Straightaway Callistus swindled them (ἐξαφανίζειν) out of it, but then lost all their money. Knowing he was in for it with his master, Carpophorus, who was told about the incident, Callistus fled (φυγή) the city, boarded a ship at Portus, and prepared to sail for wherever the vessel was headed. Carpophorus was again, somehow, informed of this. He hurried to Portus and was ferried over to Callistus's ship, but before he reached it Callistus jumped into the harbor trying to drown himself. The sailors leaped into boats and fished him out. Callistus was then handed over to his master, taken to Rome, and put to work on a grinding mill (*pistrinum*).

He suffered there for a time until one day some of the brothers came to Carpophorus and begged him to release the fugitive (δραπέτης). Callistus, they cried, had indicated that he had their money laid away in credit, and they also thought they were depositing their money with Carpophorus when they entrusted it to Callistus. Carpophorus was persuaded and let Callistus out. Callistus, though, having nothing to give them, unable to flee this time, and still suicidal, decided to go to a Jewish synagogue on the Sabbath, where he tried to pick a fight. The Jews obliged. They then dragged him before the urban prefect (ἔπαρχον τῆς πόλεως) Fuscianus. They said Callistus had disturbed them while "saying he's a Christian" (φάσκων εἶναι Χριστιανός). Yet again, Carpophorus was told of the events. He sped to the bema and pleaded with Fuscianus not to believe Callistus, declaring, "He is not a Christian (οὐ γάρ ἐστι Χριστιανός). He's just looking to die because he made away with a lot of my money (χρήματα πολλά)." The Jews thought this was all a ruse to liberate Callistus, so they clamored against Carpophorus before Fuscianus. He was persuaded, had Callistus whipped, then sent him to work the Sardinian mines.

The story continues. Next Hippolytus relates that after Callistus was in Sardinia for a while a concubine (παλλακή) of the emperor Commodus named Marcia, who was a god-lover (φιλόθεος) and desired to do a good deed, summoned the "blessed Victor," a bishop (ἐπίσκοπος) of the church at that time. She asked Victor what martyrs (μάρτυρες) were in Sardinia. Victor gave Marcia all the names, but did not give her Callistus's name because Victor knew what he had done. Marcia requested and received from Commodus a letter of release (ἀπολύσιμος ἐπιστολή), which she gave to one Hyacinth, who was an elderly eunuch (σπάδος ὄντος πρεσβύτερος). After receiving the letter Hyacinth sailed to Sardinia and handed over the letter to the governor of the territory, who released the martyrs, but not

Callistus. Callistus then fell on his knees in tears and begged (ἱκετεύειν) that he also be released. Overcome by Callistus's importunity Hyacinth requested that the governor release Callistus as well, saying that he (Hyacinth) had raised (θρέψας) Marcia, and he guaranteed no risk would come to the governor. The governor was persuaded and released Callistus. When Callistus showed up again in Rome Victor was quite disturbed (πάνυ ἤχθετο) at what had happened. Since he was good-hearted (εὔσπλαγχνος) he did nothing. But because people kept reproaching Callistus, and Carpophorus was still angry about the whole affair, Victor sent Callistus to Antium, allotting him a monthly allowance of food. Finally, when Victor died, his successor, Zephyrinus, recalled Callistus and appointed him "over the cemetery" (*Haer.* 9.12).[4]

Because there seems to be such arresting historical detail in this section of Hippolytus's work (e.g., the development of the first "Christian" cemetery, the monepiscopacy in Rome, the personal background of the future Pope Calixtus I), scholars have tended to overlook the parody of the account. Rarely is the historicity challenged. No one, it seems, has ever doubted that Callistus was the slave of a Christian named Carpophorus, a member of the Caesar's household in the late second century.[5] Instead, the reference to Carpophorus is conventionally taken alongside Irenaeus of Lyons's allusion to "faithful ones in the royal court" as contemporaneous evidence for a group of Christians in the *familia Caesaris* during this time (see appendix 1). Others have suggested that Carpophorus was a Christian imperial freedman at the same time as the powerful Christian chamberlain Marcus Aurelius Prosenes (see chapter 5), with both representing the Christian community at the imperial court. Carpophorus's status as a "rich imperial freedman" would also suggest that Roman Christians were now in a prominent economic position, says Mario Mazza.[6] Some have been so assured of the historicity of Hippolytus's story about Callistus and Carpophorus that they augment it by citing an inscription from Rome for a certain Marcus Aurelius Carpophorus. This Carpophorus, the thinking goes, is identical to the Carpophorus recorded in the *Refutation* (see appendix 2).

Yet the account in the *Refutation* is one of the great smear campaigns of ancient literature. And the description of Callistus, which includes a reference to Caesar's household, is the climax of the entire polemical project.[7] It comes directly after the author has already categorized Callistus's teachings as heretical. So the ensuing description of Callistus was meant to "explain his life (βίος)." The audience was then supposed to read the "biography" of this "wannabe martyr" as the stereotypical behavior of a heretic (*Haer.* 9.11).

Indeed, the vitriol of the story is so pervasive that even those who accredit this account still struggle to make historical sense of the details.[8] Some scholars have reasoned that the author of the *Refutation* must have deployed the account from a geographical distance and only after the death of Callistus.[9] It is also clear that the author himself was on the outside of a Christian community looking in. The polemicist was crying out for recognition, but was doing so by brandishing a "heresiological blacklist" with Callistus as the most imminent example. The author's sole objective, in no uncertain terms, was to expose his bête noire Callistus as a heretic, a fraud (γόης), and a knave (πανοῦργος).[10] If this were not enough, his feud with Callistus was deeply personal (*Haer.* 9.12.15, 21). That the author goes so far as to claim, through Carpophorus, that Callistus was not even a Christian says a lot about the animosity that this author harbored and the underlying tensions between "factionalized" Christian communities in Rome during this period.[11]

Despite any verisimilitude, therefore, one cannot assume that the story about Callistus in the *Refutation of All Heresies* is a "historically valid" account. The story that the author tells about Callistus is satirical and fictionalized. The tale that this polemicist spins about his opponent is rife with stereotypes about slaves and slave owners. Dishonest slaves who steal, flee, and attempt suicide—as Callistus allegedly does—and slave owners who search out their fugitive property and expose them as frauds—as Carpophorus allegedly does—are tropes of Roman comedy and satire, not to mention features of the New Testament Gospels (e.g., Luke 16:1–8).[12]

The account of Callistus and Carpophorus in the *Refutation* is remarkably similar to two satires by Lucian of Samosata (ca. 125–80 CE). In Lucian's *The Runaways*, the goddess Philosophy bemoans how slaves leave their work and disguise themselves as would-be Cynic philosophers, then go around taking money (χρυσίον) from whomever they can, collecting tribute, and trying to pass themselves off as those truly (ὀρθῶς) practicing philosophy (*Runaways* 12–15, 22). By thievishness (ἁρπαγή) and by always hanging around tables (τράπεζα)—that is, banking counters and/or dining tables—these slaves acquire fortunes (πλοῦτος; *Runaways* 16). But they are frauds (γόης), and Philosophy prompts Hermes and Heracles to go expose the fake philosophers and reveal the genuine ones (ὀρθῶς; *Runaways* 17). As the story concludes, the divine posse together with certain slave owners find and expose the fugitive slave (δραπέτης) frauds (γοής), who are then punished and sent back with their owners.

In the prequel to this satire, *The Passing of Peregrinus*, Lucian likewise recounts the life of a Cynic philosopher named Peregrinus, whom Lucian exposes as a fraud (γόης; *Peregrinus* 13). According to the account, some of Peregrinus's premier exploits included patricide, adultery, and pederasty. He also beguiled a group of Christians to support him while he was in prison. Much money came to Peregrinus, so that he acquired not a little revenue from it and lived in prosperity, despite being a fugitive (φυγή) on account of his crimes (*Peregrinus* 10, 13, 16, 20). Peregrinus eventually came to Rome. But once there, he was so belligerent in his Cynicism that he was brought before the city prefect, who kicked him out of Rome (*Peregrinus* 18). The denouement of the story is when Peregrinus eventually commits "suicide" at the Olympic games by throwing himself—albeit less than enthusiastically—onto a funeral pyre.

At the level of authorial intent, plot, and descriptive vocabulary the account about Callistus and Carpophorus from the *Refutation of All Heresies* and the satires of Lucian are in close concert. Even more striking, the two authors not only use identical terms to impugn their opponents (γόης, χρῆμα, τράπεζα, δράπέτης, φυγή, ὀρθῶς); they even use synonymous phrases. Callistus was entrusted with χρῆμα οὐκ ὀλίγον and made away with χρήματα πολλά, while Peregrinus received πολλὰ χρήματα and procured πρόσοδον οὐ μικράν. Both authors also level similar charges against their respective opponents, including thievery, greed, dishonesty, sexual deviancy (*Haer.* 9.12.20; *Peregrinus* 14, 17), and hoodwinking Christians out of money. Both authors were concerned with "orthodoxy" (ὀρθῶς; *Haer.* 9.12.15) and false teachers and their followers (*Haer.* 9.12.24; *Peregr.* 24).[13] And to discredit the views of their opponents both authors participated in the ancient discourse of slavery by using a standard rhetorical ploy: they pointed up their opponents' slavishness.[14]

Apart from the sheer vitriol and personal animosity of Hippolytus the parallels with Lucian cast serious doubt on the historical credibility of this portion of the *Refutation*. After all, by casting Callistus as a slave the author could really sling some mud. Portraying his opponent Callistus as a slave would directly question Callistus's morality, since Roman slave ideology already constructed the slave as morally deficient and dishonored. But the account's utter conventionality also shows the portrayal of Callistus as a slave was certainly an artifice, if not entirely artificial. It was *literary* more than social description.[15] Taking a page right out of Lucian, the methods and aims of this Christian polemicist were not truth but the characteristic exaggerations of satire. "If any charlatan (γόης) and trickster, able to profit (χρῆσθαι) by occasions comes among the Christians," Lucian says, "he quickly acquires sudden wealth" (*Peregrinus* 13). Callistus, a domestic slave of Carpophorus from Caesar's household, was an archetypal character of Second Sophistic satire.[16] By acknowledging the parody, even fictionality, of this portion of the *Refutation* both Carpophorus and "Caesar's household" appear equally contrived.

Carpophorus, Caesar's Household, and Christians in Third-Century Rome

In the *Refutation of All Heresies,* both Carpophorus and Caesar's household were constructed to legitimate the author's own position at the expense of his opponent. The author marshals "Caesar's household" as an ancillary piece to dig up his opponent's past and tarnish his reputation in the eyes of the community. Within that polemical context, the reference to Carpophorus as a "faithful man from Caesar's household" was not simply the author's expression of social reality, but a strategic example of social typification. Like a puppet, Carpophorus was used to expose Callistus as a conniving, thieving, fugitive slave, and then—just like that—Carpophorus was retired. The Carpophorus from "Caesar's household" never again appears in the annals of Christian literature.[17]

The "Caesar's household" mentioned in this account was also not an independent reference to yet another example of Christians in the *familia Caesaris.* The reference is caught up in a referential loop stemming from Paul himself. The Greek phrase used to describe Carpophorus as a faithful man "from Caesar's household" is ἐκ τῆς Καίσαρος οἰκίας. In general, this phrase is quite rare. It appears in only two other early Christian texts: the *Martyrdom of Paul* and Philippians (4:22). The author of the *Refutation* uses exactly the same Greek phrase as these two texts, preposition and all. But the author parallels even more closely the text from the *Martyrdom of Paul,* since he uses the word πιστός in conjunction with Καίσαρος οἰκία, rather than "saints" (ἅγιοι) as Paul did. The author of the *Refutation* was writing precisely when the story about Paul's martyrdom was blossoming in Rome. So it appears that the polemicist "Hippolytus of Rome" reappropriated the phrase "Caesar's household" from what is now known as the *Martyrdom of Paul,* a text that in turn depends on the apostle Paul's use of that same phrase.

The verbatim use of this key phrase, which is found only in two interrelated Pauline texts, was intentional. The image of Paul stands closely behind the *Refutation*'s attack on Callistus, as the author was trying to move Callistus outside of an ostensible orthodox line that originated from the apostle Paul. This is why "Caesar's household" is on the front line of the attack. For when the author composed his satire about Carpophorus and Callistus, the phrase "Caesar's household" evoked a historiographic allusion to Pauline tradition.[18] Indeed, I would argue that it was precisely because of a presumed "positive" apostolic tradition about Caesar's household in Rome that the author could then paint Carpophorus in a certain comparative light against Callistus. This heretic was not a member of Caesar's household, says the author, merely a domestic slave and fraud of one of its members. The broader implication is that the traditions about Paul and Caesar's household in Rome were not restricted to commemorations of his martyrdom. The traditions could be reframed in new ways. The satirical nature of the story about Callistus and Carpophorus, combined with the tradition about Paul and Caesar's household in Rome, largely obscures any historical core that the account might have. The story of Callistus and Carpophorus does show, however, what at least one Christian polemicist could reasonably imagine about Christians and the imperial household in third-century Rome.

Recovering a Historical Situation

If the Christian community that Hippolytus describes did have some ties to a *familia Caesaris* in the imperial capital the connection appears to have been only secondary, through the slave (Callistus) of another imperial personnel (Carpophorus). In this case, the domestic slave Callistus was a far more important figure in Roman Christianity than Carpophorus from "Caesar's household." Callistus was later known as a pope, after all. There are also other, more nuanced ways to understand Carpophorus's relationship to Roman Christianity. The term translated as "faithful man" (πιστός) that singles out Carpophorus from Caesar's household is syntactically a mirror reflection of the *Martyrdom of Paul*, as I mentioned above. But the historical situation of Carpophorus appears more open and fluid in light of the broader semantic range of the phrase "faithful man."

By calling Carpophorus an ἀνήρ πιστός, commonly translated as "faithful man," the author was not necessarily identifying him as a Christian. As a matter of fact, in the only other instances in which the author of the *Refutation* uses a combination of πιστός and ἀνήρ, the phrase denotes his *opponents*.[19] Considering this trend, it is difficult to make the case that, in using πιστός and ἀνήρ, the author was specifying Carpophorus as a man of "Christian faith."

Instead, it is more likely that the author was merely describing Carpophorus's reputation as a "trustworthy" moneylender. The economic meanings that the term πιστός carries—such as "genuine," "trustworthy," or "worthy of credit"—would square much better with the premise of the story, since it pivots on money, profit, investment, and loss.[20] The use of the term πιστοί throughout this section of the treatise also emphasizes an economic meaning. After losing their money, for example, the brothers entreated Carpophorus for help, saying that they thought they were "investing" (lit. "placing a trust," πιστεύεσθαι) with Carpophorus when they had invested (πιστεύεσθαι) with his slave Callistus (*Haer.* 9.12.6). When Hippolytus later calls Carpophorus εὐλαβής, often translated as "devout," the same economic undertone is evident. After the brothers entreat Carpophorus, he agrees to release Callistus, saying that "he could care less about his own property" (ἴδιος ἀφειδεῖν)—that is, his slave Callistus!—but was thinking about the deposits (παραθήκη). Carpophorus responds this way not because he is "devout," as in a dedicated Christian, but because he is "cautious" or "shrewd" with money (ὡς εὐλαβής).[21] Portraying Carpophorus as a trustworthy and shrewd member of Caesar's household provides just the kind of contrast the author needs to discredit the thief Callistus.

In the story, moreover, the character Carpohorus acted as a financial broker for a specific segment of Roman Christians. As such, he could have been counted as one of the "faithful" precisely because of his trustworthy banking activity on behalf of those Christians. By comparison, the epigraphic record attests that imperial slaves and freedpersons in Rome had many different roles within socioreligious groups (*collegia*) devoted to particular gods. They could be devotees of the deity and participants in the group, and/or primarily financial sponsors who would help supply, furnish, or restore a meeting place; gift money or little goodies in wicker baskets (*sportulae*); or provide burial for group members and/or for outsiders on their own property.[22]

At the very least the language (πιστός, εὐλαβής) that Hippolytus uses to describe Carpophorus is vague enough to warrant caution. The upshot is that even in a polemical project meant to marginalize other opinions, exclude Callistus, and articulate the "true" meaning of the designation Christian, a member of Caesar's household was evidently accepted in a gray area. Whichever way Hippolytus intended to cast Carpophorus—as a Christian, a sympathizer, or merely an outlier—what mattered more was the ability to shape "Caesar's household" to police the boundaries of Hippolytus's community and to bolster his own position within a particular Christian faction.[23]

A similar historical situation lies behind two other characters in this section of the *Refutation*, Marcia and Hyacinth. According to the author both had ties to the imperial palace. Hippolytus says that Marcia, the emperor Commodus's concubine, was a god-lover (φιλόθεος) who desired to do a good deed. Because of her intercessory role on behalf of condemned Christians, and her interaction with Victor and Hyacinth, the concubine Marcia has been identified in some scholarship as not just a god-lover, but a Christian. Likewise, others have proposed that the eunuch Hyacinth was really a "presbyter" or "priest" of the church in Rome who exercised a certain amount of influence there, even carrying on "diplomacy" for the Roman Christians.[24]

To be sure, both Marcia and Hyacinth were undoubtedly imperial personnel.[25] But their particular roles in, much less their commitments to, a Christian group in Rome are far more unsettled than the current interpretations might indicate. Hippolytus wrote the whole story in the *Refutation* from memory, after the fact. He was thus (re)constructing Marcia and Hyacinth in his present situation for his own purposes. A passage commonly cited to inform the interpretation of Marcia as a Christian comes from the Roman historian Dio Cassius; it comments that Marcia "greatly favored the Christians and rendered them many kindnesses." Yet this comment was added only later by Dio's eleventh-century epitomator, Xiphilinos.[26] This addition was made long after Marcia had already taken her place in Christian memory as a god-lover who saved a future Pope. By contrast, other Roman sources that mention Marcia, such as Herodian and the *Historia Augusta*, provide some racy details—including how she helped murder Commodus—but say nothing about her apparent Christian leanings.[27] That she was clearly the emperor's sexual partner turned assassin only raises further questions about her possible Christian affiliations—questions that the *Refutation* has no interest in answering.

Indeed, the designation of Marcia as a φιλόθεος who desired to do a good deed was an idealization. If the account is true, Marcia's original connection with a Christian community was entirely derivative. Reading between the lines of the *Refutation*'s account, Peter Lampe has rightly suspected that the connection between Roman Christians and Marcia was most likely the eunuch Hyacinth.[28] It was Hyacinth, the imperial eunuch, not Marcia herself, who appears to have set up for Victor some kind of introduction with Marcia in order to solicit help in releasing certain Christian prisoners. The introduction and help that Marcia rendered must originally have been a favor for her de facto foster father Hyacinth, and was not intended as an act of Christian piety. The connection that Hyacinth had with Marcia is also why the author of the *Refutation* describes Hyacinth as a πρεσβύτερος. He was more simply an elderly man who had raised Marcia, not a "presbyter" of the church. But because Marcia was apparently able to request and secure the release, she would be remembered among Roman Christians as a "god-lover" who had done a good deed. For his part, Hyacinth's influence was not so much with the imperial court itself but with Marcia, the emperor's concubine. Beyond his connection to both Victor and Marcia, the details of Hyacinth's Christian piety are unknown, though he certainly seems to have been involved in a Roman church.

The underlying reality, therefore, is that there probably were imperial personnel like Carpophorus, Hyacinth, and Marcia who in various ways were connected to Christians in Rome during the late Antonine period. But reading the account in the *Refutation* critically and within its context reveals that those in the imperial household had a much more ambiguous Christian status than many have allowed. To my thinking, it did not matter so much to Hippolytus whether Carpophorus, Callistus, Marcia, or Hyacinth was Christian. What mattered more was that he could convincingly shape their connection to Caesar's household for his polemical project. Hippolytus's contemporary Tertullian of Carthage takes a similar approach in his apologetic works.

The Palace, Proculus, and Christian Milk

As one writer was using "Caesar's household" to police an internal conflict at Rome, another Christian writer from North Africa was using the imperial household in Rome to guard against a perceived external conflict. In 212 CE Quintus Septimius Florens Tertullianus (ca. 160–220 CE), Tertullian for short, penned an open-letter apology to Scapula, the proconsul of Africa Proconsularis.[29] Apparently, it had been an ominous year: droughts, fires on Carthage's walls, and a solar eclipse. Scapula had gotten antsy, it seems, and started trying and torturing Christians. In response, Tertullian's brief letter *To Scapula* tries to combat the usual suspicions that Christians are responsible for natural calamities because they are treasonous, sacrilegious (*sacrilegium*), and incestuous and that Christians refuse to sacrifice or swear by the emperor's *genius*. Tertullian argues that all of these charges are false. Christians are loyal to the emperor, paying reverential homage (*colere*) to him. They sacrifice by praying for the emperor's safety, health, and well-being (*pro salute*).[30] Consequently, Tertullian argues, it is counterproductive to persecute Christians, since they are innocent, peaceful, and beneficial for Carthage.

Near the end of his apology Tertullian becomes more direct in his argument. He reminds the proconsul of the official precedents concerning the treatment of Christians. Tertullian does this by citing a particular Christian who had served the emperor in Rome's palace: "Even Severus himself, the father of Antoninus [Caracalla], was mindful (*memor fuit*) of the Christians; for he sought out the Christian Proculus, surnamed Torpacion, the steward of Euhodia, who once cured him by anointing, and he kept him in his palace (*palatium*) until the day of his death. Antoninus, too, brought up as he was on Christian milk, had known him well" (*Scap.* 4.5).[31] On its face, this passage seems to offer yet two more examples from the Severan period of potentially influential Christians in Rome's imperial household. Torpacion was a Christian physiotherapist serving on the emperor Severus's permanent staff, probably as a freedman. The then-current emperor, Caracalla, had also known him well, says Tertullian.[32] I will return to Torpacion momentarily.

In addition to the identification of Torpacion as a Christian, several scholars have inferred from the phrase "brought up on Christian milk" (*lacte Christiano educatus*) that Caracalla had a Christian imperial slave as his wet nurse.[33] Some have then hypothesized that this slave woman would have come from the "strong Christian community at Lugdunum" (Lyon) where Caracalla was born in 186 CE while Severus was the provincial governor. And since many of Lugdunum's Christians had emigrated from Asia Minor, Anthony Birely stated, this wet nurse was "likely to have been an immigrant Greek, perhaps even from Syria."[34] This Greek-speaking woman from the East, Lampe added, would have attracted the interest or curiosity of Caracalla's mother, the future empress Julia Domna. When Caracalla's younger brother Geta was born in Rome in 189 CE, the Christian wet nurse would also have sojourned there. After Severus was proclaimed emperor in 193 CE she probably numbered among the imperial family, Lampe concludes.

There has even been speculation that this Christian wet nurse in the imperial palace had a Christian son. According to the fourth-century *Historia Augusta*, as a boy Caracalla had a playmate who was Jewish (*Iudaicam religionem*; *Caracalla* 1.6). Lampe construes this obscure biographical nugget like this: Jews and Christians could still be confused by pagans, therefore the "Jewish boy" could have been the Christian son of Caracalla's wet nurse. So Caracalla, it would appear, "had a personal relationship with at least three Christians," Lampe says: his wet nurse; his freedman chamberlain, Marcus Aurelius Prosenes; and Torpacion.[35] If the Jewish boy was really a Christian then the number would be four, one must suppose.

Tally aside, the whole idea that Caracalla had a Christian slave as his wet nurse is a mistake.[36] To get technical for a moment, some manuscripts of Tertullian's text (*Ad Scapulam*) read *lacte Christiano educatus*, which would indicate that the one "brought up" (*educatus*) on Christian milk was Caracalla. In the conventional reading of this manuscript, *lacte Christiano* is thus interpreted as a roundabout phrase for Christian wet nurse.[37] Notwithstanding Tertullian's penchant for playing on words, he does not use the standard term for "wet nurse" (*nutrix*). Nor is that Tertullian's claim. Here he uses "milk" (*lac*; Gk. γάλα) metaphorically to mean Christian teaching—a common idiom in early Christian writings. So if one follows this manuscript tradition, a better interpretation would be that because Caracalla knew Torpacion well, Caracalla was—by osmosis—also brought up on Christian doctrine.[38]

Although this interpretation is possible, I think it is unlikely. Another manuscript of Tertullian's text reads *lacte Christiano educatum*. This reading (*lacte Christiano educatum*) matches the clause that begins with the accusative pronoun *quem* and clearly indicates that the one "brought up" on Christian milk was actually Torpacion.[39] More recently scholars have preferred this manuscript reading as the more syntactically and historically intelligible. In this case, Tertullian claimed that Caracalla knew *Torpacion* had been a Christian from birth (*educatum*), but the emperor nonetheless allowed him to live unmolested in the imperial palace.[40] And here, I suggest, is the real focal point of Tertullian's anecdote.

Torpacion and a Plea for Tolerance

Within his apology, one of Tertullian's strongest pleas for tolerance comes when he tells Scapula about Torpacion's service in the palace. As a powerful rhetorical example, Tertullian ushers the emperor-serving Torpacion before Scapula to change how the magistrate views North African Christians as a whole. Here the apologist tries to cut to the bone by claiming that the emperor Severus, the principal magistrate and "the human being next to God," was himself mindful of Christians (*Scap.* 2.7). The chief evidence, according to Tertullian, was the emperor's treatment of Torpacion.[41] The then-reigning emperor Caracalla was also forbearing of Torpacion, Tertullian argues. He knew Torpacion had been brought up as a Christian yet did nothing. To mistreat Christians in Carthage, therefore, is to contradict the policy of the emperors themselves, who allowed Christians to live peacefully right beside them.

But Tertullian also says nothing about what Torpacion's Christian-*ness* was like. Nor does the apologist mention anything about Torpacion's political influence, his social status, or his economic potential as part of the palace staff.[42] Instead, Tertullian's strategy is to highlight Torpacion's spatial proximity to the imperial power-center. As the emperor's physiotherapist Torpacion had regularly touched Septimius Severus. In Tertullian's mind this intimate contact bestowed a certain importance and trustworthiness on Torpacion—and by extension, upon other Christians as well. The body of Torpacion, in other words, is a surrogate body for the wider Christian community. And like the story of Paul and Caesar's household in the *Martyrdom of Paul*, the image of a Christian so close to the emperor attempted to break and then reframe the perceived boundaries of cultural space. In this way Torpacion functioned in Tertullian's argument as a geopolitical figurehead. Tertullian spotlighted this servant of the emperor in order to open up representational space for North African Christians. Because of Torpacion, they too should be allowed to enter the cultural record as legitimate people who were deserving of fair treatment, even esteem.[43]

Tertullian, however, was also writing about Torpacion from a distance and retrospectively. Tertullian gives no evidence that he personally knew Torpacion. And how Tertullian knew that within the private, labyrinthine complex on Rome's Palatine Hill a former emperor's personal physiotherapist had been a Christian is unknown. Not only that, but how Tertullian could have known that the emperor Caracalla had known that Torpacion was a Christian is also unclear.

One possibility is that Torpacion was a native of, or had lived in, Carthage and was once part of a Christian community there. This scenario would make sense of Tertullian's use of *educatum* to mean that Torpacion was brought up on Christian milk. Another possibility is that Torpacion accompanied Severus in 202 CE when the emperor visited Africa Proconsularis on a trip (*adventus*) with Julia and their two sons, Caracalla and Geta.[44] As part of what would have been an extensive retinue, this visit could have been an occasion for Torpacion to connect with a local Christian group in Carthage. The answer will probably remain elusive, and the lack of knowledge should also caution against some hypotheses that "Christianity reached Africa" with members of the imperial household.[45]

Whatever the case, it is likely that Tertullian had previously heard about Torpacion from other Christians who once knew him. To manufacture cultural cachet for his community, the memory of Torpacion that Tertullian shared with a Christian group was then brought to bear on the current sociopolitical and ideological structures of Roman North Africa. In this way, the very act of calling up Torpacion before Scapula was an ideological appropriation of the past.[46] The reference to Torpacion and the palace was part of a similar process already witnessed in the *Martyrdom of Paul*, in which Christians were defined largely through their spatial connections with the imperial center. From his Carthaginian location Tertullian looked across the Tyrrhenian Sea to the imperial palace in Rome, and moved Torpacion from imperial center back to provincial periphery.[47]

By 202 CE it thus seems that Torpacion had become the local face of an apologetic tradition about believers in Rome's imperial palace. Fifteen years earlier Tertullian had asserted in his lengthy *Apology*, which likewise responded to a recent persecution of Christians (*Apol.* 1.1), that Christians even fill (*implere*) the imperial palace in Rome. The apologist sneers: "Oh, sure, the Mauritanians, the Marcomanni, and the Parthians—or other races (*gentes*), however great, of but one region with their own borders—are more numerous than the whole world (*totius orbis*)! We are only recent, and we have filled (*implevimus*) everything you have—cities, blocks, forts, towns, market-places, camps, tribes, town councils, palace, senate, forum (*palatium, senatum, forum*). We have left you only the temples" (*Apol.* 37.4).[48] Apart from sheer apologetic exaggeration, the claim about Christians "filling" the imperial palace has roots in the *Martyrdom of Paul*. Tertullian not only knew key details about Paul's martyrdom story that are found only in the *Martyrdom of Paul*—for example, that Paul was beheaded in Rome.[49] But Tertullian's apologetic use of the imperial palace as a hub of Christians and as a mark of their territory in the world echoes the apologetic use of the imperial palace in the *Martyrdom of Paul*. In this story, after all, the palace is one of the most dominant ideological features. But even the language Tertullian uses apropos of the palace (*palatium*) is similar to that of the *Martyrdom of Paul*. When Nero began to systematically kill off the Christians it was the Romans' protest in front of "the palace" (τό παλάτιον) that prompted Nero to halt his killing spree and to then establish the more restrained policy that none of the Christians should be killed without due process. The presence of so many Christians (πλῆθος πολύ) in the emperor Nero's realm, not least in his own palace, was also part of the claim that there were Christians throughout the whole world (οἰκουμένη ὅλη) and they should not be marginalized.[50]

As in the *Martyrdom of Paul*, the North African apologist was not claiming that literally every person serving in the emperor Severus's palace was a Christian. In articulating the image of a Christian or Christians serving the emperor in the palace, Tertullian was trying to redefine the spatial field and the boundaries of the Christian "race" (*gens*) as a whole. As geographer Doreen Massey once explained, it is not just that space is political, but "thinking the spatial" in a particular way can "shake up the manner in which certain political questions are formulated, can contribute to political arguments already under way, and can be an essential element in the imaginative structure which enables in the first place an opening up to the very sphere of the political."[51] By thinking spatially about both Torpacion and the palace, Tertullian ultimately hoped to reset the political climate, halt violence, and promote tolerance for all those Christians living outside of the palace. Whether Tertullian was successful in his endeavor is another question. But his method of presenting Christians as a race with a Christian territory that even encompasses Rome's imperial palace lays the groundwork for later apologetic historiography about precisely such Christians in the Severan period (see the conclusion of this book).

In all, what both Hippolytus and Tertullian did in their respective projects was to shape individuals from within the imperial household as representatives for their own causes. Both authors did so to safeguard their communities against perceived threats—internal and external. At the time that they were writing, there certainly seem to have been people from the imperial household who were Christians, or who were involved with Christian groups, though the nature of their piety and the extent of their participation are less clear. The variation in the diversity of the references—Carpophorus, Callistus, Marcia, Hyacinth, and Torpacion—probably reflects the various positions that those Christians from the imperial household were thought to have in relation to Christian communities. But the references were also carefully constructed. To make their case, Hippolytus and Tertullian utilized a story about Christians in Rome's imperial household that the *Martyrdom of Paul* had already established. In the second half of the third century the same kind of work continued. Christian writers linked individuals from the imperial household to stories about Paul and Caesar's household. The authors again did so to protect their communities from perceived threats. Only here the perceived threat was far more pervasive and, for some writers, even more ominous.

CHAPTER 4

CHRISTIAN PIETY AND A

MARTYRED SLAVE OF CAESAR

I was once a slave of Caesar, now I am a slave of Christ.

—EUELPISTUS

When the emperor Decius decreed in January 250 CE that all inhabitants of the empire must sacrifice to the Roman gods before a magistrate and receive a certificate of proof (*libellus*), the response from the majority of Christians was predictable. They simply complied. According to Cyprian, Carthage's third-century bishop, many Christians by an "overwhelming impulse" rushed eagerly into the Forum to offer sacrifice and to receive their certificate. Other Christians, to comply with the edict in other ways, offered incense to the emperor or swore by his *genius;* some sent proxies, while others compelled all their dependents—their tenants and clients (*inquilinos vel amicos*)—to sacrifice. Some bribed the magistrates to obtain a certificate, and others sacrificed only to protect wife, family, and children. Still others fled altogether, including Cyprian himself, who went into hiding. There were certainly recusants. They were punished by imprisonment, torture, or execution and were later remembered as martyrs. But when the dust had settled, enough Christians wound up with certificates of sacrifice that Cyprian's church evidently had to grant counter certificates of peace (*libellus pacis*) to restore to communion all those who had "lapsed" by obeying the emperor's edict. Even Cyprian the bishop had to justify his "self-exile" to his critics.[1]

All told, the Edict of Decius had a profound effect on third-century Christians. Many would look back on Decius's short reign as a time of outright persecution, when Christians were forced to "apostatize or die." And yet from the diverse responses that Cyprian describes, the choice for the majority was not simply between two opposing alternatives. For many Christians before and after Decius, honoring the emperor (βασιλεύς; 1 Pet 2:17) by performing the patriotic duty (*pietas*) of loyal citizens of the Roman Empire is what Christians were supposed to do.[2]

In the aftermath of Decius's edict, amid the inevitable damage control and finger pointing, several Christian writers worked furiously to counteract this practice of sharing piety between Christ and the emperor. These writers set out to make the exclusive worship of Christ a defining characteristic for Christians. The process would involve rewriting the past and inventing new stories about earlier martyrs who, in their worship of Christ, had refused to conform to imperial edicts that demanded worship of Roman gods. A new story about a martyred slave of Caesar, found in a text called the *Acts of Justin and Companions* (Recension B), was integral to that revisionist process.

In the second half of the third century, an editor (or editors) refashioned a character named Euelpistus from an earlier version of the *Acts of Justin and Companions* to redefine Christian piety as an exclusive enterprise. Besides drawing from an ideology of Roman slavery to make the case, the editor(s) found creative material to shape the character Euelpistus as a resilient martyr by using the stories about Paul's martyrdom in Rome. Particularly important was Paul's connection with the emperor's slaves. The use of Euelpistus as a paragon of Christian piety, however, did not reflect reality so much as refract it. The available epigraphic and archaeological evidence frequently attests that imperial slaves were active in worshipping the Roman gods, specifically the emperors themselves. While the character Euelpistus was cogent precisely because—through the work of the editor(s)—he acted against cultural assumptions of slave piety to become a "slave of Christ," he was ultimately a fictional character. Euelpistus's piety was idealized in Christian commemoration. The Euelpistus character in the *Acts of Justin and Companions* (Recension B) thus raises crucial questions about material culture and the lives of some imperial personnel who may have worshipped Christ and the emperors simultaneously.

Date and Context

In one account of Justin Martyr's death (ca. 165 CE), Rome's urban prefect Quintus Junius Rusticus, known as a Stoic philosopher and friend and instructor of the emperor Marcus Aurelius, questions the Christian apologist Justin along with his companions. Rusticus asks these suspected Christians about their doctrines, their practices, where they meet, and who their parents are. During Rusticus's interrogation he comes to a certain

Euelpistus, whose name means "a good hope." The narrator identifies Euelpistus as a slave of Caesar (δοῦλος Καίσαρος). Like Justin and the other companions, this imperial slave openly confesses, "I too am a Christian" (*Acts Justin* B 4.3).[3] Emboldened, Euelpistus then refuses to yield to the emperor's edict and sacrifice to the gods. So like the rest of the companions, Euelpistus is led away to be scourged and beheaded as one of the "holy martyrs" (*Acts Justin* B 6.1).

This trial scene is one of the best-known among scholars of early Christianity and Roman history alike. By and large, the text is usually read as historical evidence that a Christian imperial slave named Euelpistus was the companion of Justin Martyr in the 160s.[4] In his collection of historical essays on Antonine Rome, the eminent social historian of slavery, Keith Bradley, simply stated that Euelpistus, one of the martyred companions of Justin Martyr, went to his death as a slave. Peter Lampe claimed the same. As part of a diachronic section on the social level of Christians in Rome, Lampe listed Euelpistus as a Christian member of the *familia Caesaris* "at the time of Justin." Before Lampe, in the widely acclaimed and now reprinted book *Pagans and Christians*, Robin Lane Fox asserted that "when Justin was brought to trial in the 160s, he was accompanied by Euelpistus, 'a slave in Caesar's household' who had parents in Cappadocia, probably before he passed into the Emperor's service." Reading the text as it is, others have echoed these descriptions of Euelpistus.[5]

Yet Euelpistus the slave of Caesar, turned martyr for Christ, was not a historical figure of second-century Rome. Nor does the version of the *Acts of Justin and Companions* that records Euelpistus that way reflect a second-century situation.

The *Acts of Justin and Companions* is preserved in three distinct Greek recensions: A, B, and C. The shorter version, also considered the earliest, is Recension A. The best-known and most-used version of Justin's martyrdom is Recension B. The longest and most theologically developed version, Recension C, was composed long after the other two. When describing Euelpistus as an imperial slave, most commentators correctly specify in their notes Recension B of the *Acts of Justin and Companions*. But Recension B derives from and thus postdates A. This means that the description of Euelpistus as a slave of Caesar was not the "original." It is only in the later recensions (B and C) that Euelpistus is identified as an imperial slave.[6]

Though establishing absolute dates for the recensions is difficult, tell-tale signs suggest that Recension B was much later than the 160s. The opening mentions that "impious decrees (προστάγματα)" were posted against the Christians "in town and country alike to force them to offer libations to empty images (σπένδειν τοῖς ματαίοις εἰδώλοις)." For purists, this line is a potential problem. It seems anachronistic for an authentic, mid-second-century text. In his classic *Martyrdom and Persecution in the Early Church*, W. H. C. Frend even admits in a note that "we know nothing of 'impious decrees' being issued 'in town and country'" in the time of the emperor Marcus Aurelius (161–80 CE). Because Frend wanted to preserve the historical integrity of the martyrdom account, long thought to be the best example of an authentic Roman trial (*commentarius*) of Christians, he then found it necessary to preemptively counter suspicions of "forgery." Frend says that the opening "must obviously be attributed to a later, perhaps post-Constantinian, editor."[7] But this view of the text ignores the fact that the reference to an imperial edict is repeated later. In the climax of the account, Rome's urban prefect Rusticus passes judgment on those who "refused to sacrifice to the gods (θῦσαι τοῖς θεοῖς) and yield to the emperor's edict" (προστάγμα; *Acts Justin* B 5.8).

Besides the opening, however, other details of Recension B indicate a time far beyond the mid-second century. In particular, the compulsion to "sacrifice to the gods" and "sacrifice to idols" is repeated throughout Recension B while it is entirely lacking in Recension A (*Acts Justin* B 2.1, 5.4, 5.7, 5.8). And unlike Recension A, the dialogue in Recension B opens with Rusticus demanding that Justin "submit to the emperors" (βασιλεῖς). The reference to an imperial edict, and the compulsory language combined with the repetition of sacrificial expectations, point to a milieu after the emperor Decius had specifically decreed that all inhabitants of the empire should sacrifice and pour libations.[8]

In fact, the language in the *Acts of Justin and Companions* Recension B reflects the formulae of Decius's edict, which has now been reconstructed from the extant *libelli*, preserved in papyri from Egypt. The crucial line from the reconstructed wording of Decius's edict would be the following: "That all men together with all women and members of the household [i.e., slaves—οἰκέται] and infants [or children] sacrifice and pour libations (θύειν καὶ σπένδειν), and accurately taste the same sacrificial meats." In the extant *libelli*, the participants in the rite record their "piety (εὐσεβής) to the gods," and that they "in accordance with the decree (προσταχθέν) poured libations (σπένδειν) and sacrificed (θύσειν)."[9]

The objects of the prescribed piety were the Roman gods, but this included the emperors as well. Decius's prescribed universal *supplicatio* involved the divinized emperors (*divi*) and Decius's own *genius* right alongside the traditional Roman deities. The purpose was not to persecute Christians but to legitimize Decius's power amid the turmoil of the previous fifteen years. The "religious" element was supposed to secure divine favor by restoring traditional Roman piety, uniting the empire in religious observance under Decius.[10] Tucked into Decius's demand for a formal rite of sacrifice, therefore, was also a call for the whole population of the empire to prove its loyalty—and its piety (*pietas*)—to him.

While the Decian legislation is a fitting backdrop for Recension B, it is only the terminus post quem. The text of Recension B well reflects an even later date in the third century. Less than a decade after Decius's edict the emperor Valerian, with his coemperor son Gallienus, again issued an edict. The emperors posted letters (*letterae*) throughout the empire mandating that "those who do not make the Roman cult the object of their worship should nevertheless acknowledge Roman rituals (*caeremonia*)." The content of this edict was directed against Christians, though only a particular swath of them—church leaders and high-status Roman citizens whom the emperors ordered "to turn to that which is according to nature (φύσιν) and worship (προσκυνεῖν) the gods who preserve their Empire."[11]

The edict seems to have failed. A second, harsher letter then followed in 258 CE. This second edict outright condemned bishops, priests, and deacons. It stripped senators and high-ranking officials of their property, and if they continued to be Christians (*Christiani esse*), it condemned them as well. Matrons would lose their property and be exiled. Finally, the letter states, "the *Caesariani*, whoever of them had either confessed before, or now confess (*confessi*), should have their property confiscated (*possessiones confiscantur*) and sent in chains to the imperial estates (*Caesarianas*)." The rescript took aim first at Christian leadership and second at the highest social ranks to discover who would perform the proper piety of Roman *religiones*, to find out who was loyal to the emperor, and to seek out "whoever" (*quicumque*) had confessed or would confess to being Christians.[12]

Then, in 303 CE, the emperor Diocletian issued a series of edicts that for the first time took direct aim at Christians en masse. Christian places of worship were to be destroyed, Christian scripture confiscated, and Christians' legal rights stripped away. Often termed the "Great Persecution," these edicts were especially concerned with imposing sacrifice (θύειν) on all inhabitants of the empire.[13] Diocletian himself had a keen interest in sacrifice, as coins minted during his reign often depict him performing the rite. As for the targets of the edict, the fourth-century Christian author Lactantius (ca. 250–325 CE) also mentions that Diocletian raged against his own household, including his domestic slaves (*domestici*) and eunuchs (*Mort. pers.* 15). Eusebius of Caesarea (ca. 260–340 CE) narrates more specifically that one Dorotheus, an imperial servant (παῖς), together with other domestic slaves in Diocletian's household (οἰκετεία), refused to sacrifice when ordered, suffered for piety (εὐσέβεια), and were martyred at Nicomedia (*Hist. eccl.* 8.6.1–6).

During the second half of the third century, therefore, there were three moments of perceived "cultural trauma" that could spur Christians to rework the *Acts of Justin and Companions* in light of present concerns.[14] And the editorial work of the *Acts of Justin* Recension B is pronounced. There are unmistakable parallels between Recension B and three imperial edicts mandating Roman sacrifice. The fact that slaves and members of the imperial household were specifically included in the Edict of Decius and the "Great Persecution," respectively, was an impetus for a new account about one of Justin Martyr's companions.

A New Kind of Martyr

In the *Acts of Justin and Companions* Recension B, Euelpistus is a momentous character. Notably, he is the only companion in this recension of the martyrdom account whose recorded status changes from Recension A to the later Recension B. In Recension A, he is simply Euelpistus. In Recension B, he is Euelpistus a "slave of Caesar." All the more striking, the editor(s) foreground the new label "slave of Caesar." It is inserted *before* Euelpistus is identified as a Christian. By contrast, in other martyr acts, Candida Moss notes, when the accused are questioned regarding their name, place of origin, and social status, their self-identification as Christian supersedes other identity markers.[15]

The editor(s) of Recension B also gave Euelpistus the slave of Caesar the loudest voice of all the companions. The other characters respond to Rusticus in almost exactly the same terms as they did in Recension A. Not Euelpistus. Euelpistus confesses in Recension B, "I too am a Christian. I have been manumitted (ἐλευθερωθείς) by Christ, and I share in the same hope by the favor of Christ" (*Acts Justin* B 4.3).[16] This is the longest and most polished response of any character, except for Justin himself.

While Recension B is generally longer and more rhetorically developed, the changes to Euelpistus are distinct and demand special consideration. The editor(s) transformed Euelpistus into a slave of Caesar in order to raise the stakes of the martyrdom account. The core issue of Recension B is piety (εὐσέβεια). The text calls on its audience(s) to resist the prescribed piety toward the emperors, the Roman gods, and their "empty images" and revere only Christ. Such narrowly restricted piety was by no means self-evident for Christians in antiquity, as Moss says. Displays of piety were not solely religious but encompassed all manner of social and identity-grounded responsibilities, reinforced social relations, and regulated networks of power.[17]

The focus on piety is one of the reasons why Euelpistus is first unveiled as a slave of Caesar. By characterizing him as a slave the text evokes the

Roman conventions of piety and raises the expectation of Euelpistus's unrelenting obedience to his master, the emperor himself. More specifically, in the ideology of Roman slave-owning, a slave like Euelpistus had been fundamentally dishonored; he had been damaged morally by the experience of slavery. Part of the "good behavior" that showed the slave's potential for moral rehabilitation and might later lead to the reward of manumission, citizenship, and a patron-client relationship was a slave's proper reverence and loyalty (*pietas*/εὐσέβεια) toward his/her owner.[18]

The editor(s) of this version of the *Acts of Justin* no less than the real audience living after Decius's edict—some of whom would have been slave owners themselves—understood these subtle mores.[19] For this reason Euelpistus's eventual refusal to yield to the emperor's edict was especially powerful. Paradoxically, it is only by betraying his master and breaking the biblical household codes that admonish slaves to obey their earthly masters that Euelpistus exhibits what the editor(s) deem to be proper Christian piety.[20]

By recasting the story of Euelpistus in this way the redactor(s) were creating a new example for the Christian audience to mimic. Indeed, the example of Euelpistus's devotion to Christ was, in some sense, even more radical than the other characters. At the same time, changing his status to an imperial slave opened a new dimension in which to commemorate Euelpistus as a martyr. When Recension B was composed, some communities had already been commemorating the Euelpistus figure. What changed for the audience of the new version (B) was that the "public moment and public identity" of confessing Christ was now bound up with a slave of Caesar.[21]

This revised Euelpistus character thus represented a new development in ancient Christian martyrdom accounts. For although other ancient martyrdoms feature Christian slaves, and the *Martyrdom of Paul* features several slaves of Caesar, the *Acts of Justin and Companions* Recension B is the first and only account that features a slave of Caesar who was actually martyred for Christ. Just as the *Martyrdom of Paul* at the end of the second century used "Caesar's household" to create a tradition about Paul in the first century, the new story of Euelpistus as a martyred slave of Caesar was also multitemporal. Responding to a third-century situation, the editor(s) recast Euelpistus as part of a second-century past. Simultaneously, if Recension B was responding to developments after Decius's edict, then the new Euelpistus character probably reflected the reality that, by the end of the third century, there almost certainly were Christian slaves in the imperial household.

But in Recension B the memory of Paul's martyrdom also influenced the new formulation of Euelpistus. As Moss observes, a number of suggestive family resemblances between the *Acts of Justin and Companions* and the *Martyrdom of Paul* point to a shared "martyrological grammar" and eschatological perspective.[22] Both stories were set in Rome, both present an imperial edict aimed at Christians, both share the belief that the "whole world" will be consumed by fire, and both discuss ascending to heaven after beheading. The death of Paul was also exemplary for other texts long after the *Martyrdom of Paul* had materialized.[23] Moss rightly cautions that it is difficult to press too firmly on the textual and conceptual connections between the *Acts of Justin* and the *Martyrdom of Paul*, since they were probably produced around the same time. But such caution is more appropriate for Recension A than for Recension B.

Because Recension B most likely dates to the second half of the third century there is much more chronological distance from the *Martyrdom of Paul*. In this case, one can more confidently assert that it is the *Martyrdom of Paul* that was influencing the *Acts of Justin* Recension B. Besides, Recension B demonstrates another parallel to the *Martyrdom of Paul* that is lacking in the earlier Recension A—the use of a Christian imperial slave in martyrological grammar. The description and dialogue of Euelpistus in Recension B correspond to the portrait of the Patroclus character in the *Martyrdom of Paul*, who, as an imperial slave, also challenges the authority of the emperor and confesses to being a soldier of Jesus Christ. And if many of the parallels between the *Martyrdom of Paul* and the *Acts of Justin* were already present in Recension A, then the editorial changes to Euelpistus in Recension B suggest that, as it related to "Caesar's household," a more conscious memory of Paul's martyrdom was at work. The revised Euelpistus character would tilt the interpretive lens of Recension B back toward the example of the apostle Paul's martyrdom.

To take this one step further, when Recension B was composed the Christian audience appears to have already accepted the earlier story about Christians in the imperial household. Adding Eulepistus to a second-century past then bolstered that story. There was an ideological, even cosmological, component to this, again reminiscent of the *Martyrdom of Paul*. By altering their texts to place a Christian in the imperial household, the Christian editor(s) and audience also imagined that through Euelpistus, they, too, had infiltrated the system of power at an earlier time. Recension B helped reshape the collective past of its audience.

The process of revising the past continued in a second iteration. As the editor(s) of Recension B appropriated and incorporated an "interpretive *topos*" into their martyrdom project—a Christian in the imperial household—they preserved a martyrological motif for future generations. And if martyrdom is a "practice of dying for god and talking about it," as Daniel Boyarin says, then clearly some Christian editors kept "talking" about slaves of Caesar.[24]

Later on, another editor (or editors) continued crafting the account and refining the martyred imperial slave character Euelpistus. In Recension C, Euelpistus is even more poetic in his response to Rusticus: "I was once a slave of Caesar, now I am a slave of Christ, winning freedom by his favor" (*Acts Justin* C.3.4).[25] Along with several new features—including a liturgical closing, the commemorative date of the martyrdoms (June 1), and gruesome details of the scourging—Recension C also has Justin refer to Mary as the "all-holy mother of God" (θεοτόκος; *Acts Justin* C 5.1–2). The latter detail in particular seems to date this recension to the fifth century at least, perhaps sometime around the Council of Ephesus in 431 CE, as Herbert Musurillo suggested.[26] The editorial activity means that a Christian community, well into the fifth century, continued commemorating Euelpistus as a slave of Caesar who, as an example of unshakable faith, withstood persecution to uphold the ideals of Christian piety.

Piety Practices

Despite Recension B's claims about the exclusive worship of Christ through the example of Euelpistus, a pious Christian martyr, the reality was more complicated for flesh-and-blood slaves of Caesar. Even if imperial slaves considered the exclusive worship of Christ necessary, they did not always have the freedom to take exclusive stances about their piety. The emperors' slaves were not under the constant eye of a taskmaster, to be sure. Yet the kinds of duty (i.e., piety—*pietas*) that the slave system presupposed would govern the reverential responses of those within the system. Considering some of the other forms of piety that were expected from, or characteristic of, imperial slaves helps explain why the new Euelpistus character was so exemplary in a project that tried to redefine Christian piety as an exclusive activity.

The piety that a slave was expected to show toward his/her master went beyond simply obedience or gestures of deference. In the typical Roman household slaves and freedpersons were expected to participate in the domestic cult, which would include rituals for the household deities and the guardian spirit (*genius*) of the slave master. The best-known indicators of this household piety were the *lararia*, the shrines for household gods. These shrines could take several forms and be located in several different areas of a house at once, including within the slave quarters. But the typical worship of the *genius*, accorded to any head of household, in no way entailed divine status for him/her. With the emperors and their households, however, the situation was a bit different.[27]

In contrast to the situation in other Roman households, the master or patron of imperial personnel was worshipped across the empire—in the grandest provincial temples and in the smallest open-air shrines—as a living, divine being. The emperors were worshipped as Roman gods, with sacrifices, prayers, offerings, and so on.[28] Imperial personnel were expected to show the proper reverence to their imperial master or patron. But the cultural expectation was that imperial slaves and freedpersons would also honor, revere, and worship the living emperor himself by performing household rituals that upheld the emperor's divine authority.[29]

The cultural expectations regarding a slave's duty (*pietas*) toward the emperor continued even after the imperial master died. When an emperor died, he was officially made a deity (*divus*) in a grand ceremony called *apotheosis*. His *genius* ascended to heaven where it was worshipped with the other gods of the Roman pantheon. The son of this god (*divus*) was also ushered in as the new emperor.[30] Slaves and freedpersons of the imperial household would continue to worship their former master as an official *divus*, while simultaneously carrying on the expected household piety toward their new imperial master.

The reality of the domestic cult of emperor worship has always been lost in previous discussions of Christians in the imperial household. And yet enslavement certainly constrained, even prescribed, piety toward the divine emperor. A cogent example is an inscription from Ostia Antica, ancient Rome's bustling port city. The inscription records that a place was assigned on an imperial estate (*praedia Rusticeliana*) for the worshippers of the *lares* and images (*cultores Larum et imaginum*) of "our lords the most unconquered emperors." The place was assigned by an imperial freedman procurator named Callistus. The emperor worshippers had evidently petitioned Callistus for a place on their estate to be consecrated for the well-being of "our lords the emperors." The petition was granted, and the site was dedicated during the reign of Caracalla, 205 CE to be precise. The association of worshippers, as others have noted, was composed mainly of imperial slaves who worked on the estate.[31] One Maximinianus, a house-born slave (*verna*) of the emperor, was then put in charge of the group by the imperial freedman Callistus, who instructed Maximinianus to "take the matter in hand."

But the inscription records that Maximinianus, who was to preside over the imperial estate's *cultores Larum et imaginum*, was also the manager (*vilicus*) of the imperial slaves who lived and worked at the estate.[32] In other words, this imperial estate kept imperial slaves who lived and worked there under the authority of an imperial slave who was also the overseer of a group that worshipped the emperors and consisted of the same imperial slaves from the estate. It is difficult to envision any scenario in such a setting when a slave could politely decline the conventions of the household cult or sidestep the group that worshipped the emperors.

In addition to this expected piety toward the household cult, the emperor's slaves and freedmen often on their own initiative in their own cultic associations worshipped the emperors, either jointly with other gods or solely. A plethora of examples survive. One example from Rome in the time of Justin Martyr himself records that a cultic space was assigned by the procurator of the patrimonial estates of Caesar for a *collegium* dedicated to worshipping Asclepius, the god of healing, in conjunction with the health of the emperors and the "numinous imperial house." The heads of the *collegium* were Felix, Aspergus, Regianus, and Vindex. Felix and Vindex were both house-born slaves of the emperor, but all of the *collegium*'s heads were also slave managers (*vilici*) at the Galbana estate (*vilici praediorum Galbanorum*). This is the same warehouse district that would have included the Horrea Galbana (see chapter 2). The roster of the *collegium*, comprising fifty-three names, included two slaves of Felix, presumably the same Felix mentioned above, and seven other house-born slaves of Caesar.[33]

Besides corporate worship, individual imperial slaves and freedpersons worshipped the emperors as well. This worship took diverse forms across the Mediterranean. One form of individual piety was a small shrine-house (*aedicula*) that held a statuette of the emperor to which the practitioner could make a libation or supplication. These shrines, which appear to have been manufactured and sold in the vicinity of temples, were transportable receptacles that the slave could move from one locale to another or place on an altar in the home or other building.[34] During the reign of Nero, for instance, a slave of Caesar named Fausius, with his own resources, had an *aedicula* made to house the images of "Nero Caesar Augustus and sacred Silvanus" (fig. 6). Another form of individual worship was an altar to an emperor upon which imperial personnel could make offerings and

FIG. 6 A portable shrine (*aedicula*) of Fausius, a slave of Caesar's, for an image of the emperor Nero and the god Silvanus. The statuettes of Nero and Silvanus would have sat atop the shrine. Mid-first century CE. Museo Nazionale Romano—Terme di Diocleziano, Rome, Sala V.

sacrifices or burn incense. One dated to the Flavian period is an altar "for the health of the masters, the *genius* of the *horrea*." The altar was erected by Saturninus and Successus, who were *horrearii* at the *horrea*.[35] Still other forms of such piety were the more modest plaque dedications to the *genius* of an emperor, such as the one Corinthus, a slave of Caesar, made in Rome for the emperor Trajan (98–117 CE).[36]

Though the material record presented here is primarily from the second to early third century—nearly all extant epigraphy falls within this range—the thematic connections between this material and the *Acts of Justin* Recension B are still quite cogent. In the third and fourth centuries, imperial slaves were still honoring their imperial masters as they had in previous centuries.[37] So the vignettes I have offered above challenge, if not belie, the exclusive piety of the imperial slave Euelpistus in the *Acts of Justin and Companions* Recensions B and C.

The material culture of imperial personnel shows just how pointed, but contrived, the new story about Euelpistus really was. More than any other character, a slave of Caesar who defied the imperial decrees and the emperors themselves by refusing to sacrifice to the Roman gods—or even to the emperor to whom he belonged—intensified this account's call to resistance and exclusive Christian piety. The character Euelpistus shattered cultural expectations of piety, ignored moral/legal obligations of slave to master, and undermined the hegemony of imperial power.[38] As for loyalty and "good behavior," this slave character essentially gives his imperial master the proverbial finger. He has already been manumitted by Christ, he says.

Yet as important as Euelpistus is for Recension B, and as inspiring as his memory might have been in Christian commemorative narrative, the reality was more complicated. Any real imperial slave who worshipped the god Christ would also be expected to, and in one way or another most likely did, worship Roman gods, including the emperors themselves. Euelpistus, the slave of Caesar who would worship only Christ and show no piety toward other gods, or the emperors, was a decidedly constructed character. He was an idealized figure of Christian commemoration.

While it is certainly possible that some slaves in the imperial household worshipped only Christ—Eusebius relates that several imperial slaves from Diocletian's household were Christian martyrs—the piety of most must have been more adaptable, hybrid, and acculturated. Though this may seem distasteful to the modern palate, for imperially owned persons it was more likely an established fact of life. It was the imperial slaves, after all, who had to adjust their cosmologies, and adapt to and/or adopt the religious practices of their overlords and the dominant culture, not vice versa.[39]

When tested by the grind of everyday life, devotion to Christ was not always the zero-sum game that ancient Christian authors wanted it to be. The case of Euelpistus in the *Acts of Justin* Recension B and the nature of piety within the imperial slave system point to a more flexible definition of "Christian" during the third century. And when trying to identity Christians in the imperial household from the archaeological record there is a similar need for flexible categories of analysis.

CHAPTER 5

MATERIAL EVIDENCE FOR A

CHRISTIAN IMPERIAL FREEDMAN

> Thus even a Christian, if he possessed the confidence of the
> emperor, could become a man of importance in the empire.
>
> —ADOLF VON HARNACK, *THE MISSION*
> *AND EXPANSION OF CHRISTIANITY*

In March of 1830 there was a marvelous discovery in Rome. A half mile west
of Castello di Torrenova, on a road in the Borghese estate on the north side
of the Via Labicana, some road workers uncovered a huge sarcophagus. It
had "a remarkable" Latin inscription "in good letters." The English reads:
"For Marcus Aurelius Prosenes, freedman of the Emperors, chamberlain
to the Emperor, procurator of the treasury, procurator of the imperial
estate, procurator of gladiator-shows, procurator of wines, appointed to
the service by the divine Commodus, and a most dutiful and well-deserving
patron, his freedmen from their own money caused this sarcophagus to
be adorned." The notice of the find, signed by the commissioner of antiquities, Carlo Fea, emphasized that this Prosenes was an important person
in ancient Rome. Fea noted that Prosenes, as a former slave, had held
some of the most prestigious positions of administration and was personal
attendant to the emperor—a powerful figure in the palace.[1] The next year
a second notice for the monument appeared. Again the Latin inscription
was recorded, but this time the author of the notice, Giorlamo Amati, also
called attention to two defective lines on the sarcophagus's upper right
band. The first expert editors of the sarcophagus, Amati says, did not think
to read the Latin. But, Amati related, both he and the illustrious Emiliano
Sarti did so, and they provided the secondary Latin inscription in their
publication. The English reads: "Prosenes, gathered to god on the 5 Nones

. . . nia in the consulship of Praesens and Extricatus for the second time, as he was travelling back to the city from the expedition. His freedman Ampelius wrote this." Not only was Prosenes a major political figure, Amati notes, but his promotions in the service led to major military dignity as well since he traveled in the expedition's retinue.[2] So end the notices.

A decade later the legendary Italian archaeologist Giovanni Battista de Rossi (1822–1894), the renowned father of "Christian archaeology," first saw Prosenes's sarcophagus perched at the then-new entrance to the Villa Borghese. The timing was fortuitous. De Rossi was in the midst of compiling his mammoth collection of all Christian inscriptions found in Rome and its surroundings, the multivolume *Inscriptiones Christianae Urbis Romae*. The phrase "gathered to god" (*receptus ad deum*) that occupied the side of the sarcophagus was perfect. De Rossi must have immediately understood the significance. Here was a Christian inscription. But it was no ordinary Christian inscription. It was the earliest example of a Christian inscription from Rome (182–217 CE). And even more extraordinary, the person recorded as an imperial freedman, once manager of the entire imperial household and the right-hand man of the Roman emperor Caracalla, must himself have been a Christian.[3] De Rossi displayed the inscriptions at the front of his collection (*ICUR* 1.5).

Since then the Prosenes monument has been especially valuable to the pioneer narrative because it explains how early Christianity, in coming "out of the shadows" onto the world stage, made a profound social ascent. Prosenes, it is thought, demonstrates the changing social composition of Christianity during the third century. This imperial freedman has come to exemplify how "successful" Christianity was even prior to Constantine, attesting that Christians were "a persistent presence in the palace" from the time of the apostle Paul.[4] In the battle between "pagans and Christians," A. D. Lee writes, Prosenes shows that Christianity "penetrated the administrative ranks of the imperial palace" earlier than expected and "to quite a high level."[5] Like a weathervane Prosenes signaled the new world order of late antiquity.

In many ways Prosenes is representative of the modern narrative and its quest to find Christians in the imperial household. His case also reveals the pitfalls that accompany efforts to excavate those Christians from the material record of the early third century. For this reason, Prosenes and his sarcophagus deserve special attention. The following chapter will then turn to other inscriptions from the imperial household that have a similar pedigree in epigraphic and archaeological catalogues.

Despite being featured for over a century and a half in the most authoritative collection of Christian inscriptions from Rome (*ICUR*) the

Prosenes material demands a more careful interpretation. The sarcophagus monument defies the pagan-Christian taxonomy that has long been used to identify Prosenes as a Christian. The ostensible Christian content on the sarcophagus, rather than a covert profession of Prosenes's faith, is an example of commemorative discourse. Above all, Ampelius's inscription expressed piety toward Prosenes, his deceased patron. The sarcophagus and the inscriptions were also quite Roman. The monument reflects the burial customs, commemorative practices, and ritual world typical of Roman slaves and freedpersons, so much so that Prosenes's freedmen and slaves were actually participants in the cult of the dead. They honored both their deceased patron and their "divine" patron, the emperor Commodus.

To appreciate the monument in its original cultural context first requires exposing some of the methods that have guided previous interpretations of Prosenes and his sarcophagus. Once the problem areas are identified, a "reexcavation" of the monument can commence. The reinterpretation involves contextualizing the sarcophagus inscriptions as part of a three-dimensional memorial in a particular commemorative setting and drawing from other, analogous inscriptions of imperial personnel. In so doing, the method I use sets the monument on a continuum of material culture discourse shared by many groups in Rome.

Problems with Method

Since De Rossi first labeled the Prosenes monument a Christian artifact there have been few dissenters. Most commentators have simply assumed that the powerful high court official named Marcus Aurelius Prosenes had been a Christian.[6] The assumption has fermented, even allowing scholars to reconstruct a biography for Prosenes, which is then redeployed in historical reconstructions of early Christianity. It is stated without qualification that "Prosenes converted to Christianity"; that Prosenes entered "into the Christian catechumenate" and that Prosenes's position as overseer of the gladiatorial games may have kindled the Church Order (*Traditio Apostolica*) against such activity in the third century; and that during his lifetime at the imperial court Prosenes may have cultivated a façade so as not to "betray his Christianity." Prosenes has been described as a "respected figure" among the "Christian community" of imperial personnel and courtiers in Severan Rome.[7] He has even been associated with the Carpophorus from Hippolytus's *Refutation of All Heresies* (see appendix 2). More recently others have entertained the idea that Marcia, the concubine of Commodus (see chapter 4), helped the Christian Prosenes advance in the imperial administration.[8]

And yet all of this hangs on a later, laconic, and allegedly Christian phrase that Ampelius scratched on the band of a perfectly ordinary Roman sarcophagus. For this very reason, some scholars have voiced doubts about the traditional interpretation of the monument. Barbara Borg has noted that it is far from certain that the phrase *receptus ad deum* refers to the Christian god. Carlo Carletti has likewise observed that the "formula" (*receptus ad deum*) cannot be constituted as a sure attribution. In second- and third-century epigraphy, Carletti explains, "there are no shortage of pagan funerary attestations" that use analogous phrases with Roman chthonic deities—for example, *dei manes receperunt*.[9]

Added to this, the term *deus* was not simply a code word for Christ. Even a reference to one god was not exclusive to Christians, since during the Severan period in particular focus on one god or divine unity ("monotheism") was the zeitgeist. This period saw the cult of Sol Invictus come into its own, producing a universal solar monotheism embracing all other deities, and enabling divine power to be focused on the emperor (see appendix 2).[10] What is more, other epigraphic phrases similar to Ampelius's that have been designated as positively "Christian locutions" (*receptus in pace* or *accepta ad deum*) do not appear in inscriptions before the fourth century, and most are even later.[11] This chronological fact has led defenders of Prosenes's Christianity to fitfully circular explanations. Peter Lampe admits that comparing Ampelius's inscription with the later Christian comparanda is "anachronistic, "but," he says, "it must remain, because there is hardly any comparable Christian material for comparison in this early period. In the area of recognizably Christian epigraphy, Christians are still newcomers."[12] In other words, what constitutes Christian content is narrowly defined by comparison with other, and inevitably later, inscriptions that have already been classified as Christian. Any sense of parity with non-Christian materials is largely unknown.[13]

Just as problematic is the methodological hedging that often accompanies the standard explanations of the monument. At the same time that Ampelius's formula *receptus ad deum* is claimed to be recognizably Christian, it is also claimed that the monument is *clandestinely* Christian. According to conventional explanations, Christians of the early third century did not dare publicly display their "Christianity" on a stone. Because of Rome's usual legal practice that persecuted and martyred Christians merely on the grounds of the "name Christian" (*nomen christianum*), they instead composed epitaphs that gave nothing away. Ampelius's additional inscription would show that Christians hid behind plainly pagan, or at least neutral, epitaphs.[14] Ampelius etched an "almost hidden confession of faith," a "veiled profession of Christian allegiance," an "undeniable hint" on the upper band, and an otherwise religiously "neutral" sarcophagus covered his tracks.[15]

But the notion that Prosenes's monument was intentionally clandestine, arcane, deceptive, or invisible to non-Christians then runs headlong into contradiction.[16] For those who say that the monument is neutral ultimately conclude that it is really Christian. Likewise, many have suggested that Christians of the imperial household, because of their solid occupational status, prominent place in Roman society, and personal relationship of patronage to the emperor enjoyed a privileged protection from legal denunciation and the empire's "outbreak" against the Christians.[17] So while Prosenes is affirmed as someone who was protected and powerful, his Christian identity is described as veiled, almost hidden, and hinted at. "No-one was flaunting Prosenes's commitment," writes one scholar, "but it is explicit."[18]

All of this is mystifying. In certain times, in specific places, and for certain reasons, some followers of Christ were persecuted and killed. Yet such persecution does not apply to Rome during the Severan period and certainly not to imperial slaves and freedpersons of that time. In fact, the opposite seems to be the case.[19] Christian apologists like Tertullian and later Eusebius—neither of whom was ever shy about pointing out persecutions and martyrdoms—looked to Severan Rome as a model of tolerance. And both apologists underscored that there were known Christians who served the emperors without difficulty (see chapter 3 and the conclusion).

Besides, a persecution narrative cannot explain epigraphic content. If Ampelius was at legal risk, why then would he explicitly identify himself by signing the inscription with his own name? If Christian imperial slaves and freedmen were protected from legalities, why is the monument still "neutral" and Ampelius's inscription "veiled"? And if there was little risk for Prosenes—he was dead, after all—why was Ampelius not more explicit: *Prosenes Christianus*? What real purpose would it serve Ampelius, anyway, to only sort of identify Prosenes as a Christian? In reality, the idea of concealment in neutrality, expressed with bewildering descriptors like "phanero-Christian" or "crypto-Christian," has more to do with modern misunderstanding of ancient epigraphic intentions and stylistic conventions than anything else.[20]

The inherent problem is the category of analysis. The majority who have analyzed the Prosenes monument have used a pagan/Christian taxonomy that simply does not hold up to scrutiny.[21] The idea is that early Christian funerary dedications demonstrate "deep ties with pagan epigraphy," distinguishing themselves only, and not always securely, by "a few clues" like "Christian symbols," "forms of salutation or acclamation," a "communal element," and a "basic attitude." For this reason, an inscription consigning a person to the Roman chthonic deities (Di Manes) but also recording that the person "sleeps in peace" might still be categorized as a "Christian inscription."[22] The internal "religious" indicators are weighed against each other to determine if the overall content is pagan or Christian. The Prosenes monument combines "pagan" and Christian elements, but the *receptus ad deum* is thought to be the "clue" that "tips the scale in favor of the Christianity of the text."[23]

Yet weighing epigraphic content as if on a scale is a facile way to understand an inscription. It breaks up an object into supposedly "Christian" and "pagan" elements, gives more "weight" to the "Christian" elements than it does to the "pagan" ones, and assumes that an object from antiquity, despite the composite semiotics, should ultimately have a single "religious" meaning. This is not the case. The absence of a Dis Manibus formula on the sarcophagus does not by default make it Christian either. Examples of "the Divine Shades" appear on inscriptions in conjunction with Christograms well into the fourth and even fifth centuries.[24]

Even if *Christianus* had been etched on the Prosenes monument, what "Christian" meant—especially for a figure like Prosenes—would still be open to question. The meaning of "Christian" in the Severan period, as in any period, depends on whom one asks. As Justin Martyr once said, not all who call themselves Christians are Christians.[25] Certainly, devotees of Christ including some imperial personnel could have set up epitaphs or tombs just as devotees of other gods did. And yet the search for specifically Christian "identity elements" and religious credos in the epigraphic medium is likely doomed if Christian*ness* was fluid.[26] The search would be equally doomed if the artistic content, especially of the early third century, was meant to reflect a broader commemorative practice rather than merely Christianness. This is all the more reason to resist making monolithic claims about the Christian identity of Prosenes, or any other person from the imperial household for that matter. Because in the end, binary religious categories such as "pagan" or "Christian," which have so often been used to brand a religious identity onto the material, obscure rather than elucidate the breadth of significance that an artifact could have in its specific environment. For what is irretrievably lost to the modern investigator is the belief of the subject involved.[27]

More recently the problems with using time-honored religious categories for epigraphic analysis have been acknowledged, even if new terminology has not yet been adopted. Recent scholarship has also emphasized the need to evaluate so-called Christian epigraphy and burials within a broader epigraphic and cultural context.[28] I take up these tasks below.

I begin by first reexcavating the Prosenes monument within its original archaeological setting.

Reexcavating the Prosenes Monument

The famed sarcophagus of Marcus Aurelius Prosenes is located a few hundred meters east of the Flaminio entrance to the Villa Borghese. Elevated on a pediment, in De Rossi's day it would have dominated the view of those entering the gardens. Now the sarcophagus is hidden from view. Enclosed within a high-walled construction zone, it sits awkwardly before a stagnant pool of muddy water. Scrap metal, pylons, fencing, and construction shelters encroach upon it. The overgrown vegetation that surrounds the monument has now made its way through the cracks in the once pristine sarcophagus face. Grime and mildew cling to the surface. To add insult to injury, a vandal even tagged the back with spray paint. The current state of the sarcophagus is a far cry from its antique setting when the monument on the Via Labicana was nestled among the rolling fields of suburban Rome.

During the imperial period, southeast of the city, villas and funerary monuments were strewn along the north and south sides of the Via Labicana. In 1983, following the installation of a sewer that had destroyed massive walls near Torre Maura at mile eight of the ancient Via Labicana (present-day Via Casilina), an emergency excavation unearthed one of the ancient villas. Over a number of seasons, excavators articulated the different phases of the complex, which was partly agricultural, partly residential, and in use from the Late Republic to late antiquity. The third phase (C) of the villa saw, among other additions, a new atrium that included a black-and-white mosaic in a geometric pattern and a water basin (*vasca*). Just before the initial excavations of this area began in 1983 a small water pipe (*fistula*) was recovered from that basin. The stamp on the pipe reads: Aurelius Prosenes. The proximity of the two finds—the Prosenes sarcophagus and the *fistula*—combined with the rare cognomen Prosenes makes the identification nearly certain.[29] Marcus Aurelius Prosenes, the imperial freedman of Caracalla, most likely owned a vast villa estate (*praedium*) between the sixth and eighth miles of the Via Labicana, today's Torre Maura and Torre Nova. When, and how, Prosenes obtained the estate is unknown, though his freedmen apparently installed his open-air sarcophagus on his estate between the sixth and seventh miles of the Via Labicana, presumably where passersby could see it.[30]

Ampelius's secondary inscription offers some clues about what prompted the freedmen's commemorative activity. Prosenes had accompanied Caracalla on his Parthian campaign (216–17 CE). On the way back

from the campaign to Rome Prosenes had died. The portion of the sarcophagus upon which Ampelius chiseled has been damaged, so the name
of the location where Prosenes died is defective. If De Rossi's restoration
of the inscription is correct, though, Prosenes died at Same in Cephallenia
(present-day Sami, Cephalonia, which is the largest of Greece's Ionian
Islands), well over a thousand kilometers from Rome. Some of Prosenes's
slaves and freedmen, perhaps including Ampelius himself, must also have
traveled in the expedition's entourage and were there when Prosenes died.

Following the conventions of kinship duty (*pietas*), this group of
dependents was then responsible for composing Prosenes's epitaph and
adorning his sarcophagus. The selection of a sarcophagus by Prosenes's
freedmen was not evidence that the freedmen sought a "Christian burial" for
Prosenes, or further corroboration for Ampelius's profession of Prosenes's
Christianity, as some have claimed. There is also no reason to assume that
Prosenes's flesh-eater actually had his flesh. Based on a circular logic, some
have argued that the sarcophagus itself suggests a Christian activity, since
"burial, not cremation, was cherished by the Christians."[31] By the third
century, however, interment was increasingly popular among Romans. In
Roman funerary practice it also was possible to "bury" an absent body in
an imaginary funeral (*funus imaginarium*), and some sarcophagi were even
used for cremation burials.[32] In my view, this was likely Prosenes's fate.

It would make more sense that Prosenes was either buried on the
island of Cephalonia and his bones later returned to Rome, or cremated on
the island and his remains returned to Rome in due time.[33] The sheer difficulty of transporting Prosenes's quickly rotting corpse over such a great
distance (1,000 km), even if he had been embalmed, makes an immediate
interment on the Via Labicana impractical. After arriving in Rome with
a decomposing corpse the freedmen would still have to select and install
the sarcophagus.

Examples among other imperial personnel prove to be insightful
in this respect. Marcus Ulpius Phaedimus was a freedman of Trajan.
Like Prosenes, he, too, rose through the slave system from cupbearer (*a
potione*) to *lictor* nearest the emperor, and then to the right arm of the
emperor—"keeper of privileges granted by the emperor" (*a commentariis
beneficorium*). He even had a slave, Valens, in charge of his clothes (*a veste*).
Phaedimus was one of Trajan's favorites. He accompanied Trajan on his
long Mesopotamian campaign (113–17 CE). During the return in 117 CE,
Phaedimus died, just a few days after Trajan, at Selinus in Cilicia, near
present-day Gazipaşa, Turkey. Upon Phaedimus's death, Valens became
Phaedimus's freedman and even managed to become an imperial freedman himself. It was also Valens who brought his patron's remains back to

Rome. However, Valens did not do so until over a decade later, in 130 CE. He inscribed this detail on the epitaph that he later erected for Phaedimus in Rome. The interval makes it likely that Phaedimus had originally been cremated in Selinus, and his ashes, rather than his bones, later returned to Rome.[34]

Similar circumstances befell the imperial freedman Titus Aelius Titianus, guardian of the priestly archives. Titianus died at Carnuntum on the Danube sometime between 170 and 172 CE, probably accompanying Marcus Aurelius, who was there campaigning against the Macromanni. Titianus's wife, Flavia Ampelis, then received permission from the emperor to return Titianus's remains (*reliquiae*) to Rome. But only later did Ampelis return them, as she inscribed this information on her husband's urn.[35]

These examples help tell Prosenes's story. Ampelius and the other freedmen, by retrieving their patron's remains and furnishing his sarcophagus, acted as other Roman freedmen would have. The sarcophagus that the freedmen chose was also adorned with standard funerary imagery (fig. 7).[36] On the main face, two winged putti hold the vertical dolphin handles of a tablet on which Prosenes's *cursus honorum* was engraved. Below the tablet are two crossed cornucopias. At the feet of the putti are quivers and bows. Next to them, two lit torches lean against the cornered pillars upon which is the image of an urn. Vines flow across the upper band of the box. On each acroterion a putto sleeps on a bundle of scrolls (*rotuli*). Resting griffins in midrelief occupy the short sides. Finally, the sarcophagus lid shows Prosenes lying on a dining couch (*kline*) dressed in a tunic and pallium, ready to be feted by his freedmen when they come to his monument. Unfortunately, but predictably, only Prosenes's lower half is now preserved. Previous commentary on the monument has tended to downplay the ornamentation and gloss over certain aspects that do not conform to a Christian interpretation. Hence, the dubious modern concept of "neutral" is applied. The designation "neutral" is built upon the presumption that Prosenes, and a number of his freedmen, were Christians to begin with and so would not want any explicitly "pagan elements."[37] Yet both the putti and the griffins had mythological overtones. The putti are part of a Cupid motif, which earlier interpreters had actually identified as Prosenes's guardian spirits (*genii*). These images had a range of associations from pleasure, fertility, and prosperity to the gods Venus and Dionysius to death and apotheosis.[38] Had the freedmen wanted a "completely neutral" appearance they could have picked a different sarcophagus.

In the central inscription, the freedmen also affirm the emperor Commodus as divine (*divus*). Lampe tries to explain away this "pagan element" by citing "the usual epigraphic expression" and further argues that the

FIG. 7 Sarcophagus monument of the imperial freedman Marcus Aurelius Prosenes. Front view. Villa Borghese Park (Flaminio), Rome.

freedmen "of course refrain from such other pagan religious formulas as 'dis minibus.'"[39] But the freedmen did not have to include the title *divus* in the first place. It was a usual epigraphic expression because in life and in death, Romans and imperial personnel approached former emperors as divinities.[40] As proper Roman piety dictated, the freedmen recognized "the divine Commodus" as the initiator of Prosenes's good fortune, and by extension their own. This is why they honored Commodus with the inscribed term *divus* in the first place. Ampelius was certainly included among the *liberti* mentioned on the same central inscription that recognized Commodus as divine.

Beyond the representation on the monument itself, the ritual space it occupied is significant. There is no reason to doubt that Prosenes's slaves and freedmen would have given him the traditional funerary rites, including sacrifice, libations, incense, and/or offerings to the Roman gods. The freedmen would also have regularly gathered to feast with Prosenes, who was now, according to their cosmology, part of the divine realm. Banquets at the graves of family and friends—that is, meals with the dead—were

FIG. 8 Secondary Latin inscription of Ampelius, freedman of Prosenes, showing "received to god" (*receptus ad deum*) on the upper right band of the sarcophagus.

standard among Romans and Roman Christians alike. Besides the anniversary of Prosenes's death there were other opportunities in the Roman calendar (*dies Natalia, parentalia, rosalia*) for the freedmen to enact their piety toward their patron, and to properly remember him, by sacrificing or pouring libations to his *Manes*.[41]

It was most likely on one of these cultic occasions that Ampelius, prompted by the rituals honoring his dead patron, left his mark on the sarcophagus band (fig. 8). I would suggest that the inspiration for Ampelius to add the inscription was his own manumission. Ampelius was once Prosenes's slave and was probably manumitted upon Prosenes's death (*ex testamento*)—a common practice, as the examples of Phaedimus and Valens indicate. While commemorating Prosenes, Ampelius would add the inscription to toast his own manumission, his newfound status, and his patron's generosity. After all, he signs his inscription "Ampelius, (his) freedman." The signature was a pious act. Ampelius commemorated his patron Prosenes by remembering the place and date of his death, as well as his reception into the divine realm, to (or among) an unnamed god.

The area on the sarcophagus that Ampelius chose for the inscription, however, more likely had to do with space and aesthetics than a desire to covertly profess Prosenes's Christian faith. It was common for epitaphs to have later additions, especially at the bottom of the texts. In this case, without defacing the monument there was not enough space on the tablet or the

sarcophagus face to accommodate Ampelius's inscription. But the upper
right band of the sarcophagus lid provided a long (1.5 m), flat surface for
Ampelius to work his chisel. His hand is fairly neat, and the style of his *L*s
and *A*s resemble that of the tablet. The size of his lettering (3–4 cm) is, in
fact, nearly identical to the lettering on the main inscription (3–4.5 cm).

In other words, there is nothing about Ampelius's inscription that
is surreptitious. Had he wanted to hide something, he could have chiseled less, with smaller lettering, on the back or behind the *kline*. Instead,
despite the irregular Latin grammar and the damaged portion, Ampelius's
inscription is entirely legible. Anyone who approached the right side of the
sarcophagus could have seen it.

Claiming Prosenes as a Christian

A cast of that same right side, along with a cast of Prosenes's *cursus honorum,* is now on display in the Vatican's Pio-Cristiano Museum. The display,
in all its selectivity, is a testament to the modern claim of Prosenes as an
important Christian, worthy of an esteemed place in Christian cultural
heritage. Notwithstanding that heritage, however, when Ampelius chiseled
receptus ad deum on the side of his patron's sarcophagus he was conveying
something that, in my view, cannot be readily captured by the monolithic
category "Christian." As physical forms of memory, epitaphs were idealized
commemorations of the deceased. And sometimes it is necessary to distin-
guish commemorative practices, such as the death-writing expressions,
from social or religious reality.[42]

In the case of Prosenes, Ampelius's epigraphic phrase was a commemorative discourse. Ampelius made a polysemous expression. It was open to
a plurality of interpretations and reinterpretations.[43] The secondary phrase
"received to god" may have been a discourse that Romans and Roman
Christians alike would have used or would have recognized. Or it may even
have been meant to evoke a view of death to which third-century Roman
Christians would have subscribed. But whatever Christian meaning can
be squeezed from Ampelius's "formula," that meaning would still reflect
Ampelius and *his* vision, more than it would Prosenes himself.[44]

Indeed, the composite nature of the monument and the polysemy of
Ampelius's inscription are in some sense where the stone resembles real life.
Christians were not all alike.[45] There was more than one way to display one's
Christianness. And whether in the first or the third century, any members
of the imperial household who were devotees of Christ were not *only* that.
Even if Prosenes's devotional practices were known, "Christian" would
have had a number of registers and been fleshed out in several different

ways. Moreover, any glimpse of the "cultic gestures" on the marble would have appeared within a range of *religiones* and human relationships, as Jaś Elsner says.[46] So even if *receptus ad deum* was a locution shared among certain Christians in Rome, Ampelius engineered that expression for a particular commemorative moment and published it in a particular commemorative space. It was not necessarily indicative of his piety practices in everyday life, much less of Prosenes, whose voice is entirely absent here.[47] Considering the epigraphy as a distinct mode apart from everyday reality, the temptation to make definitive claims about Prosenes's Christianness should also be resisted. To take such a step goes beyond the evidence.

Although in the present discussion I have emphasized the limitations of knowledge, all is not lost. The Prosenes monument affords the opportunity to think about what "Christian" could have meant in Severan Rome. If Prosenes was devoted to Christ at all, there were multiple "category memberships" and alternating piety practices, with various saliencies and intermittent hierarchies. He could have provided money, banquets, a meeting space, or access to his estate, from which a group of Christians might have benefited. But Prosenes's Christianness—whatever that might have been—would not have always been activated, given priority or even significance, simply because it may have been available.[48] The emperors' slaves and freedpersons inhabited a religious landscape—work, theater, racetrack, arena, crossroads, civic buildings, urban festivals, and the halls of the palace—that constrained their loyalty to the Roman gods, and to "the divine Commodus" himself. There is every reason to believe that Prosenes fulfilled his duty, just as other members of the imperial household did. For some that meant their loyalty to Christ would also be stretched or, in some cases, torn.[49]

So those who wish to measure Christianity's sociopolitical rise in the Roman Empire by divining the presence of Christians in the imperial household would do well to remember that for imperial personnel like Prosenes, the meaning of "Christian" would always have been conditioned and variable. This is an especially appropriate check on investigating Christian members of the imperial household. The lives of imperial slaves and freedpersons were fundamentally defined by their relationship to the emperor and all the duties (*pietas*) that such positionality required. "Christian" was a polynomial expression in the same way that "Roman" was a discourse of possibilities.[50] Even Tertullian, arguably the most hard-line apologist of this period, articulated the terrific idea of "almost Christian" (*paene Christianus*). And it is no coincidence that Tertullian used this phrase to describe a high-ranking political official, Claudius Lucius Herminianus, governor of Cappadocia, whom, Tertullian says, died almost a Christian (*Scap.* 3). Perhaps Prosenes, too, died "almost a Christian."

Prosenes's monument is thus an important reminder that in antiquity, what it meant to be a Christian—if the "to be" verb is even appropriate—was never as clear-cut as the strokes of stonework.[51] Particularly in expressions of material culture, "Christian" and "Roman" were also intertwined more tightly, and for much longer, than is often acknowledged. And as the following chapter illustrates, the ability of modern interpreters to identify Christians in the imperial household by citing inscriptions, even from Rome's catacombs, is equally complex as the Prosenes monument.

CHAPTER 6

CHRISTIANS AND IMPERIAL PERSONNEL
IN ROME'S CATACOMBS

> Sometimes epigraphic pitfalls emerge as windfalls. More
> often, they deceive the unwary into believing things that are
> not so.
>
> —JOHN BODEL, *EPIGRAPHIC EVIDENCE*

Besides the Prosenes sarcophagus, in the remainder of the nineteenth century, and into the early twentieth century, several other notable inscriptions naming slaves or former slaves of the emperors were found in Rome. These inscriptions, which were discovered in the reexcavated catacombs, lent themselves even more readily than Prosenes's sarcophagus to finding Christians in the imperial household. For in addition to their presence in what was thought to be an exclusively Christian burial setting—the catacombs—many of the inscriptions were epitaphs that also bore symbols like the fish and the anchor, long thought to be definitive signs of the ancient Christians who had once populated Rome's underground hollows. The inscriptions were then catalogued, in some cases reidentified, as Christian artifacts by the notable founders of "Christian epigraphy": Giovanni Battista de Rossi, Orazio Marucchi (1852–1931), Ernst Diehl (1874–1947), and the indefatigable Antonio Ferrua (1901–2003).[1] As some of the first fruits from the new field a number of these inscriptions recording imperial slaves and freedpersons were circulated for a wider audience in the *Bulletino di Archeologia Cristiana* (1863–94), begun by De Rossi, and in the *Nuovo Bulletino di Archeologia Cristiana* (1895–1922). Along with being circulated for mass consumption in newly available catalogues and periodicals, several of these inscriptions began appearing in the earliest handbooks on "Christian epigraphy" in which they were often grouped under natural headings like "imperial civil servants" or "slaves and freedmen."[2]

What was once a relatively random collection of a few inscriptions from Christians in the imperial household grew and morphed. Now the inscriptions are considered to be a full-blown corpus of at least a dozen examples, with some being added and others dropped over time. The Prosenes monument remained the crown jewel.[3] But taken together and in light of the Prosenes monument, the inscriptions suggested a particular group—some would even say acquaintances—of influential Christians in the imperial household during the early third century. The material also appeared to verify the literary references to Christians in the *familia Caesaris* during this period and so added a further testimonial to the modern narrative of Christians in Caesar's household.

Although some inscriptions that have been catalogued and cited as the products of Christians in the imperial household are dubious (see appendix 2), others found in Rome's catacombs do indeed reflect an emergent Christian material culture. By that, I mean that the epigraphic material likely expressed fundamental elements of a Christian group's cosmology, at least in the context of individualized, commemorative funerary rituals.[4] However, these commonly cited inscriptions from the catacombs are not hard evidence for Christians in Rome's imperial household during the early third century.

Previous classifications of these inscriptions, largely indebted to the transcriptions of the epitaphs in catalogues, have traditionally operated with a narrow view of the catacombs and a static view of the epitaph stones themselves. Yet Rome's underground hollows were ever shifting sites for Christian and non-Christian burials throughout late antiquity. The epitaphs of the interred—including the epigraphy and iconography so vital to identifying Christian burials—were also frequently made of reused material from the plundered tiles and marble fragments of earlier monuments.[5] Here the inscriptions recording imperial slaves and freedpersons come to the foreground.

The Roman Empire's most epigraphically attested slave group was located in the imperial capital. Thousands of inscriptions mentioning imperial slaves and freedpersons, the vast majority epitaphs, filled Rome's landscape, from the cavernous columbaria of the early imperial period to the house tombs and monuments along the roads leading to and from Rome to the hypogea of the catacombs themselves. In several cases, the land on which certain catacombs developed and the hypogea within which bodies were interred were originally dominated by the funerary activity of imperial slaves and freedpersons. It is in this earlier epigraphic activity that

Rome's imperial household was implicated in the emergence of Christian material culture.

Some of the most commonly cited inscriptions for Christians in the imperial household, inscriptions found in the catacombs with a fish or anchor symbol and catalogued as Christian artifacts, were stones reused at a date well beyond the early third century. The original epitaph stones recording imperial slaves or freedpersons were recut and refitted to cover the burial niches (*loculi*) of other individuals in late antiquity. This activity was part of a broader trend in late antiquity in which earlier inscriptions of imperial personnel were spoliated in different ways and for different ends. But the reusing and reframing of epigraphic content was, in some cases, meant to create new expressions of Christian commemorative discourse at the beginning of the fourth century or later.

While I cannot possibly assess all the relevant inscriptions here, by examining the history of several exemplary epitaph stones and articulating the archaeological context of those epitaphs, a new profile of material evidence for Christians in Caesar's household comes into view. The emergence of a Christian material culture in late antiquity often developed through, and sometimes quite literally on, the bones of the emperors' slaves and freedpersons. Recent currents in catacomb study allow for a richer diagnostic discussion about the reuse and reworking of inscriptions from imperial personnel in Rome's funerary contexts. One inscription in particular is worthy of detailed examination—the influential epitaph of an imperial slave named Atimetus located at San Sebastiano ad Catacumbas takes us to the core of the catacombs and the beginnings of Christian material culture in late antiquity.

Currents in Catacomb Study

It was once standard to view the miles of catacomb galleries beneath the streets of Rome as the exclusive burial ground for ancient Christians. This view, which predated but intensified in the "rediscovery" of the catacombs in the sixteenth century, continued during the nineteenth century with the veritable explosion of interest in the catacombs. The reasons for understanding Rome's underground hollows as exclusively Christian sites are nearly as old and as complex as the catacombs themselves.[6] But apart from an overt apologetic approach, textual sources such as the medieval *Liber Pontificalis* and especially a single sentence from Hippolytus's *Refutation of All Heresies* were foundational to understanding the catacombs. According to the traditional interpretation of Hippolytus's text, at the beginning of the third century Pope Zephyrinus put Callistus, the slave of a Christian from Caesar's household, in charge of "the cemetery" of the Christian community (*Haer.* 9.12). De Rossi, for his part, identified this cemetery as the Catacomb of Callixtus on the Via Appia, even though Callistus himself was evidently buried elsewhere (see appendix 2). De Rossi's reading of the text from the *Refutation of All Heresies* then bolstered the view that Rome's other catacombs were also collective and exclusive Christian burial spaces that the ecclesiastical authorities oversaw.[7]

Within this framework, the epigraphic, iconographic, and artistic material unearthed from the catacombs was presumed a priori to be Christian. Exceptions could be noted, though they were often purposefully ignored. The burden of proof was to show that an inscription was *not* a Christian one.[8]

A classic example of this is Orazio Marucchi's analysis of an inscription that records an imperial freedman. The inscription was found "in the cemetery of Priscilla" on the Via Salaria Nova in northern Rome. The marble, which was broken in three places, was a plaque (*titulus*) for a family tomb. The owner and dedicator was the imperial freedman—the name is lost to the lacuna—who was also president of a tent-makers association (*Aug(usti) lib(ertus) praepositus tabernaculo[rum---]*).[9] The plaque was found only a short distance from another inscription that enclosed a burial niche (*loculus*) and commemorated a wife named Bibia Corinthia. The cognomen Corinthia suggested to Marucchi that the wife was probably from Corinth originally. Marucchi could not "help but run with the thought" that Aquila and Priscilla (or Prisca), the companions whom the apostle Paul met in Corinth, were also buried in the same cemetery. On De Rossi's hypothesis, based on Romans 16:3–5, it was thought that the couple had returned to Rome, where they founded a house church on the Aventine Hill. The church was later known as La Chiesa di Santa Prisca, and was connected to the large cemetery on the Via Salaria named after Priscilla. The inscription for an imperial freedman in charge of tent-makers, combined with an inscription for a woman from Corinth, both of which were discovered in a cemetery that was ostensibly connected to Priscilla and Aquila, who like Paul were tent-makers, led Marucchi to exclaim: "Who would deny some probability that the inscription [of the imperial freedman] now discovered belonged to the descendants of companions of Aquila and Prisca?"[10] The implication is that the imperial freedman, like Prisca and Aquila, may have been a follower of Christ.

The above sample of early Christian archaeology illustrates the power that the catacombs had to shape the epigraphic material found within. Other inscriptions recording imperial slaves and freedpersons that were merely found near the entrances to known catacombs were initially classified as Christian, then later erroneously recorded as coming *from* or found *in* the catacombs themselves—a provenance that only sustained the classification of the object as Christian (see appendix 2). Unfortunately, some of those inscriptions originally documented as Christian artifacts from the catacombs have gone unquestioned.

Yet the traditional assumptions about the catacombs have more recently been entirely undercut. Simply put, the catacombs were not exclusive Christian cemeteries that a central Roman Church instituted and maintained.[11] There is now undeniable evidence for "contemporary burial side by side, throughout the third and fourth centuries, of Christians and pagans, not only within a single tomb monument but in adjacent subterranean spaces."[12] And the catacombs, which had begun as private burial plots, continued to be controlled and managed by families at least through the mid-fourth century.[13] The work of Éric Rebillard has also shown that the word "cemetery" used in the *Refutation of All Heresies* (εἰς τὸ κοιμητήριον κατέστησεν), and which has propagated the traditional picture of the catacombs, did not designate a communal burial ground in the more modern sense of a churchyard until the sixth century. At the end of the second century CE, the term in both Greek and Latin (κοιμητήριον/ *coemeterium*) referred more precisely to a "tomb," and in the coming centuries the word began to refer to martyrs' tombs or the shrines surrounding them (*martyria*). A single "tomb" could be established for a collectivity of people, such as a family or a *collegium*, but the collective space was available because an individual owned the tomb and/or surrounding area and gave access by gift or purchase.[14] So it was that several of the early nuclei of catacombs (hypogea) were developed on private land (Catacomb of Priscilla), while others developed on imperial property (Catacombs of Domitilla, Sebastian, Praetextatus, and Pamphilius).[15] The distribution of property reveals much about those inscriptions of imperial slaves and freedpersons that were discovered in the catacombs.

Along with the catacombs the epigraphic material that was discovered has also been guided by the same set of assumptions. Conventionally, whether an inscription was discovered within or above the catacombs, if content that seemed to be Christian appeared on the stone, then the inscription, and by association the person(s) recorded on it, are also identified as Christian.[16] Content such as the anchor and fish images were viewed as a kind of imprimatur of Christian faith. One enduring example is a family tomb inscription (*titulus*) belonging to the early third-century imperial freedman named Lucius Septimius Severinus. The inscription says he "built the tomb (*munimentum*) with the enclosed field (*agello*) for himself, and his freedman and freedwomen and their posterity." The stone is headed with two fish facing an anchor. Both symbols have been interpreted as proof that Severinus was a Christian, and his *titulus* has been singled out as a very early attestation of such Christian symbolism.[17] In the early twentieth century, the inscription was even cited as a nice example of "Christians at Court and among the Governing Classes" during the period of 180–250 CE. This method of epigraphic analysis categorizes an inscription as Christian simply because it carries a symbol that evinces Christianity.[18]

And yet the tautology of this method often rests on the time-honored tradition about the "Christian" catacombs. The thinking is that recognizable and discrete Christian epigraphy and iconography began to develop in the early third century. This is precisely when Christian communities, it is thought, were able to own their own collective cemeteries, the most famous of these being the catacombs in Rome. It was then and there that "open expressions of Christianity" in "secure" burial locations were not only possible but became common.[19] Consequently, the analyses of epigraphy within the catacombs have been proleptic. It is assumed that even at the beginning of the third century there were figurative manifestations, such as a fish or an anchor, that could "already" be considered "precocious vectors" of a specifically Christian epigraphic tradition.[20]

In the third century, however, the fish and anchor were not exclusive Christian symbols and were not necessarily theological ideograms. The fish and anchor were the stonecutter's stock and trade. The images frequently appear in Greco-Roman art into late antiquity, and they had long functioned as metaphors for reaching a safe harbor at the end of one's journey.[21] The transformation of such iconographic images from one spectrum of metaphors to a more specific Christian spectrum—a metamorphosis usually termed the "Christianization of epigraphy"—was slow, irregular, and incomplete.[22] The beginnings of a distinctly Christian artistic repertoire, as many now increasingly argue, materialized no earlier than the end of the fourth century, though even then the older imagery remained functional, while new combinations of Christograms and Di Manes continued to appear together.[23]

Perhaps the best example of a Christian epigraphic expression from a member of the imperial household also dates to the mid- to late third century. An imperial freedman bookkeeper (*tabularius*) named Aurelius Primus, along with his wife, Cocceia Athenais, set up an epitaph for their daughter Aurelia Procope, who lived thirteen years, three months, and fourteen days (fig. 9). The epitaph stone, which came "from the cemetery of Hermes" on the Via Salaria Vetus, is headed with the date of Procope's death (*XVIII Kalendas Septembres*) and ends with the salutation "Peace be with you" (*pax tecum*).[24] Both epigraphic expressions—the date of death and salutation—reflect Christian commemorative discourse known

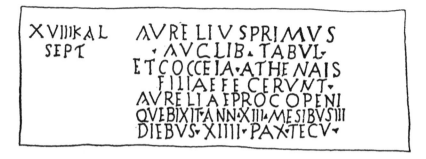

XVIIIKAL AVRELIVSPRIMVS
SEPT ·AVCLIB·TABVL·
ETCOCCEIA·ATHENAIS
FILIAEFECERVNT·
AVRELIAEPROCOPENI
QVEBIXITANN·XIII·MESIBVSIII
DIEBVS·XIIII·PAXTECV·

FIG. 9 Latin epitaph of Aurelia Procope, daughter of the imperial freedman Aurelius Primus, showing *depositio* and peace salutation. Mid- to late third century CE. Originally from Cemetery of Hermes, Rome.

elsewhere in late antique Rome. Still, it is unknown whether the imperial freedman, Primus, or his wife, Athenais, was a Christian, just as it is unknown whether it was Primus or Athenais who chose this particular funerary language. What makes interpreting this inscription as a Christian one more challenging, however, is that the other examples with the peace salutation range anywhere from 200 to 299 CE, while examples that record the date of death or *depositio* plus the *pax tecum* date to even later; the ornate script of the epitaph of Procope also suggests a date around the fourth century; and finally, Primus's imperial *gentilicium* "Aurelius" was used by emperors until Diocletian and Maxentius (307–12 CE).[25] All of the indicators on this epitaph point to the end of the third, if not the fourth century, for its commission.

The upshot is that neither the funerary context of the catacombs nor such funerary iconography as a fish or an anchor is a secure criterion for identifying deceased Christians from Caesar's household, especially not at an early third-century date. Rather than a label for an individual's religious affiliation, the material evidence from the catacombs reflects a more complicated calculus: the commemorative message that those commissioning the burials wished to convey according to their tastes and abilities to pay, the availability of subterranean "real estate," the location of other family burials, and the work and inclinations of the gravediggers (*copiatae, fossores*), who were responsible for siting and completing the burial.[26]

The cases of imperial slave and freedperson epigraphy help solve some of the calculus. Several inscriptions from imperial slaves and freedmen found in the catacombs illustrate some of the connections between the desired message, the processes of installing an epitaph, and the final reception of the monument.

Reusing Inscriptions from Imperial Personnel

At the end of the third and the beginning of the fourth century, epitaphs commemorating imperial slaves and freedpersons were being reused. In the process, some were also being transformed into newly made Christian material culture. Consider the following example. The epitaph recording an imperial freedman named Aurelius Sozon is from Rome's catacombs. It seals a specific *loculus,* in the galleries of the Catacombs of Priscilla (Gallery H, corridor 49) on the Via Salaria in ancient Rome's northern outskirts. In 1925, the epitaph naming Sozon was catalogued as a Christian inscription in Ernst Diehl's popular collection. The entry reads: *[. . . et] Aur(elius) Sozon, Augg. lib(ertus), cognatus, bene merenti posuerunt (ancora).*[27] The identification of the inscription as Christian is due principally to the anchor symbol that is carved onto a marble piece at the far right end, along with the fact that the inscription was discovered in a catacomb.[28] The epitaph naming Sozon has also been cited as part of a corpus of inscriptions that seemingly evince the growing presence of Christians in Rome's imperial household at the beginning of the third century.[29]

However, this interpretation of the Sozon inscription makes a crucial methodological mistake. The Sozon inscription is fragmentary. The marble (173 × 19 cm) is divided into three pieces, as it encloses a *loculus.* The center piece names Aurelius Sozon as an imperial freedman (*Augg. lib.*), but records that the inscription was dedicated by at least one other person, hence the plural *posuerunt.* As Marucchi originally detailed when he saw the inscription, two of the missing words in the Sozon epitaph can be reconstructed, since traces of letters from the preceding line are also visible. The missing words are *incomparabili et* (fig. 10). The more complete text should read: [*incomparabili et*] *Aur(elius) Sozon, Augg. lib(ertus), cognatus, bene merenti posuerunt.* What this means is that Sozon was a *commemorator* of this epitaph, not the one commemorated. Sozon and someone else (pl. *posuerunt*) set up an inscription for their well-deserving kin.

Even more important, Marucchi's observation, along with the drawing (*ICUR* 9.25009), indicates that the current epitaph is the last portion of an inscription that has been broken off, or deliberately cut off, and later reused to cover the present *loculus.* The person behind the epitaph, therefore, was not Sozon, and had no relation to the imperial freedman Sozon or to his kin. In fact, both Marucchi and the editors of this inscription in *ICUR* volume 9 state plainly that the stone had been reused.[30] In a surprising twist, it is only the most recent treatment of this inscription that has not voiced serious doubts about its Christian character.[31]

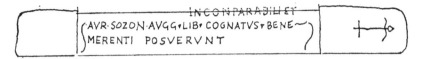

FIG. 10 Latin epitaph naming the imperial freedman Aurelius Sozon, with an anchor (right). Reused in the fourth century CE. Priscilla Catacombs, Rome.

Although the *loculus* itself does not belong to a Christian imperial freed-man named Aurelius Sozon, the current configuration of the monument teaches us something valuable about burial practices in late antiquity. When Marucchi discusses the reuse of the Sozon inscription in the *loculus* he relates that there were about ten other similar examples of spoliation and reusage in that same gallery. Marucchi cites, in particular, a tile that enclosed a *loculus* but had the name Fundanos written on the *inside* of the panel—that is, on the side closest to the remains and thus hidden from view. Oftentimes the *loculus* tile was painted over anyway.[32] But the examples that Marucchi mentions testify that the gravedigger (*fossor*) who reused the Sozon inscription and who was acting on the wishes of the family or friends of the deceased, cared more about burying the body and marking the site with a particular symbol than about the epitaph's text or even the name of the deceased showing on the marble.[33] It is certainly possible, even probable, that the anchor was intended to evoke a Christian commemorative discourse. But if this was the case, the image's discrete resonance belonged to a period later than Sozon himself. The gallery system in which the Sozon stone was reused (Gallery H) is a "fish-bone" pattern at the lower level of the Priscilla complex. This level began to be used only in the fourth century.[34]

Sozon's stone is a cautionary tale. One cannot automatically link the content of an enclosure slab with the identity of the person lying within the *loculus*.[35] On the one hand, modern investigators have precious few controls by which to determine when any of the opening, reclosing, or reuse of the material in the catacombs may have happened. The catacombs have been sites of looting since antiquity. But beginning in the seventeenth century, the catacombs were also thoroughly cleaned up in the interest of the Catholic Counter-Reformation.[36] So, as is the case with the Atimetus epitaph that I treat below, whether the current configuration of the Sozon slab is even ancient can be questioned. On the other hand, the *fossores* of antiquity often had to work quickly, and they were known to be thrifty.[37] The plentiful epigraphic material that imperial slaves and freedpersons left throughout Rome was ripe for the taking.

The distribution of property and burial space in Rome made imperial slave and freedperson epitaphs continuously available for reuse in the
catacombs. The hypogea of San Sebastiano, Pamphilius, and Praetextatus
developed on imperial property, according to Barbara Borg's study. The
large nuclei of these catacombs were primarily created for, though not
exclusively used by, the slaves and freedmen of the imperial house and the
aristocracy. Changes then occurred in the nuclei during the fourth century,
when Christians increasingly opted for burial in the catacomb galleries.[38]

At San Sebastiano ad Catacumbas there is abundant evidence for the
burial of imperial slaves and freedmen from the Flavian period onward
both above and below ground. An inscription for an imperial freedman
named Elpisius, for example, commemorating him to the Divine Shades,
was discovered in the second-century Mausoleum Y (Innocentiores) of
the *piazzola* area. In the same area, the lower chamber of Mausoleum Y
(*Innocentii*) also appears to have been a separate burial space reserved for
children, probably an association of boys and adolescents, within the imperial *familia*.[39] Similarly, throughout the second century, whole sections of
what would be known as the Praetextatus Catacombs were likely reserved
for imperial slaves who worked in the palace kitchen. This area of the
Praetextatus complex is known as the "region of the cooks" (*regio cocorum*).
At the same time, several tomb plaques (*tituli*) found above the catacomb
originally belonged to the families and kinship networks of imperial freedmen who were the head chefs (*archimagiri*) in the palace kitchen.[40]

As the hypogea of these catacomb systems were used and reused over
time, inscriptions of imperial personnel were also reused, whether for
Christians or not. A *titulus* from the ground tomb of an imperial freedman
cook named Eustathes was broken into six pieces but later reused in the
"main hall" (the Magna Spelunca) of the Praetextatus Catacombs.[41] The

FIG. 11 Latin epitaph
(*titulus*) of the impe-
rial freedman cook
Eustathes. Reused in
the Praetextatus Cata-
combs, Rome.

letter *D* of the dedication to the "Divine Shades" (Dis Manibus) is still pre-served on the stone (fig. 11). Another inscription from the palace staff, this time of the imperial freedman chef Hermes, was also reused in this same area during this period. Again, the letter *D* and a portion of *M* from the dedication to the "Divine Shades" (Dis Manibus) is still preserved. Though Antonio Ferrua does not explain how it was reused, these documented cases indicate a rich environment of spoliation.[42]

Besides the fragmentation of inscriptions, other inscriptions were reused on the back and witness a more explicitly Christian funerary dis-course. A *titulus* discovered "in the cemetery of Praetextatus," for instance, belonged to the tomb of an imperial freedman named Marcus Aurelius Secundus. The inscription for Secundus dates to the late second or early third century. The backside of this stone was reused to make an epitaph for one Hercules, recording the date of his *depositio* with a farewell *in pace*. This secondary Latin inscription for Hercules has since been cross-catalogued as Christian. It, too, dates to the fourth century.[43]

The act of reusing inscriptions that were first commissioned by or for imperial slaves and freedpersons was not even limited to the original hypogea, but could spill over into other catacomb systems. The Praetex-tatus Catacombs, for instance, developed contemporaneously with the Catacomb of Callixtus a few hundred meters away on the west side of the Via Appia. There in the Catacomb of Callixtus is an epitaph of an imperial freedman and palace chef (*archimagirus*) named Symphorus. The stone was discovered by De Rossi who did not catalogue the inscription as Christian, most likely because he noted that Symphorus's epitaph had been reused to enclose a *loculus* in the catacomb. But based on the comparanda of the imperial kitchen staff, the Symphorus stone had undoubtedly belonged to the Praetextatus complex nearby.[44]

These examples illustrate that not only were Rome's house tombs, columbaria, and catacombs works in progress throughout antiquity; the epitaph stones could be as well. Some inscriptions were fragmented or recut and then reused piecemeal (Sozon, Eustathes, Symphorus). Other stones were reused on the back. Still other inscriptions could also be reworked in other ways to reframe preexisting content.

Perhaps the most instructive case is the well-known epitaph of Licinia Amias, commissioned at the beginning of the third century and long thought to be one of the earliest Christian inscriptions from Rome, if not *the* earliest (fig. 12). It is now clear, however, that over at least a century the inscrip-tion underwent no less than *three stages* of modification. On the acroteria the dedication to the Divine Shades, the *corona lemniscata* with the ribbon bands (*vittae*), as well as the fish and anchor images, were part of the original

FIG. 12 Latin and Greek epitaph of Licinia Amias. The inscription was reworked in at least three stages over the course of a century. Third to fourth century CE. Museo Nazionale Romano—Terme di Diocleziano, Rome. Inv. 67646.

FIG. 13 Latin epitaph (*titulus*) of the imperial freedman Lucius Septimius Severinus (*CIL* 6.26259), reworked to preserve fish and anchor (top). West wall, Sala XIX of the Monastero di San Paolo Fuori le Mura, Rome.

inscription. The previous epitaph inscribed below these items was then erased to make room for the secondary inscription for Licinia Amias. Lastly, the Greek phrase "fish of the living" (ιχθύς ζώντων) was added in between the Dis Manibus and the fish and anchor.[45] It was only in this last stage of reuse, in the fourth or fifth century, that the inscription took on a Christian tenor.

The inscription I mentioned above from the imperial freedman Severinus now at San Paolo Fuori le Mura is similarly in a secondary or even tertiary form. The stone, which is embedded in the cloister wall of the church, has clearly been cut down. It lacks the typical bands and a textual margin so that the edges of several letters (e.g., *S* at the end of line 5, and *O* at the beginning of line 6) are diminished. At the top of the stone the tip of the anchor is running off of the epigraphic sheet (fig. 13).[46] These features indicate that as the inscription was reworked its first line(s) were cut off.

Someone in antiquity must have excised the initial line(s). By default, this act preserved and emphasized the fish and anchor heading. If this inscription was ever a Christian inscription, therefore, it is because the stone had been reframed at a time and in a setting in which the maritime images functioned as, and were perceived to be, Christian emblems. The reiteration would certainly have been at a time later than when Severinus himself had lived.

Atimetus at San Sebastiano ad Catacumbas

The practice of modifying and reusing inscriptions from imperial slaves and freedpersons comes to a head with the epitaph of the imperial house-born (*verna*) slave named Atimetus. He was commemorated by his parents, both of whom were also most likely imperial slaves. At the third-mile marker of the Via Appia, beneath the south-central nave of the Basilica di San Sebastiano Fuori le Mura (ad Catacumbas), in an area known as the *piazzola,* the epitaph records that Atimetus "lived eight years and three months. Earinus and Potens made the epitaph for their son." In its current form, the stone—carved on a poorly cut marble block—is a closure slab (55 × 29 cm) for a *loculus* (*lastra di chiusura*). On the epitaph an anchor is inscribed on the left side and a fish on the right. The epitaph is also framed by a continuous fresco on three sides. The left panel shows trees, deer, a donkey ridden by a person who seems to hold a baby in their arms, a large tree with red fruits, and two nude persons under the tree. On the right is a naked person, an arch, a nude man, an arch with a scale above, and another nude character (fig. 14).[47]

Because of the fish and anchor iconography in this catacomb-like context, the Atimetus epitaph has been catalogued and is often cited as a clear Christian inscription. Paul McKechnie's frequently cited article "Christian Grave-Inscriptions from the *Familia Caesaris*" compares the Atimetus epitaph to the Christian epitaph of the imperial freedman Aurelius Sozon. For McKechnie, Atimetus's Christian epitaph, like Sozon's, is evidence that both Atimetus and his parents, Earinus and Potens, had been Christians in Rome's imperial household during the Severan period (212–34 CE).[48] As such, Atimetus and his parents were individuals in a "social unit," attesting to the "solid occupational status of Christians in the *familia Caesaris* and the degree of confidence they seem to have had in publicising their allegiance in an innovative way."[49] Others have echoed this interpretation.

Just as we have seen in many cases throughout this book, the Atimetus epitaph attests to the resources that some imperial slaves had. Earinus and Potens, no doubt grieving their young slave son, were able to afford to commission a fairly large epitaph stone with an inscription and with symbols. Yet the epitaph of Atimetus is more complicated than it might

FIG. 14 Latin epitaph of eight-year-old house-born imperial slave Atimetus, set up by his parents Earinus and Potens, with surrounding fresco. Reused in mid- to late third century CE in the *piazzola* beneath the Basilica di San Sebastiano Fuori le Mura / Basilica Apostolorum, Rome.

seem. Unlike many other inscriptions discovered in Rome's catacombs, this inscription has been debated.[50] Not only that, the whole *piazzola* area is distinctive. Since the early twentieth century it has been recognized as a "mixed" environment that was never an exclusively Christian burial setting. The debate is over which inscriptions should be deemed Christian and how much of a Christian presence there was.[51] For notable archaeologists like Paul Styger, the Atimetus epitaph was more likely a "pagan" grave. Others, such as Antonio Ferrua and Franz Joseph Dölger, withheld judgment altogether after noting the difficulty of deciding between pagan and Christian.[52]

To further complicate matters the fresco and its relation to Atimetus's epitaph have received divergent interpretations as well. Some see Christian imagery where others see Roman tropes. Stefano Tortorella argues that, without a doubt, the fresco represents the triumphal entrance of Jesus into Jerusalem as in the Gospel of Matthew. This imagery, Tortorella relates, appears for the first time on Christian sarcophagi of the fourth century, and in paintings it seems to be unknown in the Christian repertoire prior to the first half of the fifth century. Nonetheless, for Tortorella, the painting around Atimetus's epitaph is special precisely because it shows this Christian imagery *already* in the first decades of the third century. If Tortorella's interpretation of the painting around Atimetus's epitaph is correct, however, then the painting would precede its comparanda by nearly two centuries.[53] To me that is unlikely. Either Tortorella's interpretation of the painting is off or the assigned date of the monument is too early.

By contrast, Roberta Casagrande-Kim has argued that the epitaph is very generic, and formulaic, and does not provide any information on the deceased's "credo," since fish and anchors were used elsewhere in the *piazzola*. The alleged Christian iconography that Tortorella sees, Casagrande-Kim continues, is completely absent from the scene on the right panel, and is tenuous at best on the left one. Instead, Casagrande-Kim proposes that the painting depicts Atimetus's movement through one region of Hades to the next. The motifs in the painting around Atimetus's epitaph would echo other, contemporaneous paintings—such as those from the Tomb of the Nasonii and the Hypogeum of the Aurelii—in depicting scenes of death and underworld journeys, but of a traditional, non-Christian form.[54]

And yet the problem with interpreting the monument as either Christian or Roman ("pagan") is that the epitaph, the fresco, and the *loculus* are all assumed to be contemporaneously connected developments that were installed de novo to represent the early third-century imperial slave Atimetus sealed within the *loculus*. This is not necessarily the case.

Indeed, the immensely complicated archaeological context of the *piazzola* suggests a far more fragmented history for the Atimetus monument.[55] Let me explain. The *piazzola* area was initially a pozzolana quarry during the early imperial period. From the second half of the first century, while mining underground was still going on, columbarium tombs began to be executed above ground approximately five meters to the north. These tombs were mostly used by imperial slaves and freedmen. At the beginning of the second century (Phase I), the adits of the mine started to be used for *loculus* burial in the walls. Again, this funerary activity was primarily related to imperial slaves and freedmen.[56]

After the roof of a large chamber of the mine had caved in sometime in the mid-second century, the cavities were filled with leveling materials, raising the ground level three meters from the older sandstone floor (*arenario*). Three tombs were then developed on the vertical tufa faces around the newly created sunken courtyard, which was dubbed a *piazzola* by G. Mancini (Phase II). This *piazzola* was now situated six meters below the surface but was open to the sky. The three tombs on the northwest perimeter of the *piazzola* are designated Mausoleums X, Y, and Z, and identified as those of Claudius Hermes, the Innocentiores, and the Axe, respectively.[57] Beneath these tombs, hypogea were dug out for *loculus* burials. Mausoleum Y, that of the Innocentiores, was in use at least through the 240s CE. In the lower chamber of this mausoleum, there were covered *loculi* for three children, named in Greek after the eponymous emperors of the year 238

CE, Gordianus, Pupienus, and Balbinus, each with the epithet "innocent" (*ILCV* 3995a–c).

Then according to the standard phasing of the area, around the mid-third century the floor level of the *piazzola* was raised again, probably because new galleries and grave recesses were excavated within the restricted area (Phase II₁). As a result, the small vaulted room on the southeast side of the *piazzola* where the Atimetus epitaph was set shows two levels of *loculus* burials, one lower and one superimposed approximately two meters higher. The Atimetus inscription belongs to this upper level.[58]

In the second half of the third century (Phase III), the *piazzola* was filled in with six meters of earth as construction of a new cult area (*memoria*) for the apostles Peter and Paul, what the discoverer Paul Styger called a *triclia*, began immediately above. The *triclia* became a paved courtyard with a dining room and benches along three walls where devotees gathered for funerary banquets (*refrigeria*) in honor of the two apostles. Finally, in the early fourth century (Phase IV), the whole area was buried under the foundations of the new basilica (Basilica Apostolorum Petri et Pauli).[59]

The relative chronology of the *piazzola*'s phases means that the *loculus* that the Atimetus epitaph covers belongs to the later or last phase of the *piazzola*'s usage before it was buried. So rather than the early third century, a conservative date range for the installation of the Atimetus epitaph in the *loculus* would be between 240 and 270 CE, if not later.[60]

However, the *piazzola*'s protean context also indicates a more disrupted arrangement of Atimetus's epitaph stone in the *loculus*. As Paul Finney once noted, following what Dölger hinted at fifty years prior, the Atimetus inscription was "evidently introduced as a *secondary* feature into the center of a loculus."[61] The epitaph stone indeed shows telltale signs of being cut down and reused from a once-larger inscription. The stone is oblong on the left and top, while relatively straight on the right and bottom. But on the bottom right side, the tail of the vertical fish also runs off of the smooth epigraphic surface and onto the roughly hewn marble beneath the sheet. The lettering of the inscription is then crowded at the top, while there is still ample space below. More conspicuous, at the end of the top line of the inscription the head stroke of the letter N (in VERN) is cut off. In the earliest available photograph, published by Styger in 1935, this feature is clearer than in the more recent photographs.[62] The stone's awkward shape, and its asymmetrical and diminished lettering, bespeak an epitaph that was originally commissioned for another burial setting.

If, as I have suggested, the current configuration of the Atimetus epitaph was not original, but the stone has been reused, then it is only in this last iteration that the inscription should be interpreted as a Christian burial monument. In all likelihood the Atimetus stone was reused in a similar way to the Sozon and Severinus inscriptions. The reuse also makes it less likely that Atimetus, the young imperial slave, was actually himself interred in the *loculus*. The "Christian inscription" was for someone else. Yet, in another sense, it is precisely the recycling of the imperial slave's epitaph that brings the fish and anchor images into sharper focus.

Because the archaeological context of the *piazzola* obviates the usual criteria for distinguishing a Christian inscription from a "pagan" one—such as a single and secure topography, Christian names, or typically Christian expressions—the only items that could be cited to interpret the Atimetus epitaph as a Christian artifact are the fish and anchor images.[63] Without allowing a more fluid reconstruction of the Atimetus monument, this limitation can lead to anachronistic and circular interpretations. The Christian "clues" offered by the inscription—namely, the fish and the anchor—confirm the interpretation of the painting as a Christian scene and then demonstrate the "Christianity of the *loculus*."[64] But the presence of imperial slaves and freedpersons in the area, coupled with the broader trends of reusing inscriptions, suggests that the fish and anchor images were later targeted and then harvested by the *fossor*. The remaking was done according to the wishes and finances of the family or kin who commissioned a burial for their departed loved one in that *loculus* beneath the *trcilia*.[65]

If the fish and the anchor are the litmus test for Christian iconography, then the reuse of the Atimetus epitaph by Christians would have been most intelligible closer to the fourth century, rather than the early third. The later era would align the epitaph more closely with the sarcophagi that Tortorella cites as comparanda and with the available epigraphic comparanda I surveyed above. The late third or early fourth century is also the date for the epitaph of Aurelia Procope by Aurelius Primus, probably the clearest example of Christian epigraphic habits from a member of the imperial household.

While the Atimetus stone likely belonged to an imperial slave who lived in the third century, only a later development would have influenced the remaking of the epitaph into a Christian piece.[66] That later development was most likely the cult for Peter and Paul. In the waning years of the third century at the earliest, the commemoration of the famous apostles in the *triclia* above the *piazzola* occasioned the creation of a Christian burial in the *loculus* below.[67] For even after the *piazzola* was buried for the above construction of the *triclia* around the mid-third century—a process that occurred in at least two phases (designated III and III$_1$)—and even after a tiled pavement was installed at this level, the upper portions of the *piazzola*

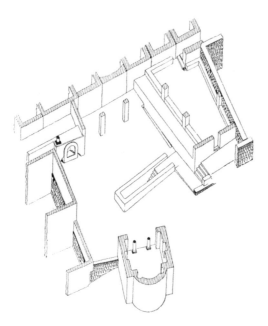

FIG. 15 Isometric reconstruction of the fourth arrangement of the *memoria apostolorum* (*triclia*) for Peter and Paul beneath the Basilica Apostolorum, showing the descending staircase to the *piazzola*. Late third to early fourth century CE.

underneath continued to be accessible (fig. 15). Visitors to the *triclia* set up for Peter and Paul could descend into the darkness below by a staircase that led down to a well (*la scala del pozzo*).[68] It is in this later, and increasingly Christian, context of the late third century when the martyrdoms of Peter and Paul were feted by devotees (on June 29) that the fish and anchor symbols would take on new valences.[69] It is thus fitting that beneath a cult site for Rome's two famous apostles—known for converting members of the imperial household (see chapter 2)—an epitaph of an imperial slave would be remade into Christian material culture.

In sum, the invention of a distinct Christian material culture in late antique Rome owes a debt of gratitude to the earlier epigraphic activity of imperial slaves and freedpersons. Out of grief for and piety toward their loved ones they furnished original material that *fossores* would later reuse to bury Christians and non-Christians alike. New Christian expressions were born and articulated even while Roman traditions of commemoration continued.

CONCLUSION

The Memory of Imperial Slavery in Early Christianity

> You will think it a joke—or an outrage, but a joke after all—
> if you read this.
>
> —PLINY THE YOUNGER

One day in the early second century the Roman senator Pliny the Younger was traveling to Tibur. Outside the city, a half mile east of Rome along the Via Tiburtina, a monument caught his eye. The monument was for Marcus Antonius Pallas, a freedman of the emperors Claudius and Nero. Also included on this monument was an inscription recording honors that the Roman Senate had decreed for Pallas. Pliny was astonished. This was a joke, an outrage. Even half a century after Pallas had been executed by Nero, this imperial freedman still made Pliny seethe. He soon vented his frustration to his friend Montanus in a letter. "How ridiculous! What a farce!" he wrote, that honors could be thrown away on such "dirt." But after leaving the monument along the road and passing on to Tibur, Pliny apparently just could not let it go. He later took the time to search the archives and look up the actual decree that the Senate had granted Pallas. He then disparaged Pallas all over again in a second letter to Montanus.[1] The idea that Pallas, a former slave of Antonia Minor, could rise from that peripheral position to powerful heights as the treasurer and secretary of an emperor, worth hundreds of millions of sesterces, was still—even eight emperors removed from Nero—almost too much for Pliny to bear. But then to grant him the rank of praetor, a decurial post carrying senatorial honor—that was just shameful.

For Pliny, the memory of Pallas stoked an aristocratic, condescending anger. He no doubt wished that the monument could be taken down and the memory erased. It was an affront to his aristocratic sensibilities and his own patriarchal instincts as a slave owner. Several of Pliny's aristocratic contemporaries, Tacitus and Suetonius, echoed these sentiments when writing about individual imperial slaves or freedmen from the past. As Roman elites living in the Flavian period—which must have felt serene compared to the chaos that closed the Julio-Claudian dynasty—perhaps their attitude is to be expected.

But the memory of imperial slaves was equally bitter for the Alexandrian Jew Philo, who lived half a century earlier. On an embassy to the emperor Caligula in 40 CE, Philo's diplomacy was hampered at every turn because, he recalls, Caligula and his slaves were always joking around. To make matters worse, says Philo, most of Caligula's slaves were Egyptian, a people constantly menacing the Jews. Philo despised them. He remembers the imperial slaves as "wicked men," "crocodiles and asps." Worse yet, says Philo, the ringleader of the brood was Helicon. Philo does not even stoop to call him a slave, but uses instead a derogatory word basically meaning "chattel." Philo calls him a "damnable and abominable creature" (ἀνδράποδον). Helicon, Philo relates, was attached to Caligula's hip day and night—playing ball with Caligula, exercising with him, bathing with him, eating with him, and when the emperor went to bed, Helicon was there, too. The whole time, Helicon was apparently at the emperor's ear defaming the Jews. Philo's other rival ambassadors, the Alexandrians, knew this full well, says Philo. So they bribed Helicon with both money and future honors, which, they hinted, they would soon bestow on him when Caligula came to Alexandria. Philo remembers his experience with the emperor's slaves as an unmitigated disaster, one that spelled failure for his mission and trouble for the Alexandrian Jews.[2]

Whether among Pliny and his aristocratic circle, or Philo and his Jewish commission, imperial freedmen and slaves were often remembered as upstarts and foils to a properly functioning government. Their undue authority beyond their station, and their ability to influence an emperor or even the workings of the empire, meant black marks on that emperor's record, and clouds over that age of Rome's history. In short, an imperial slave or freedman symbolized dishonor.

The memories that Pliny and Philo recount stand in contrast to how early Christians often remembered members of the imperial household. Over centuries, Christian groups seemed to cherish individual imperial slaves or freedmen. More than that, the idea of Christians in Caesar's household would become a mark of exaltation in Christian cultural history. But why? Why did early Christians link their story so closely to the imperial household?

Imperial slavery offered a powerful "cultural discourse" through which Christians could construct meaning and, ultimately, project themselves imperially.[3] For early Christians Rome's imperial household was both a collective memory about the apostle Paul's testimony in Philippians 4:22 and an ongoing framework for generating a cultural repertoire. As a result, the emperors' slaves were used in early Christianity as core emblematic symbols. The memory of Christians in Rome's imperial household expressed fundamental elements of Christian cosmology and, collectively, summarized the identity of Christians as a cohesive and influential ethno-cultural unit within the wider world.[4] Imperial slavery and early Christianity came into alignment.

Ultimately this book explains what the memory of Christians in Caesar's household did for early Christians. The collective, socially constructed memories of Christians in Caesar's household—selective, idealized, and distorted memories—helped Christian communities create a cultural history and geography, police community boundaries, and define their piety. Beyond that, memories about imperial slaves and freedpersons were also part and parcel of Christian material culture. In many ways, therefore, the memory of Christians in Caesar's household allowed Christians to make a place for themselves in the empire's cultural landscape.

The end of the second and the beginning of the third century mark the start of a crucial phase in early Christian memory-making, one that saw shifting notions of clerical and textual authority, group boundaries, interpretive strategies, ritual practices, and narrowing definitions of what it meant to be Christian. This era also shaped the story of Christians in Caesar's household for the past, present, and future. As the raw material for memory work, Paul's greetings from "those saints from Caesar's household" (Phil 4:22) were a wellspring of creativity, especially in directly connecting his martyrdom with "Caesar's household" in Rome.

The Caesar's household that Paul mentions in Philippians 4:22 was not a semi-elite, civil service institution of the empire with upwardly mobile slaves and freedmen, collectively and conventionally called "the" *familia Caesaris* (see chapter 1). "Caesar's household" was a specific group of the emperor's slaves—*a particular familia Caesaris.* As a group of slaves, they were akin to public slaves, migrant groups, and *collegia*—all of whom were intermingling in the Roman world. One such *familia Caesaris* was living in Roman Asia, the locus of Paul's letter to the Philippians and his encounter with a *familia* of imperial slaves. Based on a similar profile in Paul's other letters, the imperial slaves of that *familia Caesaris* worked in semiskilled positions in the financial realm. The "saints" were particular individuals who were also devoted in some way to the Judean god. Paul passed on their greetings not because he had converted them but because they already knew the Philippians. The two groups were connected over the northern Aegean region by common family and labor networks.

Once this historical background comes into focus any hint of a continuous line of Roman Christians in "the" *familia Caesaris*—whether in the time
of Paul or later—evaporates. With it, the basis for a triumphalist narrative
about the rise of Christianity also deteriorates. Some have detected Christian
imperial freedmen in *1 Clement*, for instance. There are none (see appendix 1).
Others have interpreted Irenaeus's comment about faithful ones in the royal
court as a reference to Christians in the *familia Caesaris* or in Rome's imperial
palace. Irenaeus claimed something different. Despite attempts to explain
Christianity's rise in the empire through "Caesar's household," there was
no historical connection between Paul's reference and any later individual
Christians in Rome's imperial household. The only real connection is a mne-
monic one forged long after Paul by second- and third-century Christians.

In the last decades of the second century, amid Rome's topography
and in the shadow of Paul's apostolic cult, Paul's greetings from Caesar's
household took on a new life (chapter 2). For those Christians who wove
together the story of Paul's martyrdom in Rome—a vital piece of Christian
mythology—Paul's reference to "Caesar's household" was indispensable.
Indeed, "Caesar's household" cemented the story. With the continued
focus on "Caesar's household," Nero's slave Patroclus, and the palace,
the *Martyrdom of Paul* created a Christian history and geography centered
in the imperial capital. The memory of Christians in Caesar's household,
in turn, offered an opportunity for audiences of the story—wherever they
were—to claim a past in the heart of imperial power. Such a recollection
could then become the basis for Christians in the present to contend for
their cultural place in the Mediterranean world.

Similarly, the collective memory of Christians in Caesar's household
allowed other communities to fashion the story about the apostle Peter's
martyrdom in Rome. The *Acts of Peter*—specifically, the fourth-century *Actus
Vercellenses*—shaped a new memory about Peter and Nero's slaves around
the memory of Paul and Caesar's household in Rome. The *Acts* then tied
the martyrdoms of Paul and Peter together in Rome by recalling how both
apostles had made converts among imperial slaves. The stories about the
apostles Paul and Peter making disciples among Nero's household slaves
were told and retold in many different acts of the apostles throughout late
antiquity. But because the connection between Paul and Caesar's household was so deeply rooted in Christian tradition—its original strand derives
from Paul himself (Phil 4:22)—and because the story of Paul's martyrdom
in Rome was so important for Christians' self-conception, the imperial
household would continue to inspire other stories.

Two nearly contemporaneous works at the beginning of the third
century remembered individuals who had served the emperors in Rome

(chapter 3). Both Hippolytus and Tertullian singled out a person in the imperial household: the former to ostracize an opponent and the latter to make a plea for tolerance. But both authors were engaged in memory work. They reshaped the image of their subjects above all else to shield their communities against perceived threats.

For his part, Hippolytus created a Second Sophistic satire, similar to the satires of Lucian of Samosata. He told a story about a domestic slave Callistus who acted like a prototypical heretic, and whose owner Carpophorus was, by contrast, a "faithful man from Caesar's household." To further push Callistus out of a perceived orthodox tradition, Hippolytus co-opted "Caesar's household" from the story called the *Martyrdom of Paul*. Recalling Callistus was thus meant to evoke negative memories of him. Tertullian faced a different situation, though he responded in kind. To manufacture cultural cachet for his community, halt violence, and challenge the sociopolitical structures, Tertullian reconstructed for the proconsul of Africa a certain Proculus Torpacion. This man had once had lived in the palace, served the emperors, and was known to have been a Christian. In deploying this translocal memory, Tertullian utilized Torpacion to connect provincial Christians to the imperial center. And, as in Hippolytus's work, underlying Tertullian's arguments were collective memories about Christians in the imperial palace found in the *Martyrdom of Paul*. This connection is particularly clear in Tertullian's *Apology*. Just as in the *Martyrdom of Paul*, Tertullian claims that Christians like Torpacion had already filled "the palace." Even as both Hippolytus and Tertullian recreated memories about individuals in the imperial household for their particular purposes, both, in different ways, redeveloped memories about Paul and Caesar's household found in the *Martyrdom of Paul*.

As a response to ostensible internal and external threats, the process of memory making continues in a new form in the later decades of the third century (chapter 4). In the aftermath of the emperor Decius's edict that required a universal sacrifice to the Roman gods, editor(s) reworked the earlier *Acts of Justin and Companions*—the purported martyrdom account of Justin Martyr in Rome (ca. 100–165 CE). The overarching goal of the editor(s) was to redefine Christian piety as an exclusive activity, one that could not be combined with piety toward the Roman gods or the emperors. To make this case, the editor(s) focused on creating a new memory about one of Justin's companions named Euelpistus. This character was transformed into a martyred slave of Caesar who had refused to conform to imperial edicts that demanded worship of Roman gods. The revisions of the *Acts of Justin and Companions* also involved reformulating key aspects of the *Martyrdom of Paul*, specifically in the character Euelpistus. He is made analogous to the Patroclus character in martyrological discourse and continues to be remade even into the fifth century.

Though in the story Euelpistus is a stalwart of exclusive Christian piety who would rather die than worship the Roman gods, this is a façade produced by an idealized memory of Euelpistus. In reality the lives of imperial slaves—known from the material culture that they left behind—would have in many ways constrained their piety. The emperors' slaves were expected to, and did, worship the Roman gods. This worship included the emperors themselves. The piety of those in the imperial household who may have worshipped Christ would have been much more fluid than either the *Acts of Justin and Companions* or modern commentators might suggest.

A similar pattern emerges in the archaeological evidence for Christians in the imperial household (chapter 5). The monument of Marcus Aurelius Prosenes, which has been cited as key evidence for identifying Christians in the imperial household, does not in fact provide the evidence that scholars have sought. The sarcophagus and its inscriptions do not offer posthumous proof that Prosenes was a Christian; rather they demonstrate that Prosenes's freedmen were engaged in standard Roman commemorative practices and rituals. The monument they erected was neither Christian nor "pagan," but reflects wider Roman conventions of kinship duty (*pietas*). The monument indicates that Prosenes's freedmen—like Prosenes himself and other members of the imperial household—abided by a cosmology in which the emperor Commodus was honored, revered, or worshipped as divine (*divus*). Prosenes's freedman Ampelius may have remembered his patron by utilizing a commemorative discourse that both Romans and Roman Christians would have recognized ("receptus ad deum"). Yet what "Christian" could have meant in real terms for Ampelius, much less for Prosenes, is largely inaccessible. Nonetheless, the monument is a reminder that the meaning of "Christian" was always variable for imperial personnel, whose place in the world was fundamentally shaped by their relationship to the emperor(s).

The case study of Prosenes shows how complicated the material record is. The study also mitigates against approaches that might readily identify ancient Christians by simply looking at the epitaph stones. The issue is more acute when surveying the evidence for Christians from the imperial household in Rome's catacombs (chapter 6). Although several inscriptions from the catacombs have been cited, in addition to Prosenes's, as more contemporaneous evidence for Christians in the *familia Caesaris*, the reality is more complicated. Some inscriptions found in the catacombs of Priscilla and Sebastiano, respectively, with the names of third-century imperial personnel covering burial niches, and with fish or anchor symbols on the stones, do reflect an emergent Christian material culture. These inscriptions have thus been catalogued as Christian artifacts. Yet in Rome's ever-shifting underground hollows these epitaph stones were recut and reused to make Christian burials only later, at a date well beyond the early third century, when the imperial personnel actually lived. This reuse of burial material was part of a broader trend of spoliation in late antiquity. Imperial slaves and freedpersons left behind vast quantities of epigraphic material throughout Rome's burial spaces, including the hypogea of catacombs. The earlier epigraphic activity provided the material for new, Christian commemorative language and material expressions to develop in the fourth century and beyond. In this way, the invention of a Christian epigraphic repertoire involved disremembering. New memories about deceased individuals were built on and over the older memory of Rome's imperial slaves and freedmen.[5] Memory underlies material culture (chapters 5–6). Insights from postprocessual archaeology underscore that the selected inscriptions, commonly cited as hard evidence for Christians in the imperial household, were forms of memory. Each memorial presupposed a ritual context and engaged in commemorative discourse that was ultimately meant to remember a certain individual in a particular way. The epigraphic content was, first and foremost, a reflection of the commemorators' piety toward the deceased not a religious credo.

The upshot is that imperial slaves in Caesar's household were *remembered* as Christians. Except for Paul's fleeting reference (Phil 4:22), their place in Christian communities—their signature in early Christianity—was brought to light only after they had lived, and sometimes by people who never actually knew them. The imperial slaves who were remembered as Christian were (re)constructed in particular ways to serve the current needs of the Christian community. For Christian communities, then, the significance of Christians in Caesar's household had little to do with actual flesh-and-blood imperial slaves but instead depended on what those imperial slaves were made to represent. Memory was essential.

But memory is not always a faithful recording of the past that can be replayed. Memory is, rather, an idealized and distorted image, one that is constructed at the level of individual brain function and of social performance.[6] Memory is a social process. Every memory exists through its relation with what has been shared with others—through literary, oral, ideological/symbolic, spatial, monumental, and ritual/commemorative elements.[7] By participating in the memory process individuals shape a "collective memory." This collective memory is not just a past that is shared by a group, but incorporates the constructed past that is constitutive of the collectivity. In other words, collective memory is a meaning-making, or culture-making, apparatus.[8] The memory process shapes present reality by providing people with understandings and symbolic frameworks that enable them to make sense of their place in the world. The pressing issue is always the contemporary collectivity.[9] Early Christian writers who referenced Christians in the imperial household construed the past to relate it meaningfully to contemporary exigencies, to the ongoing project of negotiating continuity and change in collective identity.[10] The current beliefs and attitudes of Christian writers like Hippolytus and Tertullian had a profound effect on how they recalled individual Christians serving the emperors in Rome (chapter 3). To mold the contours of Christian communities, memories about individual slaves or freedpersons were adjusted and transformed. Memories of imperial slaves were conformed to the authors' perspective on how they should be presented.[11] Writers and communities who evoked the imperial household in their collective memories were engaged in mythmaking, telescoping and selective forgetting, and ritual and commemoration (chapter 2). Their "complex construction" of memory was also overlaid with emotion, moral evaluative coloring, and/or theological claims. In several cases the memories were simply fabricated. And all the while the authors were not remembering those they cited as victims of slavery but as useful examples to bolster their arguments.

The writers who cited Christians in the imperial household were thus in line with their coreligionists who metaphorized slavery. The process of remembering imperial slaves as Christian and then deploying those memories as rhetorical points in early Christian texts more forcefully solidified or reduced Christian imperial slaves to symbols. Memory was part of the slavery discourse. Even if intended to be used positively or pridefully to affirm imperial slaves as historical members of the Christian community, the memory of Christians in Caesar's household contributed to the doulological repertoire.

So memory is never innocent. It has always been a central medium of power. To remember something or someone is to stake a claim on the past and in so doing control the present and future. There is also an ideological component to memory. The past is employed to explain or justify actions and to provide people with beliefs and opinions.[12] This is why memories of Christians in the imperial household were crucial pieces of rhetorical projects. Looking to the past, early Christian writers sought to find representation for their cause within Caesar's household. Although the writings were distinct—martyrdoms, polemics, apologies, and apostolic acts—they all attempted, in one way or another, to cross or mark cultural space. To make claims about how Christians "fit" in the world, about how Christians should be perceived, or about how Christians should worship, authors remembered a particular Christian slave or freedperson serving the emperor in Rome.

There was also an ecclesiastical function to memory. The imperial slaves commemorated in stories helped to augment rituals about martyred apostles (chapter 2), discipline social practice by expressing expectations of resistance to Roman piety, and even articulate theological positions, such as slavery to God (chapter 4). Yet the ways in which Christian imperial slaves were commemorated as symbols depended on the particular goals of Christian authors and their communities. In early Christian thought imperial slaves inhabited a conceptual space between the literal and the hypothetical. On the one hand, they were situated between the specific, contemporaneous slaves that Paul mentions in the earliest Christ groups (1 Cor 1:11; 16:15, 17; Rom 16:10–11; Phlm 10) and those more generally addressed in the later household codes of the Pastoral Epistles (Eph 6:5; Col 3:22; 1 Tim 6:1; Titus 2:9); and on the other, they were like the hypothetical slaves in Paul's arguments (1 Cor 7:21) and those featured so often in the parables of Jesus (Matt 18:26–32; Mark 12:1–12; Luke 12:43–45).[13]

The closest analogue to the conception of Christians in Caesar's household is Hagar in Paul's well-known allegory (Gal 4:21–31). Here Hagar was for Paul a real, flesh-and-blood slave woman of the ancient Jewish patriarch Abraham. That alone endowed Hagar with some importance. Looking back at Hagar, however, Paul understands her significance symbolically as a (negative) allegory for those who wish to be under the law (Gal 4:24). Similarly, though much closer in time than Paul and Hagar, the third-century polemicist Hippolytus negatively remembered Callistus as a representative symbol of heresy (chapter 3). By contrast, those imperial slaves who are later claimed as Christian, or at least accepted as honorary members (e.g., Marcia, Carpophorus), were remembered positively as symbolizing a characteristic that the community valued, or wished to convey—trustworthiness and peacefulness (chapter 3) or centrality and piety (chapters 2 and 4).

Meanwhile, the memory produced in the fifth-century *Acts of Justin and Companions* Recension C bridged the institutional and metaphorical forms of slavery to produce a new or alternate form of "doulological knowledge" and practice (see the introduction).[14] Euelpistus, a martyr along with Justin Martyr, renounces his status as a slave of Caesar to announce that he is now a slave of Christ (chapter 4). Euelpistus does this, the text says, because he won his "freedom" by Christ's favor. Caesar and Christ are aligned as paradigmatic slave owners. A direct conceptual and interproductive connection between God and the emperor as earthly master was forged. In becoming free, Euelpistus really becomes the slave of another, more powerful, master.

The slave of Christ Euelpistus was then willing to be loyal to his new master even to the point of death (chapter 4). So Euelpistus was a model that the Christian community should imitate by also submitting to Christ as a slave to a master, and, the text argues, they should do so over and against the emperor as imperial master. Euelpistus's transition from one master to another is what we might call a "kyriarchal exchange."[15] This exchange underlies the story of the imperial slave Patroclus in the *Martyrdom of Paul*. It underlies the story of imperial slaves in the *Actus Vercellenses* (*Acts of Peter*) as well as the related stories of converted imperial slaves in other apostolic narratives of late antiquity (chapter 2). The interaction between the classes of enslavement—horizontal and vertical—was very productive for early Christians.

The cosmological-doulological worldview of antiquity also helps account for other reasons why Christians fashioned themselves through Rome's imperial household (see the introduction). The living emperor was not only a de facto master of the Mediterranean world, with its peoples in a position of subservience. The empire was effectively the emperor's very large household. In manifold ways the emperor was worshipped, honored, and revered as a god both by his slaves and freedpersons, according to the standard cultural value of duty (piety), and by populations throughout his empire. It was generally accepted that the well-being of the empire and its peoples depended on the emperor. Indeed, the cosmic order of the world was directly tied to him. This is why, in the wake of events that might spell cosmological doom, such as eclipses and droughts, authorities like the proconsul Scapula might seek out those who, it seemed, did not properly worship the Roman gods, including the emperor. Proper worship led to the proper ordering of the cosmos. This, too, is why Christian apologists like Tertullian eagerly pointed out that although Christians did not worship the emperor, they honored him and prayed for his health and safety (chapter 3).

All this is to say that when Christians claimed members of Rome's imperial household as their own they must have understood—at least in some cases—that there was a cosmic effect. In the *Martyrdom of Paul*, Nero's slave Patroclus makes this quite clear when he declares Christ "king of the whole cosmos" (ὁ βασιλεὺς τοῦ σύμπαντος κόσμου). To remember imperial slaves as Christians was to claim to have altered the relationship between imperial slave and his/her master—the emperor, the cosmic linchpin of the empire. Christians could fashion themselves as also connected, like imperial slaves were, to the imperial household, and so as more thoroughly implanted in the network of cosmic power. And through remembering the emperor's slaves, Christians could then, in a sense, make a place for

themselves in that cosmos (chapter 2). Because of their vicarious connection to the emperor Christians actually helped sustain the cosmic order,
Tertullian argues (chapter 3). But in remembering Christians in the imperial household Christian authors and audiences were also, paradoxically,
claiming to have infiltrated that network of power, supplanting the emperor-
god with their own.[16]

Remembering Christians in Caesar's household was thus a way for
Christians to fashion themselves, by implication, imperially. Even if
Christian communities did not consciously think of the cosmic implications when they referenced Christians in Caesar's household, they surely
understood the symbolic power that such a reference might carry. Eusebius
certainly did. Like the eighth-century maghāzī literature that imparted the
struggle, advance, and triumph of Islam on the Arabian Peninsula, Eusebius's writing was "a feast of sacred memory."[17] Nostalgia permeates the
stories Eusebius tells.[18] And it was the memory of Christians in the imperial
household—now made to be symbolic of Christianity's cultural triumph—
that Eusebius used in his narrative. In every case, therefore, remembering
the emperors' slaves as Christians was generative for Christian communities who sought to invent and reinvent themselves.

Memory was a culturally appropriate activity. The Roman Empire
was a "memoryscape."[19] Many groups preserved, modified, generated, and
even invented multiple and heterogeneous memories about themselves.
As Christians in the second century began dissociating themselves from
Jews they effectively lost—in the eyes of the Greco-Roman world—the protective features of legitimacy. Unlike the Jews, who possessed an ancient
and established culture, Christians no longer had claims to a homeland.
They had no ancient history. Their piety practices were now revealed to be
strange and superstitious. Christians risked, and sometimes suffered, the
backlash that comes with being perceived as new, foreign, and illicit.[20] To
counteract this, Christians would come to understand and present themselves as a people among peoples—a self-proclaimed "new race" (*ethnos*;
genos).[21]

Ethnicity, then as now, was not a fait accompli. It was not an involuntary state derived from primordial attachments such as name, territory,
language, and culture. In the ancient world, ethnicity was a shifting, sit-
uational, subjective identification of self and others, which was rooted
in ongoing daily practice and historical experience, but also subject to
transformation and discontinuity.[22] Under the broader ancient umbrella
of cultural identity, an ethnic group was also an "imagined community," a
self-ascribing and self-nominating social collectivity that constituted itself
in opposition to other groups of a similar order. Following Jonathan Hall's

explanation, some of the "core elements" of an ethnic group are a putative subscription to a myth of common descent and kinship, the genetic reality of which is unimportant and frequently fictitious; an association with a specific territory; a sense of shared history; and assimilation and differentiation from other groups.[23] In addition to these an ethnic group might also be characterized by common piety practices or material expressions.[24] Memory, and its counterpart forgetting, were crucial to establishing these elements. The collective memory of Christians in the imperial household was likewise one way to articulate ethno-cultural indicators. Even if incomplete—Christians were still *unlike* other peoples—that collective memory offered a sense of group cohesiveness and served to integrate Christians within the broader mosaic of ancient peoples.

Unraveling the rhetoric of the texts and recovering the lives of imperial personnel show that the historical picture of Christians in Caesar's household is distinct from the memory that was created later. It is by recognizing how the two processes worked in tandem—the historical dynamic and the memory dynamic—that a new window into the makings of early Christianity opens up. Although there were Christians in Rome's imperial household by the third century, the historical evidence is overshadowed by the collective—and continually constructed—memory of Christian imperial slaves and freedpersons. That memory was as indelible as any inscription carved on stone. Despite the fact that writers like Hippolytus and Tertullian probably thought what they were writing was historical, to take their references to Christian imperial personnel at face value misses the point.

If my argument is correct, then the literary and certainly the material references to the imperial household should not be amassed as historical evidence for the growing presence and increasing power of Christians in the Roman Empire. The references should be inspected as artifacts of Christian cultural memory. The literary and material evidence relating to the imperial household that I surveyed throughout this book are traces of early Christian ethno-genesis. Whereas the modern pioneer narrative stresses that Christians in the imperial household drove the social ascent of Christianity, for early Christians the import of the imperial household was its utility in the creative process of Christian culture-making, whether it concerned a history and geography, community boundaries, piety, or later material culture.

In the end the memory of Christians in the Roman emperors' households likely would have floundered had not the apostle Paul, centuries before, remembered to pass on certain greetings at the end of one his letters. Because of that, later Christian communities could reinterpret the present and harken back to when, according to tradition, the apostle to the gentiles first opened the doors of the imperial palace for a new people to enter. The memory of Christians in Caesar's household would thus live and grow as long as communities read Paul's letter to the Philippians and commemorated Paul's martyrdom. With "Caesar's household" in their cultural repository, Christians could reinvent themselves as a people who from the very beginning were destined, like Paul once said, to inherit the world (Rom 4:13).

APPENDIX 1: CAESAR'S HOUSEHOLD (PHIL 4:22), *1 CLEMENT*, AND IRENAEUS

Since the late nineteenth century, many scholars have followed J. B. Lightfoot and linked the "saints from Caesar's household" in Philippians 4:22 to Clement of Rome, the supposed author of *1 Clement,* as well as to Claudius Ephebus and Valerius Bito, the couriers of *1 Clement.* Both the author and the couriers, it is thought, were Christian imperial freedmen in Rome in the late first century. This identification of figures associated with *1 Clement* has been based largely on the tradition that the apostle Paul wrote Philippians from Rome, where he converted members of Caesar's household. Some scholars have then cited the Christian imperial freedmen from *1 Clement* as the predecessors of the "faithful ones in the royal court" whom Irenaeus, bishop of Lyons (ca. 130–202 CE) mentions in the fourth volume of his *Against Heresies.* So these "faithful ones" were thought to be not only the later manifestation of the "saints in Caesar's household" that Paul had mentioned in first-century Rome, but also the same group that a few decades later authors like Hippolytus and Tertullian would mention. In other words, from Paul to Clement to Irenaeus to Hippolytus and Tertullian there were Christians in "the" *familia Caesaris* in Rome. The evidence suggests otherwise. Because my conclusions are largely negative, I present them here rather than in the text.

Clement

Lightfoot first suggested that Clement, known as the late first-century bishop of Rome and the supposed author of *1 Clement,* was a freedman of Flavia Domitilla and Titus Flavius Clemens, cousins of the emperors Vespasian and Domitian (see the introduction to this book). Lightfoot then proposed that Claudius Ephebus and Valerius Bito, the couriers of *1 Clement* (*1 Clem.* 65), were "retainers of the Caesars" and imperial freedmen who were likely included in the Caesar's household Paul mentions in Philippians 4:22. The link Lightfoot drew between Paul's Caesar's household and *1 Clement* would remain indubitable into the twenty-first century, even though Lightfoot's identification relied on a tenuous matching of Paul's letter to then recently discovered inscriptions in Rome that record the name Clement for imperial freedmen. In his book *From Paul to Valentinus,* Peter Lampe challenged Lightfoot's accepted interpretation. In addition to rightly locating "those of Caesar's household" (Phil 4:22) "in the east," Lampe also pointed out that there is no basis for Lightfoot's identification of Clement except for the coincidence of the name Clement in both the letter and the inscriptions.[1] However, by continuing to speak of Clement as the author of *1 Clement,* Lampe does not go far enough.

More than anything else the problem with identifying Clement of Rome, the supposed author of *1 Clement,* as a Christian imperial freedman is this: *1 Clement* is anonymous. That fact has been widely accepted among scholars. The "epistle of Clement" that Eusebius later calls "long and wonderful" never once mentions a Clement. It is not until the last quarter of the second century—almost a full century after the proposed date of *1 Clement*—that the name Clement is attached to the letter. Hegesippus (110–80 CE), who had been in Rome in the time of Anicetus (155–66 CE), mentions a letter that Clement wrote to the Corinthians during the persecution of Domitian. Around 170 CE, Dionysius of Corinth also attests to the reading of that letter during the liturgy. This information comes only from Eusebius, writing nearly two centuries after Hegesippus and Dionysius (Eusebius, *Hist. eccl.* 3.16; 4.22.1, 23.11).[2] For his part, even Irenaeus of Lyons, who claims that Clement was the third bishop of Rome and had seen and conversed with the apostles, says only that the letter was sent by "the church" (*Haer.* 3.3.1). Clement of Alexandria (150–215 CE) often cites *1 Clement* in his *Miscellanies,* attributing it in one instance to Clement (*Strom.* 1.7), and in another merely to the church in Rome (*Strom.* 5.12).

According to the letter itself, it was written by "the church" in Rome (*1 Clem.* 1.1). And despite the fact that the name Clement was used for imperial freedmen in Rome, and was the cognomen of the emperor Domitian's cousin Titus Flavius Clemens (cos. 95 CE), there is no way to make the identity of the letter's author secure. The name Clement, after all, was quite common, as others have noted.[3] From the second century to the fourth century, the bishop of Rome, the author of *1 Clement,* and the coworker of the apostle Paul (Phil 4:3) were all identified as one and the same Clement. Notwithstanding the synthetic identification, not a single ancient Christian source claims that Clement was an imperial freedman. The closest thing to such a claim comes from the fourth-century *Clementine Homilies,* in which Clement says he is "the kindred of Caesar" (12.8). The idea then that Clement of Rome was a Christian imperial freedman is modern make-believe, tout court.

While Lightfoot's identification of Clement has largely been scrapped, Lightfoot's idea that the couriers of *1 Clement* were Christian imperial freedmen from Rome has lingered in scholarship.[4] Lampe, for example, affirmed Lightfoot's argument, asserting that Ephebus was an imperial freedman and Bito was a freedman of the Valerian family. Lampe also connected what he called the "Christians members of the *familia Caesaris*" during the time of Commodus to Ephebus and Bito who "already in the first century" were such members. For Lampe, the imperial freedmen Bito and Ephebus represent the "sociological apex of Roman Christianity in the first century."[5]

And yet, as in the case for Clement as an imperial freedman, the evidence for identifying Ephebus and Bito is equally tenuous. Lampe's argument proceeds as follows: he first points out that the Greek cognomens Ephebus and Bito betray a slave background. He then turns away from Ephebus entirely—as if it were an obvious fact that he was an imperial freedman—to cite a *titulus* inscription from Rome listing freedpersons from the Valerian gens (*CIL* 6.27948). This inscription dates to the first century, says Lampe, and reveals that "Judaism and Christianity of the first century had success with more than one member of the domestic staff of the Valerian clan."

The basis of this claim is one of the inscription's recorded freedpersons. Her name is recorded as Valeria Maria. Since the cognomen Maria is found "only seven times in *CIL* volume 6," Lampe argues, it represents in this case a Semitic name. There must have been Jewish members in the Valerian clan, Lampe reasons, who gave this name to the slave girl at her birth. "This opens the possible background of Valerius Bito's Christian faith," Lampe asserts. Bito "experienced the beginnings of Roman Christianity in the synagogues," Lampe states definitively. Lampe then offers the "interesting scenario" that "Maria grew up to be a Jewish (or Jewish-Christian) freedwoman and that she could even have been Bito's mother or aunt." For Lampe, this scenario explains not only how the imperial freedman Bito became a Christian, but also how Christianity in Rome developed initially from the Roman synagogues. At least one of them—the Augustesioi—was formed, Lampe says, by imperial freedmen.[6]

Lampe's argument is built entirely on speculation. The letter *1 Clement* records only the names Claudius Ephebus and Valerius Bito. Those names are in themselves insufficient to establish that the two were freedmen, much less imperial freedmen. Even in Italy, Greek cognomens were also used by Roman citizens.[7] Moreover, there are plenty of examples of people who carried imperial nomenclature as Ephebus and Bito did (Valerii, Claudii), but who were themselves not imperial personnel and had no connection to an imperial household.[8] Given the scarce information available about Ephebus and Bito—*1 Clement* indicates only that they were elderly and from Rome—their specific identities must remain uncertain. If anything, their double names might indicate that they were Roman citizens, though even this is uncertain.[9]

There is also no indication in the letter, or indeed in any other piece of early Christian literature, that either of the two envoys sent to Corinth at the end of the first or the beginning of the second century were imperial freedmen. This is a glaring absence. Ephebus and Bito, along with one Fortunatus, formed a task force to convey authority on behalf of "the Church of God" in Rome (*1 Clem.* 59.1, 63.3). Considering the conventional image of imperial freedmen as powerful people—an image so well known that the contemporaneous Roman poet Martial could satirize it (*Ep.* 2.32)—it is surprising that the author(s) of the letter, who were attempting to exercise authority, make no mention that the two envoys were freedmen from the emperor's house.

Notwithstanding modern efforts, therefore, there are no good grounds for identifying Christian imperial freedmen in *1 Clement*. Not only is there absolutely no connection between the "Caesar's household" that Paul mentions and *1 Clement*. There is also no connection between any individuals related to *1 Clement* and later literary references to Christians in the imperial household. The total lack of historical evidence for Christians in Rome's imperial household during the first century only underscores the importance of memory making in the second and third centuries when Christians were referencing believers in the imperial household.

Irenaeus and the Royal Palace(s)

A different set of problems surrounds Irenaeus's comment about "faithful ones who are in the royal court" (*Haer.* 4.30). Typically, this comment is taken as yet another reference to believers who belonged to the *familia Caesaris* in Rome. It has also been used as support for the claim that Christianity had progressed into the upper echelons of society in Rome.[10] The phrase that Irenaeus uses to describe those persons in the royal court is *qui in regali aula sunt*. Despite the convention of using *familia Caesaris* as a catchall term for all imperial slaves and freedmen, Irenaeus's phrase is not equivalent to the ancient meaning of *familia Caesaris* (see chapter 1 above). Irenaeus was referring to a decidedly different group of people, though they also worked for the emperors. The group Irenaeus refers to seems to have been the *apparitores*. To understand this we must first take a slight detour.

Besides in his treatise *Against Heresies* (*Adversus haereses*), Irenaeus appears to mention the "royal court" one other time. In a Greek letter preserved by Eusebius, Irenaeus writes to a former companion named Florinus. This Florinus, as Irenaeus understood him, had become a follower of Valentinus and a "renegade presbyter" operating in Rome.[11] Irenaeus reminds Florinus of the history and pedigree that the two of them shared back in their homeland of Asia. "These opinions [of Valentinus]," Irenaeus writes to Florinus, "the presbyters who came before us and who accompanied the apostles did not hand on to you. For I knew you, while I was still a boy in lower (κάτω) Asia at Polycarp's feet when you were faring illustriously in the royal court (ἐν τῇ βασιλικῇ αὐλῇ) and trying to make a good impression on him [Polycarp]" (*Hist. eccl.* 5.20.1–2).

The Greek phrase (ἐν τῇ βασιλικῇ αὐλῇ) that Irenaeus uses in the letter preserved by Eusebius is the exact equivalent of the Latin phrase (*in regali aula*) that is preserved in his *Adversus haereses*. Because that work by Irenaeus was originally composed in Greek, the phrase *in regali aula* must actually have read ἐν τῇ βασιλικῇ αὐλῇ in Irenaeus's original treatise.[12]

When the Greek phrase ἐν τῇ βασιλικῇ αὐλῇ is used in other sources, it is frequently in the plural: ἐν βασιλικαῖς αὐλαῖς. It usually indicates a group of local officials who deal with imperial and provincial business (πράγματα) alongside governors, as well as indicating officials in public positions (δημοσίοις τόποις) who had some resources, even a salary (ὀψώνιον).[13] For example, when the second-century astrologer and Irenaeus's contemporary Vettius Valens (ca. 120–75 CE) describes which astrological signs determine which outcomes for particular types of people, he relates: "Those who are assigned a moderate hypostasis are trusted with royal business (βασιλέως πράγματα), are stewards (διοικοῦσι) and superintendents (διευθύνουσιν)—but are subject to ups and downs and hatred. Some become or are associated with governors (στρατιωτικοί); some receive a salary (ὀψώνιον) at the royal courts (ἐν βασιλικαῖς αὐλαῖς) or in public positions (δημοσίοις τόποις). They are not, however, elevated so high in their livelihoods as they are sunk in inglorious display and in care-worn, broken misery" (*Anthology*

9.2.73). According to Valens, those who worked in the royal courts—note the plural—dealt with imperial and provincial affairs alongside governors, could be public officials themselves, and clearly had some resources at their disposal.

The same usage of the Greek phrase ἐν βασιλικαῖς αὐλαῖς appears in Epiphanius's so-called Medicine Chest. The fourth-century heresiologist records that after the theologian Origen (ca. 184–253 CE) fled Alexandria for Judea, he met Ambrose, who was a distinguished (διαφανής) imperial official, or literally, "a distinguished person in the royal courts" (ἐν αὐλαῖς βασιλικαῖς). Once more, note the plural even when referring to an individual. Ambrose became Origen's patron. And while Origen was in Tyre, burning the midnight oil to produce voluminous works, such as the *Hexapla*, Ambrose employed Origen's stenographers and assistants (ὑπηρετοῦσιν), bought all the papyrus (χάρτην) Origen needed, and took care of Origen's other expenses.[14]

Based on these descriptions, then, Irenaeus's old friend Florinus was likely employed in some official capacity in a provincial court in Asia Minor. For this reason, Irenaeus uses official, honorific vocabulary (λαμπρῶς). Irenaeus does not specify Florinus's status as freeborn, freedman, or imperial freedman, but he had clearly achieved some local status—at least from Irenaeus's viewpoint.[15]

Taken together, the characteristics associated with those described as ἐν αὐλαῖς βασιλικαῖς suggest a group of *apparitores*. This group was comprised of *free* men. That is, they were either former slaves or freeborn and worked for the "state" (*res publica*) to aid the Roman magistrates, priests, and emperors, both in Rome and in the provinces. Representing a section of Roman society between slave and equestrian, *apparitores* worked in numerous capacities, as scribes, clerks, secretaries, amanuenses (*scribae*), and even keepers of the sacred chickens (*pullarii*). Those employed in these services, like so many other groups in the Roman Empire, formed colleges (*collegia*), ordered themselves in corporate bodies (*ordines* and *decuriales*), and assigned themselves honorific titles and ceremonial offices.[16]

Now, the *apparitores* did work with and alongside public slaves and imperial personnel in the administration. There are also cases in which imperial freedmen were themselves *apparitores,* the most famous of whom was perhaps Trajan's freedman Marcus Ulpius Phaedimus (see chapter 5).[17] But overall, *apparitores* were usually not imperial freedmen, and certainly not part of a *familia Caesaris* in any ancient sense of the phrase. Because *apparitores* were free men they were employed, apparently with a salary, as per the founding charter (*lex Ursonensis*) of the Roman colony at Urso, Spain (*colonia Iulia Genetiva*). At Urso, it is likely that the *apparitores* were also only "part-time," and like the magistrates they attended, had other income that they acquired through business (*negotium*).[18]

To summarize, then: the Greek phrase Irenaeus used originally for "in the royal court(s)" (ἐν αὐλαῖς βασιλικαῖς), his description of Florinus from the letter preserved in Eusebius, and the characteristics of the *apparitores* all match what Irenaeus says about those "faithful ones in the royal court" in book 4 of his *Adversus haereses*.[19] Here is the relevant passage from Irenaeus in full:

For there follows us in some cases a small, and in others a large, amount of property (*possessio*) that we have acquired from the mammon of unrighteousness. For from what source do we derive the houses in which we dwell, the garments in which we are clothed, the vessels (*vasa*) that we use, and everything else ministering to our everyday life, unless it be from those things that, when we were gentiles, we acquired by avarice, or received from our heathen parents, relations, or friends, who unrighteously obtained them?—not to mention that even now we acquire such things when we are in the faith (*in fide*). For who is there who sells (*vendit*), and does not wish to make a profit (*lucrari vult*) from him who buys (*emit*)? Or who purchases anything (*emit*), and does not wish to obtain good value from the seller (*vendit*)? Or who is there who carries on a trade (*negotians*), and does not do so to obtain a livelihood? And as to those faithful ones who are in the royal court (*qui in regali aula sunt fideles*), do they not have the utensils they employ from the property that belongs to Caesar (*nonne ex eis quae Caesaris sunt habent utensilia*); and to those who have not, does not each one of these give according to his ability (*secundum virtutem praestat*)? The Egyptians were debtors to the [Jewish] people, not only as to property (*res*), but as to their very lives, because of the kindness of the patriarch Joseph in former times; but in what way are the gentiles (*ethnici*) debtors to us, from whom we receive both gain and profit? Whatsoever they amass with labor, these things do we make use of without labor, although we are in the faith (*in fide*).[20]

Note the language. The "faithful ones" refers to persons in a royal court who are also associated with business activities (*negotium, vendit, lucrari, emit*). They have an undisclosed amount of materials from their trade, but they also acquire provisions (*utensilia*) from working in an official capacity under Caesar. These individuals then share with others to the best of their ability (*secundum virtutem praestat*). The language that Irenaeus uses of these "faithful ones" suggests a group of *apparitores*—most likely free men—working in one of the empire's royal courts.[21]

Be that as it may, often lost in the interpretations of Irenaeus's reference to the "faithful ones in the royal court" is his overall polemical purpose. The five-volume heresiological treatise that Irenaeus calls the *Refutation and Overthrow of Knowledge Falsely So Called* (ἔλεγχος καὶ ἀνατροπή τῆς ψευδωνύμου γνώσεως) was a decade-long project seeking to discredit the second-century Roman Christian Valentinus (ca. 100–160) and his successor Ptolemy.[22] By the time Irenaeus writes the fourth book of this treatise, he aims to refute more specific objections of his opponents—for example, the nature of the Creator, the salvation of the body, and in particular the role of Moses and his writings. The Creator and author of the law is the one god, Irenaeus argues, the father of Christ; Christ himself observed the law; the law and the gospel are not in opposition to each other as if they were from different gods, and so on and so forth.[23]

The passage in which Irenaeus mentions those in a royal court combats a charge that the god who commanded the Israelites to take vessels (*vascula*) of all kinds from the Egyptians during their exodus should be rejected, since that god promotes theft. Those who think this way, Irenaeus responds, "are ignorant of the righteous dealings of god" (*Haer.* 4.30.1). To make his argument work, however, Irenaeus needs a contemporary parallel for the ancient Israelites and the patriarch Joseph. The "faithful ones in the royal court" help fulfill this need. And as Graeme Clarke once observed, Irenaeus is arguing by analogy: the Jews are a *type* for those "in the faith," as both receive vessels (*vasa*) in their dealings with the gentiles. Irenaeus here co-opts LXX Exodus 11:2 and 12:35, which record that the Israelites took from the Egyptians items (σκεύη) of silver and gold.[24] Just as the patriarch Joseph received *res* from the Egyptians, Irenaeus argues, so now some faithful ones get *utensilia* from Caesar. Irenaeus's reference to the royal court was thus a plausible support for his analogical argument—an argument that uses a biblical allusion to assert that the faithful make a living at the very *centers* of imperial life.

Moreover, by saying "royal court," Irenaeus was not necessarily calling attention to believers specifically in Rome's imperial court, as is conventionally thought.[25] Irenaeus's *Against Heresies* had several targets in his multicentered geography that included both Rome and Asia, among others. As Jared Secord has explained, Irenaeus's map of the world had four regions, with the center of the world (*kosmos*) comprising the purported apostolic churches of Rome, Ephesus, Smyrna, and Corinth. These four are the only churches named in the entirety of Irenaeus's treatise. Notably, three of the centers are in the Greek East—perfectly understandable coming from a Greek émigré.[26]

If anything, therefore, the only precise geographic reference to a "royal court" in Irenaeus's writings is to "lower Asia" (Smyrna), not Rome. On the ground, furthermore, heresiological works like Irenaeus's assumed a wide readership and extensive geographic circulation.[27] By leaving unsaid a particular geographic reference to "the faithful in the royal court," but simultaneously aiming his project at the perceived orthodox centers, Irenaeus could intimate a worldwide, orthodox geography.[28] Wherever there was a royal court, Irenaeus would argue, "faithful ones" could be found there.

So while Irenaeus cites Christians in a royal court in a similar way to how Hippolytus and Tertullian reference the imperial household, Irenaeus's claim is distinct. He is not talking about imperial slaves or freedmen. To make his point about Christians and their relationship to the emperors, he also uses a different intertextual line than traditions from the *Martyrdom of Paul* do. What unites Irenaeus and these other Christian writers, however, is their apologetic reference to individuals working for the emperors. By citing those individuals, Irenaeus was attempting to create and police a boundary between his position and that of his so-called heretical opponents.

APPENDIX 2: EPIGRAPHY AND IMPERIAL PERSONNEL IN ROME

The three inscriptions I examine below share a pedigree similar to that of the Prosenes monument (chapter 5) and of the Sozon and Atimetus inscriptions (chapter 6). These three inscriptions are considered to be several of the earliest known Christian inscriptions. None of them contains the standard funerary dedication to the chthonic deities, the Divine Shades (Dis Manibus). Perhaps more than anything, this absence has swayed opinions about the meaning of these inscriptions and the supposed Christian proclivity of those who are recorded on the stones. While noteworthy, the absence is inconclusive, especially when the three inscriptions are studied alongside those deemed to be "pagan." Rather than compare the inscriptions with one another and with other ostensibly Christian inscriptions, I again draw epigraphic comparanda from other imperial personnel. The inscriptions should not be classified as either "pagan" or Christian, I contend, but as Roman. Ultimately, I stress the limits of knowledge. From these stones, it cannot be known whether the individuals practiced piety toward Christ as much as it can be known that their commemorative discourse included statements of piety. Like the Prosenes monument, each inscription is also instructive for understanding how imperial personnel may have interacted with Christian groups in the third century.

Alexander and Marcus (fig. 16)

Source: *CIL* 6.8987; *ILCV* 2.3872; *ICUR* 10.27126
Date: First half of the third century CE.
Location: Rome. Found in 1831 in the vineyard of the German College, where the entrance to the St. Hermes Catacombs now is, on the Via Salaria Vetus. Originally housed in the Museum Kircherianum in Rome, whose collection was dispersed in 1870. Now in the Museo Nazionale Romano, Terme di Diocleziano, Inv. 67721.
Description: Latin epitaph on white marble, broken on bottom right. H: 32.5 cm, W: 30 cm, D: 3 cm. Letters, H: 2.7–1.5 cm.

Text and Translation
Alexander / Augg. ser(vus) fecit / se bivo Marco, filio / dulcisimo, Caputa / fricesi, qui deputa / batur inter bestito / res, qui vixit annis / XVIII, mensibu

VIIII / diebu V. peto a bobis / fratres boni, per / unum deum, ne quis / (h)un(c) titelo moles[tet] / pos mort[em meam]

———

Alexander, slave of the Emperors, set up (this stone) during his own lifetime for Marcus, his sweetest son, a *Caputafricesis,* who was assigned to the tailoring regimen, and who lived eighteen years, eight months and five days. I entreat you, good brothers, by one god, that no one should damage this tablet after my death.

Commentary

Although the stone was originally discovered by Emiliano Sarti (1795–1849) in 1832, Pietro Ercole Visconti (1802–1880) provided the first extensive study of the inscription. Visconti categorized the epitaph as a Christian artifact based on two factors: context and content. Although Sarti did not include exact details of his find (near the present-day St. Hermes Catacombs), for Visconti it was "credible" that in another time the epitaph had been *in* the catacombs themselves. Like the other catacombs of Rome, the catacombs of St. Hermes were assumed to be an exclusively Christian cemetery at this time. The appeal to *fratres boni* ("good brothers") and the invocation *per unum deum* ("by one god"), Visconti surmised, were open confessions of Christianity by both imperial slaves—Alexander and Marcus.[1] The inscription was thus included in Christian epigraphic handbooks and catalogues, where it remains to this day.

Few have doubted that the father Alexander and the son Marcus were Christians.[2] Several scholars have pushed the point further by recording (incorrectly) that the epitaph comes *from* or was *in* the catacomb of St. Hermes;[3] by dubbing the brotherly language "characteristically" Christian and assuming a Christian audience;[4] and by describing the *unum deum* content as a "*doctrinal* declaration"[5] with "monotheistic axioms" that, in the words of one interpreter, were "explicit," so as to "make an ordinary pagan passerby pause a moment."[6] Because the Christian faith of the father Alexander is taken for granted, his inscription has also been used to identify another ostensibly Christian inscription—one from a certain imperial freedman named Septimius Alexander, whom it is thought, may be identical to Marcus's father Alexander.[7] The idea that Alexander and Marcus were Christians in imperial service has then made the social aspects of the inscription all the more seductive. Since Marcus appears to have been a "student" at the *paedagogium Caput Africae* on the Caelian Hill, some have highlighted the potential significance for the social advancement of early Christianity.[8]

But the inscription was found above, not in a catacomb. Even if it had been found in the catacombs, these were not exclusive Christian cemeteries but were shared by many different groups over the course of centuries (chapter 6). Although the epigraphic content (*fratres boni per unum deum*) raises the possibility that the father Alexander—not Marcus—uses a type of commemorative language typical of Roman Christians, the brotherly language (*fratres boni*) was not exclusive to Christians. Such kinship terminology was common in many group settings and Greco-Roman associations (*collegia*). The imperial slaves at the *paedagogium Caput Africae,* in fact, seem to have formed clubs, groups, or associations, and like other similar groups they would have been expected to care for their dead.[9] Moreover, the father Alexander used a distinctive group moniker for Marcus (*Caputafricesis*). This was like saying Marcus was a "West Pointer" or "Cambridgeman," as S. L. Mohler once put it.[10] All this suggests that the "good brothers" to whom Alexander was speaking were specific imperial slaves from Marcus's training center (*paedagogium*), perhaps part of a *collegium* there. Alexander assumed that they would care for Marcus's remains (*titulus*), and that when they came, as good brothers, they would commemorate Marcus with the standard rituals.

The inscription's so-called monotheistic content is not necessarily Christian either, and translating *per unum deum* as "by 'the' one god" is presumptive. On the one hand, the date of the comparanda is an issue. The next closest example of an ostensibly Christian inscription using such a phrase (*unum deum*) dates to the first half of the fourth century—well over a century after Alexander and Marcus lived.[11] This is a chronological conundrum that we encountered with the monuments of Prosenes (chapter 5) and Atimetus (chapter 6). On the other hand, as I already emphasized in the case of Prosenes, during the Severan period several religious groups might make a reference to "one god." It is unknown whether Alexander was referring to Christ, YHWH, or some other divine persona—including the emperor himself. At the *paedagogium* there were undoubtedly cultic practices for various deities, including for the emperors. The son Marcus would have been expected to practice the piety of the group. So even if his father had been a Christian—which is unknown—Marcus might not have shared that same loyalty to the Christian god.

As for the social implications for early Christianity, the *paedagogium* was not really the launching pad for brilliant careers that some have thought it was. Almost all the evidence for this particular *paedagogium* consists of epitaphs not of "students" but of the imperial personnel who worked there—either imperial freedmen or house-born slaves—who called themselves "trainers of boys."[12] Of course, some of the imperial slaves who were trained at the *paedagogium* could have gone on to important or lucrative positions. Yet there is no evidence that this was the expected outcome or that there was equal opportunity for all of the imperial slaves being trained there.[13] This fact mitigates against assumptions that Marcus was destined for a great "career."

Despite the wishful thinking of some scholars—for example, that Marcus "might have had the potential to rise to be an emperor's personal tailor"—in the grand scheme of the slavery system Marcus's labor function was purely domestic.[14] Based on the typical epigraphic idealizations, at the time of his death Marcus was more of a seamstress than anything else. Within the confines of the slavery system, Marcus was considered unskilled labor. Not to mention that his life was cut short. His father Alexander, meanwhile, who was old enough to have an eighteen-year-old son, was still enslaved. He must have been over thirty and thus past the age at which—according to accepted thinking—manumission was supposed to occur. Apart from the epitaph stone itself, Alexander's social prospects seem to have been fairly modest.

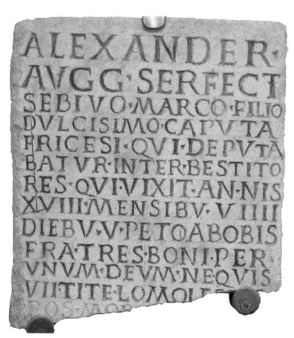

FIG. 16 Latin epitaph of the imperial slave Marcus, set up by his imperial slave father, Alexander, who entreats "good brothers" "by one god" (*per unum deum*). Third century CE. Museo Nazionale Romano—Terme di Diocleziano, Rome. Inv. 67721.

Life at this imperial *paedagogium* also had a more sinister side. The imperial slaves like Marcus were often called "Caesar's boys."[15] This was a pet name for the boys who were *delicati* or *delictissimi*—sex toys of the emperors and probably of their teachers as well. For this reason, the ancient descriptions of slaves at *paedagogia* often mention how the boys are made to look appealing.[16] Recent work on graffiti from the other imperial *paedagogium* in Rome on the Palatine Hill, for example, where the famous Alexamenos graffito was found, offers a stark picture of the sexual atmosphere at an "imperial training school." Sexual acts, it seems, were also the kinds of experiences or "training" that Marcus's social advancement might incur.[17]

Carpophorus

Source: *CIL* 6.13040; *BCAR* 1987/88, 178
Date: Second to third century CE.
Location: Rome. Original provenance is unknown. According to the editors of the entry in *CIL* 6, the inscription was in the possession of Baldwin Briello (Balduino de Briele), an antiquities dealer living at Santa Maria ai Monti.
Description: Latin epitaph of a family, with rights to tomb and garden. Dimensions unknown.

Text and Translation

M(arcus) Aurelius Augg(ustorum) lib(ertus) Carpophorus fecit / sibi et Aureliae Epictesi coniugi suae et / fili(i)s et Aurelio Paulino fratri suo et / fili(i)s

eius et Seleuco alumno libertisq(ue) / et posteris eorum item libert(is) liberta /
busque suis posterisque eorum / hoc m<o>n<u>mentum sive cepota<ph>ium /
de nomine meo alienari veto.

———

Marcus Aurelius Carpophorus, freedman of the emperors, made this for himself
and for Aurelia Epictes his wife and for (their) children, and for Aurelius Pauli-
nus his brother and for his children, and for Seleucus his foster son, and for his
freedmen and their posterity, likewise for their freedmen and freedwomen after
them. Neither this monument nor this garden-tomb of my name I allow to be
transferred to another.

Commentary
Scholars who accredit Hippolytus's information about the Carpophorus from
"Caesar's household" often state that he was an imperial freedman. Because it is
thought that Carpophorus was an imperial freedman, some have then referenced
the above inscription and suggested that the Marcus Aurelius Carpophorus of
the inscription could be identical to the Carpophorus from Caesar's household
in Hippolytus's *Refutation of All Heresies.*[18]

This is unlikely for several reasons. The name Carpophorus, meaning "fruit-
bearer," is used for many slaves and freedmen in the imperial period. It is attested
also for an imperial slave in Rome, and for other imperial freedmen of the
second century.[19] The burial inscription also "contains no Christian evidence,"
as Peter Lampe admits.[20] Moreover, the date of the inscription is not secure,
especially without an image for paleographic analysis. Thus, it is unknown if
this inscription is even contemporaneous with the Carpophorus mentioned in
the *Refutation.* The imperial nomenclature (Marcus Aurelius) is used by several
emperors from Marcus Aurelius (161–80 CE) to Severus Alexander (222–35 CE),
so the imperial freedman cannot be dated based on nomenclature alone.

If Hippolytus's details are reliable then no other information about Carpophorus's status is provided except that he was from "Caesar's household." The
locution he uses (Καίσαρος οἰκία), on a strictly historical-cultural basis, more
likely refers to imperial slaves anyway (chapter 1). Though not for this reason,
several scholars have in fact noted that the Carpophorus from Hippolytus's
account could also have been a slave.[21]

The above inscription is instructive in other respects, however, particularly for understanding how imperial personnel may have intersected with
Christian groups in Rome. Here Carpophorus and Callistus are relevant. The
titulus of Marcus Aurelius Carpophorus, for example, indicates that he had a
tomb complex. The space would likely have encompassed a typical house tomb
(*monumentum*), which could also function as the upper entrance to adjoining
hypogea. Carpophorus's tomb contained a surrounding plot of land—a garden
(*cepotaphium*; Gk. κηποτάφιον). All of this space was reserved for Marcus Aurelius Carpophorus's family network, which included a range of nonsanguine
members, including Carpophorus's slaves and freedmen, and extended to posterity, to those not yet born. Such a burial space is precisely the kind that early
Christians would have used in Rome.

The inscription provides a helpful window into the social and funerary context of Hippolytus's account. For example, Callistus, who was once Carpophorus's slave according to Hippolytus's story, was not buried in the *koimeterion* to which Zephyrinus appointed him. Instead, Callistus was apparently buried in the so-called Calepodius Catacombs just north of the Via Aurelia Vetus at the third milestone. This is on the west side of Trastevere, the area of Rome from which Callistus hailed, per the *Liber Pontificalis* (*Liber. Pont.* 1.17). Barbara Borg suggests that a private benefactor, that is, an individual owner, must have provided the original nucleus of the hypogeum where Callistus was buried in the Calepodius Catacombs, since that hypogeum was never designed to be systematically expanded for a larger community. Borg then adds that Carpophorus, the former owner of Callistus, springs to mind as the potential benefactor of the hypogeum.[22] Although Hippolytus's account is unverifiable, as are the claims of later legends such as those included in the *Liber Pontificalis,* the inscription above does illustrate how Christians in Rome during the third century would be buried, not in exclusive Christian catacombs, but in the available tomb spaces of their patron's network. In this way, Christians and imperial personnel were surely sharing burial grounds at the time when Callistus was overseeing a tomb (*koimeterion*) for Zephyrinus.

Viator (fig. 17)

Source: *CIL* 6.9077; *ILCV* I.348
Date: Second to fourth century CE.
Location: Rome. Seen and copied in the second half of the sixteenth century (Paul Knibbius) and in the first part of the seventeenth century, then lost. The inscription was rediscovered in 1917 during excavations for the foundation of two new buildings in the Piazza Colonna (present-day Via del Corso). Now in the Capitoline Museum, NCE 192.
Description: Latin epitaph on travertine marble, broken lower right, severely worn. H: 50 cm, L: 80 cm, D: 7.5 cm. Letters, H: 1.6–3.7 cm.

Text and Translation
somno aeternali / Lucretiae Hilare, coiugi karis[simae] / et incomparabili, Viator Aug(usti) n(ostri) vern(a) / adiut(or) tabul(ariorum), fecit et sibi et Lucretiae / Alexandriae et Purpurioni et Viatori et / Lucretiae Saturninae filiis et libertis / libert(orum) poster(isque) eorum. item contra se porti / cus et ariola cum memoria ad hoc moni / mentum pertinet.

———

For the eternal sleep of Lucretia Hilara, his dearest and incomparable wife, Viator, slave born in the household of our Emperor, assistant of the record-office, made this on his own behalf and for his children Lucretia Alexandria, Purpurio, Viator and Lucretia Saturnina, and the freedpersons, and for their own posterity. The opposite colonnade and the plot with the memorial are also part of this monument.

Commentary

The inscription was first classified as Christian by Ernst Diehl in 1925. According to later discussions of the inscription, the distinguishing feature that identifies the deceased and/or the dedicators as Christians is the initial phrase "eternal sleep" (*somno aeternali*). Only a Christian observer, the reasoning goes, would recognize this as a reference to the expectation of "bodily resurrection and the Last Judgement."[23]

But rather than a furtive reference to Christian belief in bodily resurrection, the *somno aeternali* phrase falls within a range of similar motifs on family tombs, especially of imperial personnel. The "eternal sleep" formulae even appear alongside dedications to the Divine Shades, as in the epitaph and family tomb of the imperial freedman Aelius Felix.[24] Besides *somno aeternali,* analogous phrases attested on inscriptions include "a house of eternal rest" and "for perpetual sleep" (*domus aeternae quietae*; *somno perpetuo*), both of which are followed by commemorations to the Divine Shades.[25] In many other cases the phrase *somno aeternali* occurs without the Dis Manibus.[26] Yet, there is no reason to suggest that these are also Christian inscriptions. If anything, the "eternal sleep" phrase on the epitaph of Lucretia Hilara seems to deny the hope of resurrection.

Instead of classifying this inscription as either pagan or Christian what is more important is the context of the commemorative discourse. The commission to "eternal sleep," which introduces the *titulus* of the family tomb (*monimentus*), is simply another expression geared toward posthumous memory (*memoria*).[27] The fact that this phrase appears on Viator's dedication and on several other similar inscriptions militates against identifying Viator and his family as categorically Christian. Without wild conjecture about belief in the resurrection and Last Judgment, it is impossible to ascertain, based on a single and common epigraphic phrase (*somno aeternali*), what "only a Christian" observer would recognize.

On the other hand, Viator's family tomb would be typical for an early Christian community in Rome during the late second or early third century. Although Viator was an imperial slave and "an undifferentiated junior assistant" in the administration, together with or because of his freeborn wife Hilara, he was able to secure a tomb complex.[28] As the inscription indicates, the monument would

FIG. 17 Latin epitaph of Lucretia Hilara, set up by the imperial slave Viator, with "eternal sleep" (*somno aeternali*) formula. Second to fourth century CE. NCE 192 Collezione Epigrafica dei Musei Capitolini, Rome. Archivo Fotografico dei Musei Capitolini.

have included a space for urns or interment, plus a colonnade (*portus*) and an *ariola* connected with the tomb. The *ariola*—a diminutive of *area*—was, most broadly, the building plot on which the tomb sat, but it could also have been an interior courtyard (*CIL* 6.13225). The term *area* is significant because Tertullian, in his open apology to the proconsul Scapula, relates that the burial places of Christians were *areae* (*Scap.* 3.1). This correlation again suggests that groups of Christians in Tertullian's North Africa, and likely in Rome as well, utilized family tombs, not cemeteries in the modern sense. Viator's tomb complex was likewise the type of private "cemetery" that Zephyrinus supposedly owned and over which he appointed Callistus, according to Hippolytus. Finally, the epitaphs erected by Viator and by Carpophorus (above) show how burial contexts in third-century Rome were likely the first meeting grounds for Christians and imperial personnel.

NOTES

Introduction

1. *Miroir Historial* X:xvi (fr. 50, fol. 314v); Davis, "Epitome of Pauline Iconography," 395–96.

2. Kyrtatas, *Social Structure*, 76, 83; Finn, "Social Mobility," 31. Similarly, Harland, "Connections with Elites," 396–98.

3. Witherington, *Paul's Letter to the Philippians*, 283.

4. Some have claimed, for instance, that Paul's family background may have been among certain powerful imperial freedmen and this is why he mentions his relative Herodion (Rom 16:11) between the households of Aristobulus and Narcissus (Bockmuehl, *Philippians*, 270; Hengel, *Pre-Christian Paul*, 4–17).

5. See Adolf Deissmann's clever response to J. B. Lightfoot's use of epigraphic sources vis-à-vis Romans (Deissmann, *Light from the Ancient East*, 279n1).

6. Lightfoot, *Philippians*, 175–77. Lightfoot cited Juvenal, *Sat.* 14.329; Tacitus, *Ann.* 13.1; Dio Cassius, *Hist. rom.* 60.34.

7. Kautsky, *Foundations of Christianity*, 65.

8. Duncan-Jones, *Economy of the Roman Empire*, 343; Cassius Dio 60.34; Suetonius, *Vesp.* 4.1; Suetonius, *Vit.* 2.5. All told, Narcissus's rise from slave to magnate was one of the most spectacular examples of disproportionate power in the early imperial period (Weaver, "Social Mobility," 4–5).

9. Lightfoot, *Apostolic Fathers*, 61–62. The identity of the Clement figure has its own tangled history, but since antiquity—thanks largely to the *Homilies* of the Pseudo-Clementine literature—this Clement had been associated with the imperial family (*Clementine Homilies* 12.8). Lightfoot admitted that the "*Clementine Romance*" was fictitious, though he nonetheless believed that the literature contained "hints" that could point in the right direction—namely, "to the doors of the imperial palace (*Apostolic Fathers*, 16).

10. Lightfoot, *Apostolic Fathers*, 20, 22, 27–28, 35n5, and 60–61. The identity of this Flavia Domitilla was debated. Both Jewish and Christian traditions claim Flavia Domitilla (see Avodah Zarah 10b).

11. Lightfoot, *Apostolic Fathers*, 21–22 (citing *CIL* 6.4923; 6.8943; 6.4548; 6.15174; 6.15304; 6.15351), 27, 29–30, and 62.

12. Lightfoot, *Philippians*, 2 (my emphasis), 19; Lightfoot, *Apostolic Fathers*, 29–30.

13. Bremmer, *Rise of Christianity*, 45. On Harnack's approach, see White, "Adolf von Harnack."

14. Harnack, *Mission and Expansion*, 45n2.

15. Harnack, *Mission and Expansion*, 46–49, 51–52; Eusebius, *Hist. eccl.* 7.10. William Ramsay and Harnack's close friend Theodor Mommsen had also voiced similar conclusions about the effect that Christians in the household of the emperors had on Christianity's spread in the Roman world. See Ramsay, *Church in the Roman Empire*, 57; Mommsen, "Der Religionsfrevel," 419n 2: "der Hof von jeher Mittelpunkt der Christianisirung [*sic*]."

16. Until the 1970s, the study of early Christian materials was characterized by an overemphasis on a literary-historical and theological viewpoint (Smith, "Social Description," 19). The interest in early Christianity as a social phenomenon was not new. See Malherbe, *Social Aspects*, 4–11. For orientation to this trend in scholarship, see also Horrell, *Social Scientific Approaches*, and for a critique, see Friesen, "Poverty in Pauline Studies."

17. Smith, "Social Description," 20. This approach, in Jonathan Z. Smith's words, has been clouded in the majority of cases by unquestioned apologetic presuppositions and naive theories.

18. Frend, *Rise of Christianity*, 1, 109–10, 132–33, 272, 293–94.

19. Kyrtatas, "Christians Against Christians," 25; Kyrtatas, *Social Structure*, vii.

20. Smith, "Social Description," 19–20.

21. It continues to be one of the most influential books on the social history of early Christians in Rome. At the 2016 Annual Meeting of the Society of Biblical Literature, as part of the *Polis and Ekklesia* program unit, a special panel was dedicated to discussing Lampe's book.

22. Lampe, *From Paul to Valentinus*, 185–86, 351. For discussion, see chapters 3 and 6 and appendixes 1 and 2 in this book.

23. Lampe, *From Paul to Valentinus*, 139–40, 351.

24. Buell, *Why This New Race*, 28.

25. Lampe, *From Paul to Valentinus*, 351n1; Finn, "Mission and Expansion," 298; Meeks, *First Urban Christians*, 63.

26. Buell, *Why This New Race*, 28n101, 29.

27. McKechnie, *First Christian Centuries*, 137–49; McKechnie, "Christian Grave-Inscriptions," 427–28. These configurations of the data evoke an "arborescent historiography" that envisions clear lines of descent, linear causality, binary opposites, and clear classifications (Concannon, "Early Christian Connectivity," 66).

28. Kyrtatas, "Christians Against Christians," 25. Similar is Rodney Stark's comment that the "connection with the imperial family, even from the 'early days,' allowed Christians to survive repression and persecution" (*Rise of Christianity*, 46).

29. See MacMullen's distinction between Christians as "behavior" and Christianity as "belief" ("Two Types of Conversion," 178). For the trend of focusing on belief as a primary criterion of religion in the Roman world, see also MacMullen, *Paganism in the Roman Empire*, 1; Hopkins, *World Full of Gods*, 77. It is often thought that the "mission to convert" is what separated Christians from other groups (North, "Development of Religious Pluralism," 191–92). On the conventional discussion of conversion and the "spread of Christianity"

vis-à-vis assent to propositions, see Nock, *Conversion*, 12, 14, 138, 193, 209. See also Bart Ehrman's emphasis on Christianity's success as a result of its exclusivity and mission to evangelize (*Triumph of Christianity*, 109, 120, more generally 105–31).

30. MacMullen, *Christianizing the Roman Empire*, 39–42. Likewise, Ramsay, *Church in the Roman Empire*, 192–93.

31. Witherington, *Paul's Letter to the Philippians*, 286.

32. Turcan, *Cults of the Roman Empire*, 4–5, 11, 15; Tripolitis, *Religions of the Hellenistic-Roman Age*, 11; La Piana, "Foreign Groups in Rome," 296.

33. Cumont, *Oriental Religions*, 149 (my emphasis).

34. Kyrtatas, *Social Structure*, 84. For his part, Harnack had also compared the spread of Christianity to the spread of other religions in the empire, especially Mithraism, by citing Franz Cumont's *Les mystères de Mithra* (Harnak, *Mission and Expansion*, 317). There are many problems with this idea of imperial slaves and freedmen as "missionaries" of cults, including racialized interpretations and stereotypes about immigrants or foreigners as servile (see McKeown, *Invention of Ancient Slavery?* 11–29). Another problem is the idea that mystery cults prepared the way for a superior religion, Christianity (Smith, *Drudgery Divine*, 85–115; Burkert, *Ancient Mystery Cults*, 2–3). On the geographic movement of people as a factor in establishing new settings for cults in the Roman world see Collar, *Religious Networks*.

35. Theissen, "Social Structure," 73. The metaphor has been especially prevalent when discussing the import of Paul's reference to Caesar's household. Reumann, *Philippians*, 739; Fee, *Paul's Letter to the Philippians*, 114; Peterlin, *Paul's Letter to the Philippians*, 150n76; Tajra, *Martyrdom of St. Paul*, 67; Hawthorne, *Philippians*, 281; Frend, *Rise of Christianity*, 326; Kyrtatas, *Social Structure*, 76. The phallogocentric language is part of a dominant discourse in the field of biblical studies. For a brief overview, see Vander Stichele and Penner, *Contextualizing Gender*, 199–202.

36. Rives, "Christian Expansion," 16, 41. On the relationship between sui generis and an ontological taxonomy, see Smith, *Drudgery Divine*, 38, 36–53; McCutcheon,

Manufacturing Religion; Pals, "Is Religion a *Sui Generis* Phenomenon?"

37. On historiography, see Buell, *Why This New Race*, 24, 27, 59–61; Concannon, "Early Christian Connectivity," 66; Nongbri, *Before Religion*, 6–7, 18–19, 95–96; See also Talal Asad's critique of Clifford Geertz (*Genealogies of Religion*, 45–48). On conversion, see Crook, *Reconceptualising Conversion*, 89, 250; Lipsett, *Desiring Conversion*. On totalizing, see Buell, *Why This New Race*, 24, 29; Smith, *Imagining Religion*, xi. On religion in the ancient world, see Nongbri, "Dislodging 'Embedded' Religion." On the meaning of "Christian," see Lieu, *Christian Identity*; Harland, *Dynamics of Identity*; Rebillard, *Christians and Their Many Identities*; Kotrosits, *Rethinking Early Christian Identity*; Boin, *Coming Out Christian*.

38. For the archaeological perspective, see Lavan and Mulryan, *Archaeology of Late Antique "Paganism"*; Boin, *Ostia in Late Antiquity*, 124–64.

39. Weaver, *Familia Caesaris*. See Morley, "Slavery Under the Principate," 281–83; MacMullen, *Roman Social Relations*, 92; Alföldy, *Social History of Rome*, 132. On the political categorization, see Boulvert, *Esclaves et affranchis*; Fabre, "Mobilité et stratification," 123; Hernández Guerra, *Los libertos*, 102; Hunt, *Ancient Greek and Roman Slavery*, 76–78.

40. See the early manifestation in Judge, "Social Pattern," 23. For perhaps the most influential use, see Meeks, *First Urban Christians*, 21–22, who cites Weaver's work.

41. So Jeffers, *Conflict at Rome*, 30–33, 88, 63–89, 102; Finn, "Mission and Expansion," 298.

42. Dale Martin could even describe "slavery as upward mobility" in Paul's context by citing Weaver's study of the *familia Caesaris* (Martin, *Slavery as Salvation*, 30–31). See also Stegemann and Stegemann, *Jesus Movement*, 70.

43. Treggiari, "Social History," 150; Treggiari, *Roman Social History*, 10–11; Peachin, Introduction, 4–5.

44. MacMullen, "Epigraphic Habit"; Meyer, "Explaining the Epigraphic Habit"; Meyer, "Epigraphy and Communication"; Woolf, "Monumental Writing"; Saller, "Family and Society"; Mouritsen, "Freedmen and Decurions."

45. Weaver, "Social Mobility," citing Hopkins, "Élite Mobility in the Roman Empire." On the recent studies of Roman slavery, see Meyer, "New Histories."

46. Bodel and Scheidel, Introduction, 2; de Wet, *Preaching Bondage*, 12–16, 28; Garnsey, *Ideas of Slavery*, 1; Finley, *Ancient Slavery*, 77, 40.

47. MacMullen, *Roman Social Relations*, 92. See de Wet, *Preaching Bondage*, 18.

48. Weaver, *Familia Caesaris*, 45–46. See Mouritsen, *Freedman in the Roman World*, 94; Millar, *Emperor in the Roman World*, 73–78; Herrmann-Otto, *Sklaverei und Freilassung*, 178–79 and n94; Schumacher, "Hausgesinde–Hofgesinde," 331–35; Panciera, "Servire a palazzo," 60.

49. Burton, "Slaves," 164; de Wet, *Preaching Bondage*, 18.

50. Bodel, "Slave Labor," 323–24; Gomez, *Exchanging Our Country Marks*, 4, 227.

51. Weaver, *Familia Caesaris*, 224, 227; Bodel, "Slave Labor," 326–30; D'Arms, "Familia Caesaris," 338.

52. Millar, *Emperor in the Roman World*, 69.

53. Meeks, *First Urban Christians*, 21–22; Jeffers, *Conflict at Rome*, 30. But see D'Arms, "Familia Caesaris."

54. Weaver can muster only a seven-page statistical chapter on the decisive moment in *familia Caesaris* upward social mobility. His fullest explanation reads simply: "Manumission of those who were 30 and over would be a more routine matter, again probably handled by a department of the central administration, according to more standardised procedures, perhaps on an annual basis, and in the financial interests of the *fiscus*" (Weaver, *Familia Caesaris*, 101).

55. For instance, to show the regularity of manumission Weaver charted a corpus of some 600 inscriptions recording the age at death of imperial freedmen. The bulk of Weaver's total sample (305 out of 440) died just on either side of thirty, between ages twenty-five and thirty-four. Yet this actually shows not how manumission operated, or the expectation for when it happened ("at age thirty"), but rather the ages at death of the imperial freedmen who had already been manumitted (Weaver, *Familia Caesaris*, 100–103).

56. Mouritsen, "Slavery and Manumission," 53.

57. MacMullen, *Roman Social Relations*, 92. See discussion in Meyer, "New Histories," 244–45.

58. De Wet, *Preaching Bondage*, 21; Bradley, *Slaves and Masters*, 80–110; Mouritsen, "Slavery and Manumission," 61.

59. Weaver, *Familia Caesaris*, 299.

60. Pavis D'Escurac, "La *Familia Caesaris*," 393. See also Winterling, *Aula Caesaris*, 195–203. For purposes of description and generalization Weaver and others had also treated imperial *familia* as a single category (Burton, "Slaves," 164). The phrase *familia Caesaris* continues to be used in the conventional way, even though others have offered specific critiques of the conventional interpretation.

61. Wallace-Hadrill, "Imperial Court," 297. Similar comments in Malina, *Social Gospel*, 75.

62. De Wet, *Preaching Bondage*, 4; Glancy, *Slavery in Early Christianity*, 25–28; de Wet, *Unbound God*, 8.

63. Patterson, *Slavery*, 18.

64. See Glancy's idea of slavery as habitus in "Christian Slavery in Late Antiquity;" de Wet, *Preaching Bondage*, 25.

65. Patterson, *Slavery*, 18.

66. Lavan, *Slaves to Rome*.

67. For example, sealed amphora stoppers bearing stamps of imperial freedmen involved in international trade from Red Sea ports along the Eastern Desert have now been found as far as the port at Berenike, roughly 825 km south of Suez. This is the outer limit of the Roman world, but even here the emperor and his freedman are represented, as Italian wine was shipped east to the Red Sea–Indian Ocean littorals. Denecker and Vandorpe, "Sealed Amphora Stoppers," 120–21 and 122. See also http://honorfrostfoundation .org/wp/wp-content/uploads/2015/03/Report -to-the-Honor-Frost-Foundation-on-the-winter -2014.pdf. For other examples, see wine dealing (*CIL* 6.8826) and shipping (*ICrete* II.20.7).

68. Patterson, *Slavery*, 37.

69. Patterson, *Slavery*, 1–9; Webster, "Routes to Slavery," 45.

70. Patterson, *Slavery*, 50, 62–63.

71. Davis, *Inhuman Bondage*, 31.

72. Patterson, *Slavery*, 38–39.

73. Davis, *Inhuman Bondage*, 31.

74. Bodel and Scheidel, *On Human Bondage*, 3.

75. De Wet, *Preaching Bondage*, 49, and more generally for the development of the concept, 26–44. See also Patterson's study of Paul's language in Romans 6 (Patterson, "Revisiting Slavery," 291).

76. De Wet, *Unbound God*, 13, 18–19.

77. For that claim, apologists had other references, such as the "men and women of highest ranks" (*clarissimae feminae et clarissimi viri*), whom Tertullian says were known Christians (Tertullian, *Scap.* 4.6). See the case of Carpophorus the "banker" (chapter 3). More information about social or economic standing is intelligible from some of the selected inscriptions (see chapter 6 and appendix 2). But except for the case of Prosenes (chapter 5), each of these aspects— the social, political, or economic—can be deduced only with caution.

78. Roymans, *Ethnic Identity and Imperial Power*, 2.

79. Harnack, *Mission and Expansion*, 36; Case, *Social Origins*, 133; Frend, *Rise of Christianity*, 272. Hengel, *Property and Riches*, 37.

80. Mendels, *Memory*, 104, 112.

81. Eusebius, *Eccl. hist.* 1.4.2; Buell, *Why This New Race*, 76–78. See also Johnson, *Ethnicity and Argument*, 1–24. According to Anthony D. Smith, long-term ethnic survival depends on the active cultivation, by specialists and others, of a heightened sense of uniqueness/ collective distinctiveness and mission, especially when ethnic communities lack political autonomy, a homeland of their own, and a common language (Smith, "Chosen Peoples").

Chapter 1

1. Harnack, *Mission and Expansion*, 43–44; Deissmann, *Light from the Ancient East*, xxi, 238 and n3, 393.

2. Only Plutarch uses ἡ Καίσαρος οἰκία to refer to the dwelling of Julius Caesar (*Caes.* 63.9; *Cic.* 28.2, 47.6). But see the unique interpretation of Standhartinger, "Letter from Prison," 129n30.

3. On the issue of provenance, see Flexsenhar, "Provenance of Philippians."

4. Ascough begins the conversation (*Paul's Macedonian Associations*, 127–28).

5. For the use of triumphant language vis- à-vis Phil 4:22, see Witherington, *Paul's Letter*

to the Philippians, 286; Smit, Paradigms, 53n95; Harrison, Paul and the Imperial Authorities, 21–23; Telbe, Paul Between Synagogue and State, 246. Older and influential iterations include Fee, Paul's Letter to the Philippians, 32; Bruce, Philippians, 158.

6. Raja, Urban Development, 55, 57; Mattingly, Imperialism, 138, 142; Zuiderhoek, Politics of Munificence, 115.

7. The designation "sub-clerical" is P. R. C. Weaver's term (Familia Caesaris, 120). For the epigraphic record, see IvE 3.696; 3.855; 6.2200a; 6.2281a; 6.2222b; 7,2.4112. Assistants: IvE 3.651; 3.680; 3.736; 4.1285; 6.2061; 7,1.3046. Bookkeepers: IvE 2.297a; 3.651; 3.820; 5.1564; 4.1138; 6.2103; 6.2480; 6.2903; 7,1.3054. Tax collectors: IvE 3.647. Underslaves: IvE 5.1948a; 5.1993; 6.2270. Cashiers: IvE 3.809; 3.861; 5.1951a; 6.2200a. Stewards: IvE 3.652; 3.809; 5.1948a; 5.1993; 6.2255a; 6.2270.

8. Strabo, Geog. 14.1.24. See Parrish and Abbasoğlu, Urbanism in Western Asia Minor; Cottier et al., Customs Law of Asia, 1–10, 26–85. Pleket, "Roman State and the Economy," 119, 121; Mattingly, Imperialism, 138–39.

9. "Caesar's household," one scholar put it, was especially "at home" in Rome, whereas one must look under all kinds of "stones" to turn up evidence for their existence in Ephesus (Fee, Paul's Letter to the Philippians, 459). This is simply untrue. But similarly, Witherington, Philippians, 287; Reicke, "Caesarea, Rome, and the Captivity Epistles," 285–86. Such reasoning misunderstands the epigraphic habits and material distribution of the Roman Empire. Rome was the epicenter of epigraphy. So the vast majority of all known inscriptions come from Rome. And while for certain reasons there were more imperial slaves and freedpersons in the imperial capital than anywhere else, they could still be found all over the Mediterranean. See Beltrán Lloris, "'Epigraphic Habit'"; Bodel, "Epigraphy."

10. Mazeus and Mithridates: IvE 7,1.3006; IvE 3.851. For various reasons most slaves left no material trace in the provinces (Bruun, "Slaves and Freed Slaves," 617).

11. Frontinus, De aquaeductu 116–17. Text from Rodgers, Frontinus. See also Weaver's comments (Familia Caesaris, 299).

12. Weaver, Familia Caesaris, 48 and 300. See Schumacher, "Slaves in Roman Society,"

591–92. Examples: CIL 6.7395; 6.23548; 6.38711; 8.12833; 10.3995.

13. In the ablative form in the inscription (NSA 1916, 395; AE 2007, 222).

14. CIL 12.449.

15. CIL 3.7380 = ILS 5682 = IK 19.29.

16. On family (οἰκία) and kinship in antiquity, see Harders, "Beyond Oikos and Domus," 15, 19.

17. Holloway, Philippians, 23, 190–91, citing Bockmuehl, Philippians, 30–31, and Weaver, Familia Caesaris, 78–80.

18. The phrase possibly including women was also noted by Stegemann and Stegemann, Jesus Movement, 391. Based on representation from the epigraphic record, at least, imperial slaves and freedpersons were predominantly male (Weaver, Familia Caesaris, 170–78). For wives and daughters, see AE 1957, 181; IG X,2 1.740; CIL 8.1129; 8.12630; 8.12629. One example from the first century of an imperial slave woman who managed a familia is from Calama, Africa Proconsularis (CIL 8.5384).

19. See the imperial slave Antiochus from late first-century Athens (fig. 2): AE 1947, 77 = SEG 21.1058. See also SEG 31.1124; MAMA 5.114; MAMA 1.29. House-born slaves: IPOstie A, 279 = ISIS 127. From Ephesus: CIL 3.436 = IvE 6.2210.

20. Weaver, Familia Caesaris, 7. There is no reason to unilaterally devalue the living conditions and prospects of these imperial slaves as does Justin Meggitt (Paul, Poverty, and Survival, 126). See also the section on the nature of imperial slavery in the introduction above. This does not mean they were at the end of their life.

21. Friesen, "Wrong Erastus," 231–56. On the relationship between imperial slaves and public slaves, see Herrmann-Otto, Sklaverei und Freilassung, 179; Schumacher, "Slaves in Roman Society," 597.

22. See Friesen, "Wrong Erastus," 249–53; Meggitt, "Social Status of Erastus," 218–23.

23. CIL 3.333; 10.1750; 6.8475. Friesen, "Wrong Erastus," 248.

24. Eutycho Caesaris dispensator: IvE 6.2255a. See Thomas and İçten, "Ostothekai of Ephesos," 340. Other examples: CIL 3.4049; 6.8578. See also Gaius, Inst. 1.122; Petronius, Sat. 30.9. For commentary, see Boulvert, Esclaves et affranchis, 429–33.

25. Weaver, Familia Caesaris, 200–11.

26. IvE 6.2270.

27. *CIL* 3.333 = *CIG* 3738; *CIL* 14.4570. Boulvert, *Esclaves et affranchis*, 433–34.

28. *AE* 1954, 194: [. . .] / Caesaris / vil{l}icus XX her(editatium) / sanctissimo / deo Silvano / aram d(onum) d(edit).

29. *CIL* 13.1550: Zmaragdo vilico / quaest(ori) magistro / ex decurion(um) decr(eto) familiae Ti(beri) Cae[sa]ris / quae est in me[ta]llis.

30. The other members were not believers (Rom 16:10, 11). See Friesen, "Wrong Erastus," 250.

31. Others have hinted at this. See Ascough, *Paul's Macedonian Associations*, 127; Thurston and Ryan, *Philippians*, 161; Reumann, *Philippians*, 739. By comparison, Rom 16:1–2 is a letter of introduction for Phoebe. See also *POxy* 2.292 (25–26 CE).

32. Klauck, *Ancient Letters*, 24–25. On the friendship motif, see Reumann, "Philippians," 83–106; Fitzgerald, "Philippians," 141–62.

33. Michaelis, *Der Brief des Paulus*, 75. For similar positions, see Bormann, *Philippi*, 211; Reumann, *Philippians*, 739; Taylor, *Paul*, 94. See also Hawthorne, *Philippians*, 281; Marshall, *Epistle to the Philippians*, 125.

34. 1 Cor 14:33, "all churches of the saints" (ἐν πάσαις ταῖς ἐκκλησίαις τῶν ἁγίων); Rom 15:25–26 and 2 Cor 1:1, "with all the saints in the whole Achaea" (σὺν τοῖς ἁγίοις πᾶσιν τοῖς οὖσιν ἐν ὅλῃ τῇ Ἀχαΐα).

35. Phil 1:12, 14; 3:13, 17. Compare with 1 Thess 2:17, 5:26; 1 Cor 16:20.

36. See White, *Social Networks*, 26–27.

37. *CIL* 3.7268 = *CIL* 5.8818 = *ILS* 1503. The inscription was found in Altinum (present-day Altino) northeastern Italy. The other inscription is *CIL* 3.556 = *ILS* 1504. See also *ICorinth* 8.3 62 = *AE* 1964, 167.

38. Kadushin, *Understanding Social Networks*, 28.

39. Menjívar, *Fragmented Ties*, 2. For a description of network theory proper, see Kadushin, *Understanding Social Networks*, 14; Prell, *Social Network Analysis*, 7–8. For a similar theory applied to ancient contexts, including early Christianity, see Concannon, "Early Christian Connectivity."

40. Some have proposed that the saints were originally from Macedonia, Thrace, or even Philippi. In this case, the imperial slaves had been, for causes unknown, severed from their compatriots or ethnic group in the Philippian community (Müller, *Der Brief des*

Paulus, 210; Schenk, *Die Philipperbriefe*, 134, 142).

41. *CIL* 3.7047 = *IGR* 4.710 = *MAMA* 4.53 = *GRIA* 61.

42. *MAMA* 4.70; *MAMA* 6.372. All the Arruntii may have been wealthy freed slaves or descendants of them. For an overview, see Christol and Drew-Bear, "Documents latins de Phrygie," 55–62, 82.

43. The people of nearby Prymnessos (present-day Sülün, 22.5 km/14 miles south of ancient Synnada), along with the "Roman residents" and the "Romans doing business there," honored Lucius Arruntius Scribonianus with a statue. Scribonianus was of senatorial rank, prefect of Rome, an augur, a descendant of Pompey the Great, and *quaestor* of the province of Asia in 50 CE, not long before Hyacinthus set up his inscription (*SEG* 36.1200). See Christol and Drew-Bear, "Documents latins de Phrygie," 59 and n77. On the idea of a Roman diaspora, see Purcell, "Romans in the Roman World," 85. Others have classified the phenomenon as a trade diaspora (Terpstra, *Trading Communities*, 176).

44. See the case of Titus Flavius Epagathus from Ephesus (*IvE* 7,1.3019) and Titus Flavius Helius (*GRIA* 144). Helius's wife, Hedone, was a member (position unknown) of the Sextilii family, which was prominent in mid-first-century CE Ephesus and also appears in Smyrna and Akmonia (*AE* 1966, 448; *IvE* 2.404; *AE* 1950, 100).

45. Harland, *Associations*, 44.

46. Laurence, *Roman Archaeology*, 125–26; Eckardt et al., "Long Way From Home," 102. Migrations happened in several stages with stops at various cities and provinces (Noy, *Foreigners at Rome*, 55). As a comparandum, see the case of nineteenth-century Chinese migrant networks in McKeown, *Chinese Migrant Networks*, 65.

47. A bilingual edict of Tiberius (ca. 13–15 CE) posted in several spots in the province of Galatia reiterates this movement (*AE* 1976, 653). See Mitchell, "Requisitioned Transport," 106–31.

48. In addition to evidence already cited for Ephesus, see, from Thessalonike: *IG* X,2 1 740 (2nd–3rd c. CE), *AE* 1993, 1396 (2nd c. CE), *IG* X,2 1 471 (3rd c. CE), and *AE* 2006, 1292 (3rd c. CE); from Corinth: *ICorinth* 8.3 62 = *AE* 1964, 167 (late 1st c. CE), *ICorinth* 8.2 76 (1st c. CE), *CIL* 3.7268, and *ICorinth* 8.3 67

(3rd c. CE); from Philippi: *Philippi* 1.282 = *AE* 1935, 47b (36−37 CE) and *AE* 2001, 1785.

49. Noy, *Foreigners at Rome*, 53. Studies of migration to Roman Spain and Gaul have also shown how important emigration from proximate provinces was, along with migration from further afield (Syria, Macedonia, Thrace, and Asia Minor). See Eckardt et al., "Long Way from Home."

50. See Brélaz, "Philippi."

51. The second part of the inscription is in Greek (*CIL* 6.29152).

52. See *CIL* 6.3309 with two different "routes" to attain Roman citizenship (Noy, *Foreigners at Rome*, 26). See also *IGUR* 2.902. Lucius Pompeius Itharus, an imperial freedman, was from Eumeneia in western Asia. Itharus apparently left home and, with the freedwoman (*conliberta*) Pompeia Gemella, acquired the Roman citizenship that his family did not possess (Noy, *Foreigners at Rome*, 25). Once his newfound status was acquired, Itharus's dispersed family left their home in Asia to join him in Rome.

53. *POxy* 46.3312; see Noy, *Foreigners at Rome*, 26−27. But compare Weaver, "'P.Oxy.' 3312," 199.

54. See Taylor, "Migration," 126−27.

55. Anticipated by Marshall, *Epistle to the Philippians*, 125. On the significance of the marketplace language that Paul uses, see Ascough, *Paul's Macedonian Associations*, 118−19, 122. For occupational networks, see Harland, *Associations*, 38−44.

56. Labarre and Le Dinahet, "Les métiers du textile," 78, no. 19, render the phrase as "préposé aux teinturiers en pourpre."

57. Sardis, Miletus, Phokaia, Hierapolis, Teos, and Kolophon, and on the islands of Rhodes, Cos, Nisyros, and Chios. See Benda-Weber, "Textile Production," 179. Cloth or weaving: Tralles, Hierapolis, Philadelphia, Smyrna, Thyatira, Pergamum, and Ephesus. For an epigraphic catalogue, see Harland, *Associations*, 39.

58. For example, Teos manufactured cloaks and overcoats from Milesian purple and wool (Benda-Weber, "Textile Production Centres," 175, 185, and fig. 115). See Cottier et al., *Customs Law of Asia*, 34−35.

59. Benda-Weber, "Textile Production Centres," 186. See Philippi 1.697 (undated); *IG* X,2 1.291 (late 2nd c. CE).

60. Witherington, *Friendship and Finances*, 137; Horsley, *New Documents*, 27−28.

61. Bormann, *Philippi*, 212−13, hints at this.

Chapter 2

1. *1 Clem.* 5. See Eastman, *Paul the Martyr*, 17; Eastman, "Jealousy," 36. For the various discussions about the date of *1 Clement*, see Lindemann, "First Epistle of Clement," 64−65; Gregory, "*1 Clement*," 227−28; Moreschini and Norelli, *Early Christian Greek and Latin Literature*, 101; Ehrman, *Apostolic Fathers*, 24−25; and Welborn, "On the Date of First Clement," 37.

2. Irenaeus mentions only that the "very great, very ancient, and universally known church [was] founded and organized at Rome by the two most glorious apostles, Peter and Paul" (*Haer.* 3.3.2). See Demacopoulos, *Invention of Peter*, 13−15; Koester, "Paul and Philippi," 63. See also Callahan, "Dead Paul," 78−80.

3. Assmann, *Cultural Memory*, 22; Kirk, "Social and Cultural Memory," 6. Geography and homeland are themselves discursively made, not foundational realities (Kotrosits, *Rethinking Early Christian Identity*, 73−76). See also Moreland, "Moving Peter to Rome," 354, 358−59.

4. Kirk, "Social and Cultural Memory," 7. See also the use of Hercules with the Batavians (Roymans, *Ethnic Identity*, 252). For discussion of Peter in Rome, see Demacopoulos, *Invention of Peter*, 13−21.

5. See Eastman, "Jealousy," 36.

6. Moreland, "Moving Peter to Rome"; Castelli, *Martyrdom and Memory*, 5, 30.

7. Eusebius, *Hist. eccl.* 2.25.7.

8. Eastman, *Paul the Martyr*, 22; Moreland, "Moving Peter to Rome," 360, 362.

9. Besides grain, a *horreum* stored a wide variety of objects, including many valuable goods, such as wine, oil, marble, ivory, etc. The buildings could be privately, publicly, or imperially owned, and typically, *horrea* consisted of a series of rooms on one or more floors, distributed around an open courtyard and enclosed within an outer wall with shops on the exterior. There were a variety of spaces available to rent within standard *horrea*, and each individual room within such a building was called a *horreum* (Holleran, *Shopping in Ancient Rome*, 70).

10. *CIL* 6.682 = *ILS* 1623 and *CIL* 6.30901 = *ILS* 1622. Dimensions are 28 × 106 × 4 cm; letters 2–3 cm. Other imperial slaves are known to have been *horrearii* as well (*CIL* 6.8682).

11. *CIL* 6.30855; 6.33906; 6.301.

12. Moreland, "Moving Peter to Rome," 360. See also Anderson et al., *Handbook of Cultural Geography*, 7.

13. Language adapted from Johnson, *Diaspora Conversions*, 44.

14. Snyder, *Acts of Paul*, 54–55, 64, and 219; Eastman, *Ancient Martyrdom Accounts*, 123. See also Schneemelcher, *New Testament Apocrypha*, 230–31; Tajra, *Martyrdom of St. Paul*, 119–20. On the *Sitz im Leben* of the *Acts of Paul*, see Pervo, *Acts of Paul*, 41, 70–71; Klauck, *Apocryphal Acts*, 48–50; Elliot, *Apocryphal New Testament*, 357. See also Tertullian, *Bapt.* 17.5. For the *Martyrdom of Paul*, Snyder suggests a date as early as the reign of Trajan, 98–117 CE (Snyder, *Acts of Paul*, 63).

15. Compare Schneemelcher, *New Testament Apocrypha*, 232, and Koester, *Introduction to the New Testament*, 329, with Pervo, *Acts of Paul*, 67. See the summary of debates in Snyder, *Acts of Paul*, 5–16.

16. Koester, "Paul and Philippi," 64.

17. For a summary of other ancient versions of the martyrdom account, see Tajra, *Martyrdom of St. Paul*, 134–42. For some of the earliest patristic commentary on the story, see Mitchell, *Heavenly Trumpet*, 363–74, esp. 365.

18. Lieu, *Christian Identity*, 237; Perkins, "Social Geography," 119.

19. A "cupbearer" would have evoked a (passive) sexual relationship with the emperor (Pervo, *Acts of Paul*, 304, 314). There are multiple signs in the story that Patroclus was Nero's catamite, especially the description of Patroclus and Caesar's other servants as "boys" (παῖδες; *Mart. Paul* 1–2).

20. Perkins, "Social Geography," 119; language adapted from Tweed, *Our Lady of the Exile*, 136.

21. Lieu, *Christian Identity*, 235. Arjun Appadurai's term *ideoscape* is also useful for understanding this same point (Appadurai, *Modernity at Large*, 33–36).

22. In this sense, the political ideology of the *Martyrdom of Paul*, I would argue, was noticeably imperial. For discussion, see Snyder, *Acts of Paul*, 60–63. See also the conclusion of this book.

23. The rhetoric is the "fruit of propagandistic impulse," reflecting the "fierce and alienated sentiments" of small, sectarian communities, which attempted to generate superiority in a social and political reality of significant social marginality (Castelli, *Martyrdom and Memory*, 36).

24. Spatio-temporal frameworks are crucial in social memory (Kirk, "Social and Cultural Memory," 2, 5).

25. Kirk, "Social and Cultural Memory," 5. Castelli speaks of a "broad metanarrative" in relation to early Christian martyrdom stories (Castelli, *Martyrdom and Memory*, 25).

26. Item de domo Caesaris Cleobius et Ifitus et Lysimahcus et Aristeus, et duae matronae Berenice et Filostrate cum praesbytero Narcisso postquam deduxerunt eum in portum. Text from Lipsius and Bonnet, *Acta apostolorum apocrypha*, 100–101.

27. Preserved in *POxy* 6.849, the earliest portions correspond to parts of chapters 25 and 26 in the *Actus Vercellenses* (Klauck, *Apocryphal Acts*, 83). Scholars usually suggest that the *Acts of Peter* were originally composed in Greek, in Rome or in Asia Minor, and at the end of the second century or the beginning of the third century. The earliest unambiguous evidence for the existence of a full-fledged *Acts of Peter* is in Eusebius, *Hist. eccl.* 3.3.2 (Klauck, *Apocryphal Acts*, 82–83). See Elliott, *Apocryphal New Testament*, 391–92; Klauck, *Apocryphal Acts*, 84; Schneemelcher, *New Testament Apocrypha*, 283; Schmidt, "Zur Datierung der alten Petrusakten," 150–55.

28. Thomas, *Acts of Peter*, 11; Klauck, *Apocryphal Acts*, 83. For brief discussion of the text, see Hilhorst, "Text of the *Actus Vercellenses*," 148–60. Although it is clearly a translated text, the *Actus Vercellenses* is misrepresented when treated as a literal and reliable transmission of an earlier work (Baldwin, *Whose Acts of Peter?* 9).

29. Thomas, *Acts of Peter*, 22. Most scholars now believe that the opening scene of Paul's departure from Rome was a third-century addition to a Greek *Acts of Peter*. See Eastman, *Paul the Martyr*, 20–21 and n13. Thomas suggests the late second century (*Acts of Peter*, 39). See also Poupon, "Les 'Actes de Pierre,'" 4372–74. However, recent work on the *Acts of Peter* has suggested ca. 250 CE as the terminus ante quem. Compare Klauck,

Apocryphal Acts, 84, and Baldwin, *Whose Acts of Peter?* 9, 302.

30. Thomas, *Acts of Peter*, 22–23, 37. Compare also the late-fourth-century text from Pseudo-Linus, *Martyrdom of Blessed Peter the Apostle*, in which Agrippa is again the main culprit. Peter's martyrdom in chapters 16–17 makes no mention of Peter making disciples in Nero's household.

31. The manuscripts testify to the strong relationship between the martyrdom of Peter and Paul. The idea that Peter and Paul worked in close cooperation goes back to the canonical Acts of the Apostles (Thomas, *Acts of Peter*, 22–24, 37). Much of the information on Paul in the opening scene is drawn from the Pauline epistles: Rom 15:28, 16:21, 16:23; Acts 28:30–31; and Phil 4:22.

32. Klauck, *Apocryphal Acts*, 83. See Bockmuehl, *Remembered Peter*, 96–97; Reed, "Heresiology," 4–8. On the Pseudo-Clementine literature, see the two authoritative articles by F. Stanley Jones, "Pseudo-Clementines."

33. See Kelley, *Knowledge and Religious Authority*, 3; Pervo, "Ancient Novel," 707; Pervo, *Making of Paul*, 177–84. In antiquity, the Clement whom Paul mentions in Phil 4:3 was often understood to be Clement of Rome (Origen, *Comm. Jo.* 6.36; Eusebius, *Hist. eccl.* 3.4.9, 3.14.1).

34. Thomas, *Acts of Peter*, 24; Moreland, "Moving Peter to Rome," 349, 357. The relationship between the real Peter and Paul of the first century was often tense at best (Gal 1:11–2:11).

35. For debate about the relationship between *Acts of Peter* and *Acts of Paul*, see Schneemelcher, *New Testament Apocrypha*, 283; Schmidt and Schubart, Πραξις Παυλου, 127. The interrelationships have not been satisfactorily resolved (Elliott, *Apocryphal New Testament*, 390; Baldwin, *Whose Acts of Peter?* 4–9).

36. Eastman, *Ancient Martyrdom Accounts*, 104, 109.

37. Eastman, *Ancient Martyrdom Accounts*, 195.

38. Pseudo-Linus, *Martyrdom of the Blessed Apostle Paul* 1–2. On the dates, see Eastman, *Ancient Martyrdom Accounts*, 28–29 and 141.

39. Eastman, *Ancient Martyrdom Accounts*, 225.

40. Eastman, *Ancient Martyrdom Accounts*, 224.

41. See Kessler, "Meeting of Peter and Paul in Rome," 268–67; Van den Hoek, "Saga of Peter and Paul," 301–26.

Chapter 3

1. Origin myths usually define friendship or kinship relations with outside groups that are relevant for the present (Roymans, *Ethnic Identity*, 235).

2. Irenaeus of Lyons did something similar with a reference to 'the royal court' in his *Against Heresies* (see appendix 1).

3. Scholars have increasingly argued that the *Refutation of All Heresies* is anonymous. See Litwa, *Hippolytus, Refutation*, xxxii–xl; Brent, *Hippolytus*, 287–90; Cerrato, *Hippolytus*, 94, 103. Less certain are Moreschini and Norelli, *Early Christian Greek and Latin Literature*, 236. When I use "Hippolytus" it is for the sake of convenience only.

4. Greek text from Litwa, *Hippolytus, Refutation*.

5. Kyrtatas, "Christians Against Christians," 25; Frend, *Martyrdom and Persecution*, 317–18; Green, *Christianity in Ancient Rome*, 98; Brent, *Political History*, 243; Batson, *Treasure Chest of the Early Christians*, 96; Andreau, *Banking and Business*, 67. For an older treatment, see Gülzow, "Kallist von Rom."

6. Mazza, "Struttura sociale," 16, 26–27. See also Frend, *Martyrdom and Persecution*, 318. For other examples of identifying Carpohorus as a Christian imperial freedman, see Fiensy, *Christian Origins*, 197; Wheatley, *Patronage in Early Christianity*, 73; Green, *Christianity in Ancient Rome*, 98; Nathan, *Family in Late Antiquity*, 52.

7. Marcovich, *Hippolytus*, 39.

8. Lampe, *From Paul to Valentinus*, 335n13. Even Döllinger (1876), who tried to smooth out the narrative into a more palatable history—and cast the Jews as the instigators—had to speculate about how Hippolytus and Carpophorus knew all the events in the story (*Hippolytus and Callistus*, 109–10).

9. Cerrato, *Hippolytus*, 104; Marcovich, *Hippolytus*, 17, 40; Brent, *Hippolytus*, 287–89. Eusebius is the earliest extant writer to make reference to "Hippolytus" and to speak of Hippolytan

texts, including the *Refutation*, but he does not give a geographic reference (*Hist. eccl.* 6.20.2).

10. Smith, *Guilt by Association*, 15; Hippolytus, *Haer.* 9.12.16 and 20; Marcovich, *Hippolytus*, 38–39. Remarkably, Döllinger claimed that "without a doubt, Hippolytus had not the conscious intention of slandering Callistus" (*Hippolytus and Callistus*, 108).

11. See Brent, *Hippolytus*, 1; Marcovich, *Hippolytus*, 41. See also Brent, "Tertullian on the Role of the Bishop," 179.

12. These rhetorical uses of slaves are noted by Joshel and Hackworth Petersen, *Material Life of Roman Slaves*, 13–14; Joshel, *Slavery in the Roman World*, 154; Bradley, *Slavery and Society at Rome*, 21, 146. For examples, see Pliny the Elder, *Nat.* 33.26; Juvenal, *Sat.* 11.191–92. For the application in the New Testament, see Harrill, *Slaves in the New Testament*, 61–84; Glancy, *Slavery in Early Christianity*, 9–38, 102–29.

13. A similar method of assimilating to a philosophical model to disenfranchise claimants appears in Justin Martyr, *Apol.* 26.6; *2 Apol.* 7.3, 13.1–4 (Lieu, *Christian Identity*, 258).

14. This is what Chris de Wet calls "doulomorphism"—that is, a certain subjectivity will be provided with or assume the subjectivity of a slave (*Preaching Bondage*, 3). See the conclusion of this book.

15. Mouritsen, *Freedman in the Roman World*, 24; Joshel, *Slavery in the Roman World*, 156. As recent studies of Roman slavery have discussed, the primary Roman axis of understanding slaves and freedpersons is one of gradated (dis)honor and morality (Meyer, "New Histories," 244–45). See also Harrill, *Slaves in the New Testament*, 83.

16. Edwards, "Satire and Verisimilitude," 89.

17. Eusebius—who is the first person to attribute writings to a person named Hippolytus—never mentions a Carpophorus, or that Callistus was ever a slave of someone in Caesar's household (Eusebius, *Hist. eccl.* 6.20–22).

18. Like other heresiologists, the author takes language directly from Paul's letters to categorize his opponents: he twice calls Callistus a knave (πανοῦργος); this is the exact same word that Paul uses in 2 Cor 11:3 to decry what he calls "false apostles" (ψευδαπόστολοι). For the predominance of Pauline tradition during this period, see Cerrato, *Hippolytus*, 169–70.

19. *Contra* Lampe, *From Paul the Valentinus*, 336n15. Nor is this evidence for the prominent position of Christians during the Severan period, *pace* Mazza, "Struttura sociale," 16, 26–27. The first instance relates to Simon Magus's explanation of the Pentateuch: a "faithful man" (πιστὸς ἀνήρ) beloved by the sorceress Circe is discovered through that milk-like and divine fruit (*Haer.* 6.16.2). The second instance appears as part of Elchasai's advice about keeping the mysteries safe, since not all are "faithful men" (ἄνδρες πιστοί; *Haer.* 9.17.2).

20. LSJ, s.v. πιστός I.2–3 and II (p. 1408).

21. LSJ, s.v. εὐλαβής II (p. 720). See Plutarch's (ca. 46–120 CE) description of Peisistratos (*Solon* 29.4) and Lucian's use of εὐλαβής in the context of money (*Tim.* 29).

22. The best examples are *CIL* 6.10234 (153 CE); 6.631–32; 6.6713 (177 CE and later); 6.30983 (2nd c. CE).

23. As Judith Lieu notes, apologetic texts strive to control possession or application of the label "Christian," even while admitting the impossibility of securing any ultimate means of control (Lieu, *Christian Identity*, 258). The comment of Marcovich is also apt here, even if anachronistic (Marcovich, *Hippolytus*, 36).

24. On Marcia, see Döllinger, *Hippolytus*, 173; Green, *Christianity in Ancient Rome*, 135; Stark, *Rise of Christianity*, 99. This idea of Marcia as a Christian has been popularized by the *New York Times* best-selling and award-winning book by Diarmaid MacCulloch that states simply "she was a Christian" (*History of Christianity*, 167). For the descriptions of Hyacinth as a presbyter or priest, see Lampe, *From Paul to Valentinus*, 336; Frend, *Martyrdom and Persecution*, 318; McKechnie, "Christian Grave-Inscriptions," 440n36.

25. It has been also suggested, based on a pair of inscriptions from Agnani, Italy, that this same Marcia was an imperial freedwoman and the daughter of an imperial freedman (Strong, "Christian Concubine," 242, citing *CIL* 10.5917 and 10.5918). But see Flexsenhar, "Marcia, Commodus' 'Christian' Concubine."

26. Dio Cassius, *Hist. rom.* 73.4.7 (αὕτη πολλά τε ὑπὲρ τῶν Χριστιανῶν σπουδάσαι καὶ πολλὰ αὐτοὺς εὐηργετηκέναι); Lampe, *From Paul to Valentinus*, 336n15.

27. Strong, "Christian Concubine," 240; Herodian, *Rom. hist.* 1.17.7–9.

28. Lampe, *From Paul to Valentinus*, 336.

29. On Tertullian's personal history, see Wilhite, *Tertullian the African*, 17–24; Dunn, *Tertullian*; Barnes, *Tertullian*, 3–29, 57–59. There has been debate about which Scapula this was. For discussion, see Barnes, "Proconsuls of Asia," 202n8; Birley, "Persecutors and Martyrs," 53; Rebillard, *Christians and Their Many Identities*, 41.

30. *Scap.* 2.5 and 4.8, 2.4, 4.7, 2.5–9, and 2.5–8.

31. ipse etiam Severus, pater Antonini, Christianorum memor fuit. nam et Proculum Christianum qui Torpacion cognominabatur, Euhodiae procuratorem, qui eum per oleum aliquando curaverat, requisiuit et in palatio suo habuit usque ad mortem eius; quem et Antoninus optime noverat, lacte Christiano educatus. Latin from Dekkers et al., *Tertullianus*, 1125–32; English translation adapted from Thewall, *ANF*, vol. 3 (1885).

32. Timothy Barnes linked Torpacion with the imperial freedman Marcus Aurelius Prosenes, claiming that "Christians were already intruding themselves into positions of secret power and influence at the imperial court (*Tertullian*, 69). See also Lampe, *From Paul to Valentinus*, 337. Barnes emphasizes that the correct reading should be Euhodos, that is, the tutor of the emperor Caracalla, citing Dio Cassius *Hist. rom.* 76.2 (Barnes, *Tertullian*, 70n3).

33. Lampe, *From Paul to Valentinus*, 337; Oden, *Early Libyan Christianity*, 115; Grant, *Severans*, 80n18; Rankin, *Tertullian and the Church*, 23.

34. Birley, *Septimius Severus*, 125. In the subsequent editions of his book (1999), Birley excises the piece about Caracalla's Christian wet-nurse.

35. Lampe, *From Paul to Valentinus*, 337 and n16. See also Quacquarelli, *Tertulliani*, 111.

36. Levick, *Julia Domna*, 31n68.

37. Quacquarelli, *Tertulliani Ad scapulam*, 111. For some discussion of the manuscript traditions and the critical editions of *Ad scapulam*, see Waszink, "Some Observations," 46–57; Groh, "Upper-Class Christians," 43.

38. For examples of imperial freedwomen as wet-nurses, see *CIL* 6.4352; 6.20042; 6.14558; 6.16470; 6.20433. For milk as Christian teaching, see Clement (*Strom*

1.11.53.3); Heb 5:13; 1 Pet 2:2–3; 1 Cor 3:2. More generally, see *TLL* 7.2, s.v. *lac* C2b (p. 818). For discussion, see Eshleman, *Social World of Intellectuals*, 104. See also Instinsky, *Die alte Kirche*, 75n73.

39. Siglum N is the fifteenth-century Florence MS, Codex Florentinus BNC Conventi soppressi J.6.9.

40. See Birley, "Attitudes to the State," 258n2; Birley, "Persecutors and Martyrs," 54n131; Levick, *Julia Domna*, 31. For an older view, see Bulhart, *Tertullianus*, 14 and n30.

41. Tertullian evidently had a positive attitude toward Severus, whom he calls *constantissimus* in *Apol.* 4.8 (Birley, "Attitudes to the State," 258; Rankin, *From Clement to Origen*, 60). There is no good evidence for Septimius Severus decreeing an empire-wide persecution. See Birley, "Attitudes to the State," 257; Dunn, *Tertullian*, 17; Rives, "Piety of a Persecutor," 19. Eusebius, the Christian writer who mentions a persecution under Septimius, discusses only events in Alexandria (*Hist. eccl.* 6.1.1).

42. *Contra* Barnes, *Tertullian*, 69–70. Only in the following sentence does Tertullian point up that Severus knew some illustrious women and men (*clarissimas feminas et clarissimos viros*) who were Christians (*Scap.* 4.6). See Groh, "Upper-Class Christians," 43, 46.

43. Glancy, *Slavery in Early Christianity*, 131; Perkins, *Roman Imperial Identities*, 117, 127. On geographical knowledge, space, and imperial power, see Nasrallah, *Christian Responses*, 51–75.

44. Birley, "Persecutors and Martyrs," 45–46.

45. The hypothesis is based on allegedly Christian inscriptions from imperial personnel at Carthage, none of which are definitive. For this hypothesis, see Vössing, *Schule und Bildung*, 413–18; Schöllgen, *Ecclesia sordida?* 104–9; and especially Barton, "Caesar's Household at Carthage," 22. Compare Birley, "Attitudes to the State," 250. For alternate explanations of Christian origins in Africa, see Rives, *Religion and Authority*, 224–26; Wilhite, *Tertullian the African*, 31–32.

46. Kirk, "Social and Cultural Memory," 12.

47. The concept of memory as "translocal" I adapt from Brickell and Datta, *Translocal Geographies*, and from Chamberlain

and Leydesdorf, "Transnational Families," 227, 229.

48. Latin from Glover, *Tertullian*; my translation. The *Apology* dates to 197 CE, because it refers to the recent campaign of Septimius Severus against the Parthians (*Apol.* 37.4). For the more traditional discussion of Tertullian's writings vis-à-vis Roman persecution, see Rankin, *Tertullian and the Church*, 10–16. For the relationship between Tertullian's two apologies, see Barnes, *Tertullian*, 45, 166; and Dunn, "Rhetorical Structure," 51–55.

49. Tertullian remembers a Paul who was martyred in Rome specifically by beheading (*Praes.* 36; *Scorp.* 15). For discussion, see Snyder, *Acts of Paul*, 32–33; Pervo, *Acts of Paul*, 43. Other similarities between the *Martyrdom of Paul* and Tertullian's apologies appear as well: military language (*bello idonei*), "gladly butchered" (*libenter trucidamur*; *Apol.* 37.5), Christians killed with fire and the coming day of judgment (*Apol.* 37.2; *Scap.* 5.2, 2.3, 3.7). Compare *Mart. Paul* 4.

50. *Mart. Paul* 3; *Mart. Paul* 1 and 2.

51. Massey, *For Space*, 9.

Chapter 4

1. Cyprian, *Laps.* 7 says "the greatest number" (*maximus numerus*). See also Cyprian, *Ep.* 55.13.2. See Rebillard, *Christians and Their Many Identities*, 50; Brent, *Cyprian*, 223–47.

2. Moss, *Myth of Persecution*, 148, 150; Brent, *Cyprian*, 225.

3. Ῥούστικος ἔπαρχος εἶπεν τῷ Εὐελπίστῳ· Σὺ δὲ τίς εἶ, Εὐέλπιστε; Εὐέλπιστος δοῦλος Καίσαρος ἀπεκρίνατο· Κἀγὼ Χριστιανός εἰμι, ἐλευθερωθεὶς ὑπὸ Χριστοῦ, καὶ τῆς αὐτῆς ἐλπίδος μετέχω χάριτι Χριστοῦ. Text from Musurillo, *Acts of the Christian Martyrs*, 50.

4. For example, Georges, "Justin's School in Rome." See response by Ulrich, "What Do We Know About Justin's 'School' in Rome?"

5. Bradley, *Apuleius and Antonine Rome*, 122 and n32. Bradley is aware of textual recensions but does not include discussion of them. See also Lampe, *From Paul to Valentinus*, 276 and 351n2; Lane Fox, *Pagans and Christians*, 320; Novak, *Christianity and the Roman Empire*,

68; Kyrtatas, *Social Structure*, 80; Frend, *Martyrdom and Persecution*, 189n59.

6. See Moss, *Ancient Christian Martyrdom*, 89; Musurillo, *Acts of the Christian Martyrs*, xviii. For these recensions and their manuscripts, see Cavalieri, "Gli Atti di Giustino"; Burkitt, "Oldest Manuscript"; Lazzati, "Gli Atti di S. Giustino Martire"; Lazzati, *Gli sviluppi*, 119–27; Barnes, "Pre-Decian '*Acta Martyrum*'"; Bisbee, "Acts of Justin Martyr." Many treatments of the *Acts of Justin* do not mention Euelpistus as an imperial slave because they are using Recension A. In Burkitt's discussion of variations between the manuscripts for Recension B, he does not identify any variation on the reading δοῦλος Καίσαρος for Euelpistus ("Oldest Manuscript," 65).

7. Frend, *Martyrdom and Persecution*, 190n61. To endorse the historicity of the account further, Frend remarks that a "forger would hardly fabricate details" about Cappadocia, so overall this martyrdom account "illustrate[s] Roman imperial policy towards the Christians in the Antonine period" (*Martyrdom and Persecution*, 191). See also Bisbee, *Pre-Decian Acts*, 95, 100; Keresztes, "Marcus Aurelius."

8. Moss hints at this in a note and also suggests a date in the middle of the third century (*Ancient Christian Martyrdom*, 75, 89, and n32). On the date of the text, see Musurillo, *Acts of the Christian Martyrs*, xxix. Lazzati suggested that recension B "è probabilmente del IV secolo" (*Gli sviluppi*, 119). For arguments against this dating, see Bisbee, *Pre-Decian Acts*, 98–99.

9. Luijendijk, *Greetings in the Lord*, 170–73. On the *libelli*, see Knipfing, "Libelli." Similarly, see the discovery of a *libellus* in Claytor, "Decian *Libellus*."

10. Brent, *Cyprian*, 182. In this case some Christians who refused to offer or eat of animal sacrifices were prepared to offer incense and swear by the *genius* of Caesar, the usual minimal demand in martyr acts. See Rives, "Decree of Decius." On the coinage displaying Decius's program, see Manders, *Coining Images of Power*, 262. For general discussion, see Moss, *Myth of Persecution*, 145–51; Rebillard, *Christians and Their Many Identities*, 47; Brent, *Cyprian*, 123–28.

11. *Acta proconsularia* 1.1; Eusebius, *Hist. eccl.* 7.11.7; Brent, *Cyprian*, 19. See also Selinger, *Mid-Third-Century Persecutions*, 85.

12. Cyprian, *Ep.* 80.1; text from Migne, PL 4, cols. 429–30. Conventionally these Caesariani are identified as Christian imperial freedmen or civil servants (Frend, *Rise of Christianity*, 413; Frend, "Persecutions," 515). Others have described them as "Caesar's household" (Clarke, "Third-Century Christianity," 175). By the time of Valerian, however, Caesariani were primarily freeborn financial officials of higher station. See Corcoran, "Emperors and *Caesariani*," 267–68; Haensch, "Von den *Augusti liberti*," 162–63; Weaver, "Phaon," 251. For earlier ancient usages of Caesariani, see Martial (*Ep.* 10.73.4) and Epictetus, who describes them at one point as slavers for the emperors (*Diss.* 1.19.19, 3.24.117, 4.13.22).

13. Keresztes, "From the Great Persecution"; Eusebius, *Hist. eccl.* 8.2.5. The enforcement was more sporadic in the West than in the East (Rebillard, *Christians and Their Many Identities*, 58; Moss, *Myth of Persecution*, 154–58).

14. On the social creation of "cultural trauma," see Alexander, "Toward a Theory of Cultural Trauma," 1. The second half of the third century and the beginning of the fourth century was a period of creativity and memorialization for martyrdom accounts (Moss, *Myth of Persecution*, 153, 158). It is also significant that the *Martyrdom of Pionius the Presbyter and His Companions* was written shortly before or after 300 CE but was set during "the persecution of Decius." Like the *Acts of Justin* Recension B, the issue of sacrifice and Christian piety underlies this account's attempt to reach back into the past.

15. Moss, *Ancient Christian Martyrdom*, 93.

16. My translation. The language is also playful. The Greek could be equally rendered: "Euelpistus answered, 'I am a slave of Caesar and I am also a Christian, manumitted by Christ, and I share in the same hope (ἐλπίς) by the favor (χάρις) of Christ.'"

17. Moss, *Ancient Christian Martyrdom*, 91–92. The text is "manipulative" in this sense; it consciously seeks to inculcate appropriate attitudes but simultaneously recognizes that its audience does not fully hold these attitudes (Lieu, *Christian Identity*, 157).

18. See Harrill, "Domestic Enemy," 231, 247; Lieu, *Image and Reality*, 88; Meyer, "New Histories," 244–45.

19. The fact that on several occasions Cyprian mentions dependents of the household obtaining certificates points to this (*Ep.* 15.4, 55.13.2).

20. Col 3:22; Eph 6:5; Titus 2:9–10; 1 Pet 2:18. Hence, "slave betrayal" was a widely used topos of classical culture (Harrill, "Domestic Enemy," 231–32).

21. Lieu, *Neither Jew nor Greek?* 213.

22. A foundational concern for collective memory animates the historiographical and hermeneutical activity of the ancient martyrdoms (Castelli, *Martyrdom and Memory*, 136). Memorializing martyrs' deaths was at the center of constructing Christian identity (Lieu, *Neither Jew nor Greek?* 211). Moss, *Ancient Christian Martyrdom*, 98.

23. *Acts Justin* B 1.1 (πρόσταγμα) and *Mart. Paul* 2 and 3 (διάταγμα); *Acts Justin* B 5.2 (πᾶς κόσμος) and *Mart. Paul* 3 (ἡ οἰκουμένη ὅλη); *Acts Justin* B 5.1 (ἀποκεφαλίζειν) and *Mart. Paul* 4 (τραχηλοκοπεῖν). Moss, *Ancient Christian Martyrdom*, 97.

24. Lieu, *Neither Jew nor Greek?* 223; Boyarin, *Dying for God*, 94.

25. Δοῦλος, ἔφη, γέγονα Καίσαρος, νυνὶ δὲ Κριστοῦ, τῇ τούτου χάριτι τῆς ἐλευθερίας τυχών. Text from Musurillo, *Acts of the Christian Martyrs*.

26. To this day, in Eastern Orthodox traditions, Euelpistus is commemorated as a saint on June 1 (*Acts Justin* C 2.3). Musurillo, *Acts of the Christian Martyrs*, 57n16.

27. Joshel, *Slavery in the Roman World*, 18, 24; Parker, "Public and Private," 77–78; Bodel, "Cicero's Minerva," 265.

28. Gradel, *Emperor Worship*, 223–24, 231. Caligula was such a one according to Philo (οὐ λέγων μόνον ἀλλὰ καὶ οἰόμενος εἶναι θεός; *Leg.* 162). The phenomenon of emperor worship was ubiquitous and multifaceted. For a focus on Italy and Rome, see Gradel, *Emperor Worship*. For other areas and foci, see Brodd and Reed, *Rome and Religion*; Friesen, *Imperial Cults*; Friesen, *Twice Neokoros*; Ando, *Imperial Ideology*; Price, *Rituals and Power*.

29. Gradel, *Emperor Worship*, 99.

30. Davies, *Death and the Emperor*, 74–75; Price, "From Noble Funerals to Divine Cult."

31. Meiggs, *Roman Ostia*, 333; Gradel, *Emperor Worship*, 222–23.

32. *CIL* 14.4570. The inscription was reused in a Mithraeum near Porta Romana. It is now in the Ostia Museum, inv. 11221. The original location of the *praedia Rusticeliana* is unknown. For a similar group of worshippers,

see *CIL* 6.455 (168 CE) and 6.10267 in which an imperial slave (*Hymnus Caesaris Aug*) is the councillor of the group.

33. *CIL* 6.30983. Restored from the fragments of the *Forma Urbis Romae*: *CIL* 6.29844, 52 and *CIL* 6.29844, 36. The inscription was discovered in the Monte Testaccio area, near the present-day Via Galvani. Another *collegium* from Rome in this same period was dedicated to Aesculapius and Hygeia and included imperial personnel who met in the "Temple of the deified (*divi*) Caesars, in the shrine of the deified (*divus*) Titus" (*CIL* 6.10234). See also *CIL* 6.40415.

34. See Fishwick, "Votive Aedicula," 238–39.

35. *CIL* 6.235.

36. *CIL* 6.252.

37. The *Acts of Justin* Recension B assumed this when it transformed Euelpistus into a martyred imperial slave. For discussion of emperor worship in this late antique context, see Kahlos, "Emperor's New Images."

38. *Acts Justin* B 5.6; *Mart. Pionius* 8.4. Castelli, *Martyrdom and Memory*, 5.

39. For case studies of religion in New World slavery, see Fennell, *Crossroads and Cosmologies*; Sensbach, *Separate Canaan*; Brandon, *Santería*; Johnson, *Secrets, Gossip, and Gods*; Voeks, *Sacred Leaves*.

Chapter 5

1. Fea, "Scavi romani," 123. Fea did not mention any Christian content. Dimensions of the inscriptions are H: 1.5 m × L: 2.68 m × D: 1.54 m.

2. Amati, "Iscrizioni," 255–56.

3. Frend, *Archaeology of Early Christianity*, 77. See De Rossi's comments at *ICUR* 1, pp. 9–10. Until more recently this was still thought to be the earliest Roman Christian inscription (Frend, *Archaeology*, 77).

4. Frend, *Rise of Christianity*, 272–74; McKechnie, "Christian Grave-Inscriptions," 439–40; Markschies, *Das antike Christentum*, 27–28; Mazza, "Struttura sociale," 16; Lampe, *From Paul to Valentinus*, 330; McKechnie, *First Christian Centuries*, 141, 138–39. See especially Beard, North, and Price, who link Prosenes to Paul's "Caesar's household" (*Religions of Rome*, 334). See also Kyrtatas, *Social Structure*, 129; Clarke, "Two Christians," 121.

5. Lee, *Pagans and Christians*, 36, 40.

6. Thomas, "'Nero's Tomb,'" 138; Green, *Christianity in Ancient Rome*, 115; Grant, *Augustus to Constantine*, 175; Instinsky, "Marcus Aurelius Prosenes," 120; Harnack, *Mission and Expansion*, 48–49, though he has reservations.

7. Rutgers, *Subterranean Rome*, 86–87; Lampe, *From Paul to Valentinus*, 332; McKechnie, "Christian Grave-Insriptions," 434.

8. Kolb and Fugmann, *Tod in Rom*, 110.

9. Borg, *Crisis and Ambition*, 44n14. *Pace* Beard, North, and Price, who say that Ampelius's inscription is "explicitly Christian in phrasing" (*Religions of Rome*, 334). See also Carletti, *Epigrafia dei cristiani*, 132. See *CIL* 2.2255; 6.9633; 6.3055; 10.809.

10. Leppin, "Old Religions," 97; Nuffelen, "Pagan Monotheism," 16–33; Grant, *Severans*, 74; Brent, *Imperial Cult*, 266. See also appendix 2 under Alexander and Marcus.

11. Carletti, *Epigrafia dei cristiani*, 131–32; Lampe, *From Paul to Valentinus*, 331; Instinksy, "Marcus Aurelius Prosenes," 120. See *ICUR* 1.1426 (363 CE); *ICUR* 7.18496 (4th c.); *ICUR* 2.4892 = *CIL* 6.31977 (5th c.); *ICUR* 2.4137 (late 4th to early 5th c.).

12. Lampe, *From Paul to Valentinus*, 331.

13. For example, Testini, *Archeologia cristiana*, 329. On comparisons with non-Christian material, see Smith, *Drudgery Divine*, 85.

14. McKechnie, *First Christian Centuries*, 144. See also Rutgers, *Subterranean Rome*, 87; Lampe, *From Paul to Valentinus*, 332n6; McKechnie, "Christian Grave-Inscriptions," 433.

15. Quotations from Lampe, *From Paul to Valentinus*, 333; Lee, *Pagans and Christians*, 40; Instinksy, "Marcus Aurelius Prosenes," 114; Kolb and Fugmann, *Tod in Rom*, 110.

16. Finney, *Invisible God*, 288–89.

17. Lampe, *From Paul to Valentinus*, 334; McKechnie, "Christian Grave-Inscriptions," 439; Instinksy, "Marcus Aurelius Prosenes," 127; Frend, *Rise of Christianity*, 293–94.

18. McKechnie, *First Christian Centuries*, 142, 144.

19. Rowan, *Under Divine Auspices*, 220; Clarke, "Third-Century Christianity," 616–17; Sorti, *I cristiani*, 117–34.

20. For examples, see Kaufmann, *Handbuch*, 59–60; McKechnie, "Christian Grave-Inscriptions," 439. For a critique,

see Finney, *Invisible God*, 288–89; Chiricat, "'Crypto-Christian' Inscriptions," 198–214.

21. See Elsner, "Archaeologies and Agendas," 114–15. There were not two distinct and autonomous "epigraphies," one pagan and the other Christian, like distinct communicative discourses, differing from each other depending on the scope of religious affiliation (Carletti, *Epigrafia dei cristiani*, 9).

22. Mazzoleni, *Epigrafi*, 12; Carletti, "'Epigrafia cristiana,'" 133–34. See also Testini, *Archeologia cristiana*, 331, on the epitaph of Vettia Simplicia (*ICUR* 3.9221), which dates to the fourth century.

23. Mazzoleni, *Epigrafi*, 12, 15; Lampe, *From Paul to Valentinus*, 333.

24. See Mitchell, "Abercius," 309–10; Bodel, "Epigraphy," 25. On Dis Manibus, see Carroll, *Spirits of the Dead*, 266–67; Cooley, *Latin Epigraphy*, 232.

25. See Elsner's discussion of sectarian self-assertion, localism, and competition in early Christian art (Elsner, "Inventing Christian Rome," 74–75). See also Justin Martyr, *Dial.* 35.3–6; Lieu, *Christian Identity*, 265.

26. Carletti, *Epigrafia dei cristiani*, 22–23.

27. Boin, *Ostia in Late Antiquity*, 39–43; Bodel, "Epigraphy," 46.

28. For decades Carlo Carletti has altered the description of analysis from "Christian Epigraphy" to "Epigraphy of Christians," "Inscriptions of Christians," or now inscriptions of "Christian Commission" (Carletti, "'Epigrafia cristiana'"; Carletti, *Epigrafia dei cristiani*). See also Rebillard, *Care of the Dead*, 13–14; Panciera, *Epigrafi*; Solin, "Pagano e cristiano"; Di Stefano Manzella, "Stile, formulario, espressioni di fede."

29. Tartara, "Località S. Maria," 408, 411–12 and n13; Granino Cecere, "M. Aurelii Prosenetis Praedium," 192. For other finds from the area that help fill in the original context, see Quilici, *Collatia*, 693–709.

30. Borg, *Crisis and Ambition*, 44–45.

31. Lampe, *From Paul to Valentinus*, 332, citing Minucius Felix (*Oct.* 34.10). This passage, however, shows the opposite. The author writes: "The whole body, whether it crumbles into dust, or is resolved into moisture, or reduced to ashes (*cinerem*), or attenuated into smoke, is withdrawn from us, but the elements remain in the keeping (*custodia*) of god."

32. Bodel, "From *Columbaria* to Catacombs," 181; Carroll, *Spirits of the Dead*, 165, 166; Ewald, "Funerary Monuments," 397, 399.

33. Embalmers were not present in every town (Carroll, *Spirits of the Dead*, 164). On the other hand, sometimes only the bones (*ossa*) were returned home when a person died abroad (*CIL* 14.3777).

34. *CIL* 6.1884. See Millar, *Emperor in the Roman World*, 67–69; Carroll, *Spirits of the Dead*, 166. For other imperial freedmen who advanced from personal attendants of emperors to administrative services, see *ILS* 1942–1944; *CIL* 6.8409.

35. *CIL* 6.8878.

36. For descriptions of the monument from art-historical perspectives, see Thomas, "'Nero's Tomb,'" 138; Borg, *Crisis and Ambition*, 44–45; Deichmann et al., *Repertorium*, 387. The sheet of the tablet seems to have been worked before the execution of the present inscription. This prompted Deichmann to wonder if this is the secondary use of the sarcophagus by Prosenes (*Repertorium*, 387).

37. Lampe, *From Paul to Valentinus*, 332.

38. On putti, see George, "Cupid Punished," 159–60. On the relationship between myths, cupids, and torches on sarcophagi, see Zanker and Ewald, *Living with Myths*, 89, 96–100, 114.

39. Lampe, *From Paul to Valentinus*, 333.

40. Sometimes even the nomenclature attests to this when freedpersons identify themselves as freedmen or freedwomen of the *divine* emperor (*divi Augusti libertus/liberta*; Gk. θεοῦ Σεβαστοῦ ἀπελεύθερος / ἀπελεύθερα). *AE* 1984, 951; *CIL* 11.3805; 6.29681.

41. Scheid, "Sacrifices for Gods," 270–71; Jensen, "Dining with the Dead"; Zanker and Ewald, *Living with Myths*, 26–27; Ewald, "Funerary Monuments," 397–98.

42. Saller, Introduction, 5; Bodel, "Epigraphy," 46.

43. Mitchell, "Abercius," 310.

44. Saller, Introduction, 5.

45. Boin, *Coming Out Christian*, 5.

46. Elsner, "Archaeologies and Agendas," 126–27.

47. Harnack, *Mission and Expansion*, 49n1.

48. Rebillard, "Late Antique Limits of Christianness," 305.

49. Boin, *Coming Out Christian*, 89–90. On Commodus, see Toner, *Day Commodus*

Killed a Rhino, 26–27. On Christian emperor worship, see Rebillard, *Christians and Their Many Identities*, 25–31.

50. Revell, *Roman Imperialism*, x.

51. Lieu, *Christian Identity*, 3.

Chapter 6

1. Testini, *Archeologia cristiana*, 72.

2. See Kaufmann, *Handbuch*, 106; Marucchi, *Christian Epigraphy*, 223–29.

3. McKechnie, "Christian Grave-Inscriptions." Hans Instinsky was the first to interpret the inscriptions together and in light of Marcus Aurelius Prosenes ("Marcus Aurelius Prosenes," 113–29).

4. See Fennell, *Crossroads and Cosmologies*, 7–8. On the use of symbols as metaphors in culture groups and material culture, see also Tilley, *Metaphor and Material Culture*, 31–33.

5. See Lewis, "Reinterpreting 'Pagans' and 'Christians'"; Bodel, "From *Columbaria* to Catacombs." On reuse of material, see Mazzoleni, "Inscriptions in Roman Catacombs," 150; Carroll, *Spirits of the Dead*, 265.

6. For introduction and bibliography, see Lewis, "Reinterpreting 'Pagans' and 'Christians'"; Hirschfeld, "Catacomb Archaeology"; Bowes, "Early Christian Archaeology"; Frend, *Archaeology of Early Christianity*.

7. Bowes, "Early Christian Archaeology," 575–79. For an example, see Pergola, *Le catacombe romane*, 21. On De Rossi, see Fiocchi Nicolai, "Origin and Development," 9–13, 23.

8. A parallel methodology was used for material found in Rome's "Jewish" catacombs. See Dello Russo, "Monteverde Jewish Catacombs"; Kraemer, "Jewish Tuna and Christian Fish."

9. *CIL* 6.9054 = *ICUR* 9.25069: [. . .] Aug(usti) lib(ertus) praepositus tabernaculo[rum---] / [--- Chrys]idi sorori bene merenti quae vixit an[nis---] / [---] sorori quae vixit annis XVII Serapi[oni avo] / [qui vixit annis X]XXXV Chrysomallo patri qui vixit an[nis---] / [---] fratri qui vixit annis XXII Nicen[i filiae] / [--- e]x voluntate eiusdem Chrysidis [. . .].

10. Marucchi, "Notizie," 255–56. See Marucchi, *Le catacombe romane*, 492; Marucchi, *Christian Epigraphy*, 228. De Rossi's

idea was the product of mixing 2 Tim 4:19 and medieval traditions (De Rossi, "Della casa," 44–45).

11. Bodel, "*Columbaria* to Catacombs," 203. The only pre-Constantinian text that directly deals with the issue of where Christians should or should not be buried (Cyprian, *Ep.* 67.6.2) in fact shows that Christians did *not* avoid burial with their non-Christian neighbors.

12. Bodel, "*Columbaria* to Catacombs," 182, 188; Johnson, "Pagan-Christian Burial Practices." See also the discussion of the nuclei of the Priscilla Catacombs in Borg, *Crisis and Ambition*, 105.

13. Bowes, "Early Christian Archeology," 586.

14. Rebillard, *Care of the Dead*, 3–4, and the earlier study, Rebillard, "Koimetérion et Coemeterium." See also Bodel, "*Columbaria* to Catacombs," 186–87; Lampe, *From Paul to Valentinus*, 27. Contrary to De Rossi's thinking there were also no official Christian funerary societies (*collegia tenuiroum*) or specifically funerary *collegia* of any sort. See Harland, *Associations*, 28; Perry, *Roman Collegia*, 49–60.

15. See Borg, *Crisis and Ambition*, 75, 105.

16. Mazzoleni, "Rise of Christianity," 450; Mazzoleni, *Epigrafi*, 12; Mazzoleni, "Inscriptions," 151; Carletti, "'Epigrafia cristiana,'" 128–31. But see Cooley, *Latin Epigraphy*, 230. Onomastics has been another, often circular, way to identify Christians. For examples, see Testini, *Archeologia cristiana*, 369; Mazzoleni, "Rise of Christianity," 450–52. Paleography has also been used. See Mazzoleni, "Inscriptions," 150. For an overview of De Rossi and the "Roman school," see Carletti, *Epigrafia dei cristiana*, 17–18.

17. *CIL* 6. 26259. Di Stefano Manzella, "La raccolta lapidaria," 269.

18. Quotation from Cadoux, *Early Church*, 392 and n7. On symbols, see Testini, *Archeologia cristiana*, 329; Tabbernee, "Epigraphy," 127.

19. Carletti, *Epigrafia dei cristiana*, 24; McKechnie, *First Christian Centuries*, 142. See the comments of Carroll, *Spirits of the Dead*, 267–68; Tabbernee, "Epigraphy," 128.

20. Carletti's term (*Epigrafia dei cristiana*, 31). Two early Christian literary references have bolstered this supposition. Clement of Alexandria, *Paed.* 3.11; Tertullian, *Bapt.* 1.3. See Carletti, *Iscrizioni cristiane*, 27–28.

21. *Contra* Graydon F. Snyder, who thought early Christians created the anchor symbol de novo, and that it had very little metaphorical meaning outside Christian circles (Snyder, *Ante pacem*, 15). See Finney, *Invisible God*, 111; Cooley, *Latin Epigraphy*, 232, 234; Jensen, *Early Christian Art*, 47–48. By comparison, depictions of fish at Ostia were once interpreted as proof of the town's Christian residents, but today those images have been shown to be more multivalent than once believed (Boin, *Ostia in Late Antiquity*, 39).

22. The axiom is that "Christian" epigraphy derived from the standard "pagan," "secular," or—now appearing more frequently—the "Classical" or "Roman content," but was given new meaning that alludes to Christ and salvation. See Mazzoleni, "Rise of Christianity," 450; Carletti, *Epigrafia dei cristiani*, 30; Carletti, "'Epigrafia cristiana,'" 115; Carletti, "Nascita e sviluppo," 144–45; Di Stefano Manzella, "Stile, formulario, espressioni di fede," 307. But see Lewis, "Reinterpreting 'Pagans' and 'Christians,'" 284, and the comments of Snyder, *Ante pacem*, 13.

23. Cooley, *Latin Epigraphy*, 229, 231; Talloen, "From Pagan to Christian," 575; Solin, "Pagano e cristiano," 220; Elsner, "Archaeologies and Agendas," 125. See again the case of the rings with chi-rho symbols from Ostia (Boin, *Ostia*, 42–43).

24. *CIL* 6.9057 = *CIL* 9.539, 2 = *ILCV* 349 = *ICUR* 10.27029. Discovered in 1842. See De Rossi, "Epigrafi rinvenute," 51; Faßbender, "Untersuchungen," 134.

25. *ICUR* 4.9388; 1.900; 9.25098; 9.25133; 8.23243; 9.25210; 9.25332; 9.25385. For example: deposso eius VI kal(endas) / ianuar(ias) Florentinus / qui oduit dolens animo / fecit pax tecu(m) (*ICUR* I, 580 = *ILCV* 2248) dates to the fourth century. See also *ICUR* 9.25416 (290–325 CE) and 9.24461 (290–325 CE). Lampe, *From Paul to Valentinus*, 339. Compare McKechnie, "Christian Grave-Inscriptions," 436, 439.

26. Lewis, "Reinterpreting 'Pagans' and 'Christians,'" 274.

27. *ICUR* 9.25009 = *ILCV* I.763a = *AE* 1903, 176.

28. De Rossi excavated and edited the greater part of the inscriptions from the Catacombs of Priscilla and published them in the *Bullettino di Archeologia Cristiana* between 1880 and 1894. Others were published later by Orazio Marucchi, including this one in 1902. Ernst Diehl then catalogued it as a Christian inscription in his 1925 volume (*ILCV* I.763a).

29. McKechnie, "Christian Grave-Inscriptions," 433. The double imperial nomenclature attached to Sozon (*Augg.*) indicates that he was manumitted either between 161 and 169 CE during the joint reigns of Marcus Aurelius and Commodus, or between 209 and 211 CE during the reigns of Caracalla and Geta, which of course would mean that Sozon lived beyond these dates.

30. Marucchi, "Nuovi scavi," 227.

31. This begins with Marucchi's initial publication in 1902. Even Diehl has some misgivings, punctuating a note with an all-too-rare question mark (*num christianus est titulus?*). Instinsky includes the Sozon inscription in his corpus, but questions whether the findspot and the anchor symbol is enough to secure the inscription as Christian ("Marcus Aurelius Prosenes," 121). Similarly, Boulvert, *Domestique et fonctionnaire*, 103n622.

32. Marucchi, "Nuovi scavi," 227. The tile was in two parts (29 × 58 cm) and painted in a reddish color (*ICUR* 9.25215). See Mazzoleni, "Inscriptions," 150, and examples on 149 (fig. 155), 155 (fig. 159), and 156 (figs. 160, 161).

33. See the comments of Edwards, "Severan Christianity," 406.

34. Fiocchi Nicolai, "Origin and Development," 29, and plan of lower level on 25. See also Tolotti, *Il cimitero di Priscilla*, 322–40; Styger, *Die römischen Katakomben*, 132–33.

35. The majority of the tombs that are still intact do not have any inscription (Mazzoleni, "Inscriptions," 148).

36. Lewis, "Reinterpreting 'Pagans' and 'Christians,'" 276. To this day the vast majority of the catacomb galleries are inaccessible to visitors, and many are overseen by the Vatican's Pontificia Commissione di Archeologia Sacra (PCAS).

37. See the image of the *fossor* and enshrouded corpse (*ICUR* 2.6446). Mazzoleni, "Inscriptions," 150.

38. Borg, *Crisis and Ambition*, 79–97.

39. Borg, *Crisis and Ambition*, 278.

40. Galleries E17 and E19 preserve monumental graffiti on the vaults that read respectively "of the cooks 11" (*cocorum* XI), "of the cooks 6" (*cocorum* VI), and "of the cooks 30" ([*cocorum*] XXX; *ICUR* 5.14815.a-b).

On the early use of the area's material culture from imperial personnel, see Spera, *Il complesso di Pretestato*, 21–29. Borg, *Crisis and Ambition*, 86–87. For the inscriptions of the imperial kitchen staff, see *AE* 1937, 159; 1973, 84; *CIL* 6. 7458; 6.8750.

41. *AE* 1973, 84. See Ferrua, "Le iscrizioni pagane," 75. The stone, which measures 50 × 84 × 3 cm, was found in April 1962, in the eastern part of the corridor. Where exactly it was found Ferrua does not say.

42. *AE* 1937, 159. See Ferrua, "Le iscrizioni pagane," 28 and pl. IV, figs. 1–2.

43. *CIL* 6.13225 and *ICUR* 5.14329. For another instance, see *CIL* 6.13188 and *ICUR* 7.18785.

44. *CIL* 6.8751; Bodel, "From *Columbaria* to Catacombs," 192n28.

45. *ICUR* 2.4246 = *ILCV* 1611b. See Cooley, *Latin Epigraphy*, 234; Carletti, *Epigrafia dei cristiani*, 136 and n7; Noviello, "Stele con simboli cristiani," 568–69. The expression "fish of the living" remains to this day a unique epigraphic instance. Other inscriptions that have since been catalogued as Christian show the D. M. abbreviation was erased (*ICUR* 5.12895 = *CIL* 6.22939). The image for the latter is available at http://www.archeologiasacra.net/pcas-web/EDB/784/scheda.html.

46. The editors of *CIL* 6 do not mention the ostensibly Christian symbols, but record only the text and its location. The LIR at the end of line 1 is either a misspelling or an idiosyncratic abbreviation for *libertus*.

47. For the colored image, see http://www.edb.uniba.it/epigraph/781.

48. McKechnie, "Christian Grave-Inscriptions," 430n10, 431, 433, 436–37. This date is based on comparing the Atimetus epitaph with other epitaphs classified as Christian—with Aurelius Sozon's and with an epitaph from the Cemetery of Hermes dated to 234 CE that is decorated with a fish and an anchor (*ILCV* 2807). McKechnie's article has been cited with approval by Thomas, "'Nero's Tomb,'" 138n33; Lee, *Pagans and Christians*, 42.

49. McKechnie, "Christian Grave-Inscriptions," 440.

50. See Tortorella, "Il sepolcreto"; Green, *Christianity in Ancient Rome*, 115, 201; Carcopino, *De Pythagore*, 353; also advanced with caution by Solin, "Pagano e cristiano," 218–19.

51. Tortorella, "Il sepolcreto," 1362. See Fiocchi Nicolai, "Origin and Development," 14; Fiocchi Nicolai, "Strutture funerarie," 121; Carletti, "Pagani e cristiani," 304; Pergola, *Le catacombe romane*, 181–83; Rutgers, *Subterranean Rome*, 127. Even during the first half of the third century there is no evidence for exclusive use by Christians (Borg, *Crisis and Ambition*, 253). For some of the various positions on the *piazzola* area, see Mancini, "Scavi," 48–50; Marucchi, "Nota," 96–98; Lietzmann, *Petrus und Paulus*, 59; Dölger, *Ichthys*, 697–704; Testini, *Le catacombe*, 55; Jastrzębowska, *Untersuchungen*, 42–49; Brandenburg, "Überlegungen," 30.

52. Styger, *Römische Märtyrergrüfte*, 15; Dölger, *Ichthys*, 703; Ferrua, in *ICUR* vol. 5, p. 4.

53. Tortorella, "Il sepolcreto," 1366–67, 1373. A pictorial decoration in the attic of the nearby hypogea of Marcus Clodius Hermes, identified as the healing of the Gerasene demoniac from the Gospel of Matthew, is cited as an analogous phenomenon and also dated to the second or third century. Here, too, the next oldest comparable documentation of this artistic theme dates to the fifth century (Tortorella, "Il sepolcreto," 1373; Carletti, "Pagani e cristiani," 293–96). Lucretia Spera suggests the image dates to "around the middle of the third century" ("Christianization of Space," 26).

54. Casagrande-Kim, "Journey to the Underworld," 176–79.

55. For a helpful summary of the excavation history beneath the Basilica Apostolorum (S. Sebastiano), see Ferrua, *La basilica*, 7–10.

56. Borg, *Crisis and Ambition*, 150; Spera, *Il paesaggio*, 219–20; Nieddu, *La Basilica*, 5–6. For the proposed stratification layers, see Tolotti, *Memorie*, 69, fig. 21; Jastrzębowska, *Untersuchungen*, 45–46.

57. Tolotti, "Sguardo d'insieme," 125; Borg, *Crisis and Ambition*, 148–50.

58. On the successive raising/elevation of the ground, see Toynbee and Ward-Perkins, *Shrine of St. Peter*, 175 and n61; Totorella "Il sepolcreto," 1359. On levels of burials, see Jastrzębowska, *Untersuchungen*, 43. The marks of the ground levels are visible in the photographs.

59. Spera, "Christianization of Space," 26; Tolotti, "Sguardo d'insieme," 127–28. The *triclia* became known as the *memoria apostolorum*. For discussion of cultic practices,

see Eastman, *Paul the Martyr*, 72–74. For the invocations to Peter and Paul, see *ICUR* 5.12097–13096. For the account of Styger's fortuitous discovery of this apostolic cult shrine, see now Jastrzębowska, "Paul Styger," 6–8.

60. Jastrzębowska, *Untersuchungen*, 43; Tolotti, "Sguardo d'insieme," 127; Finney, *Invisible God*, 235.

61. Finney, *Invisible God*, 232, 233, and · fig. 6.5 (my emphasis); Dölger, *Ichthys*, 703. Neither Finney nor Dölger elaborates on this observation.

62. See also Carcopino, *De Pythagore*, table 20. In the more recently available photograph this feature is obscured somewhat because sealing plaster appears to have been applied into the margins of the epitaph, no doubt for the sake of preserving the monument (Ferrua, *La basilica*, 15, fig. 2).

63. See Solin, "Pagano e cristiano," 199, 219; and compare Finney, *Invisible God*, 235, 239. See the comments of Lewis, "Reinterpreting 'Pagans' and 'Christians,'" 279–85.

64. Tortorella, "Il sepolcreto," 1373.

65. Lewis, "Reinterpreting 'Pagans' and 'Christians'" 284. Compare *ICUR* 5.13269b also from San Sebastiano.

66. The paleography suggests a third-century date, as the hand is more florid than the block letters used on the epitaph, found in the *piazzola*, for one Elpisius. For the image, see Mancini, "Scavi," 66–67. Compare also *CIL* 6.9057 = *CIL* 9.539, 2 = *ILCV* 349 = *ICUR* 10.27029.

67. The feast evidently began in 258 CE while Bassus and Tuscus were the consuls as per the *Depositio martyrum*. See Eastman, *Paul the Martyr*, 95–96.

68. Tolotti, "Sguardo d'insieme," 127–28; Tolotti, *Memorie*, 159, fig. 38; Jastrzębowska, *Untersuchungen*, 257–58, figs. 6–7.

69. For example, a grafitto reading ΙΤΧΘΥΣ was scratched into the mortar in the upper chamber of Mausoleum Y, the Tomb of the Innocentiores (*ICUR* 5.12889).

Conclusion

1. Pliny, *Ep.* 7.29 and 8.6. See also Tacitus, *Ann.* 12.53; Suetonius, *Claud.* 28; Dio Cassius, *Hist. rom.* 61.14.

2. See Philo, *Leg.* 162–96; Josephus, *Ant.* 18.8, 19.5, 20.5.

3. Cultural discourse is a "historically transmitted expressive system of communication practices, of acts, events, and styles, which are composed of specific symbols, symbolic forms, norms, and their meanings" (Carbaugh, "Cultural Discourse," 169, 167–82). It is "complex processes of creation, contestation, negotiation and reformulation on the interactive level through which actors create and utilize powerful cultural tools for social change." Here "discourses are seen as symbolic representations that serve to communicate information." Thus the "approach makes possible a rich understanding of symbolic production and its effects" (Magnuson, "Cultural Discourse," 372, 374).

4. Fennell, *Crossroads and Cosmologies*, 7–8.

5. Lewis, "Crafting of Memory," 267–68.

6. Kloppenborg, "Memory," 98; Steinbock, *Social Memory*, v.

7. Olick, "Products," 8. Misztal, *Theories of Social Remembering*, 11. Moreland, "Moving Peter," 346. On memory, see the foundational work of Halbwachs, *Collective Memory*.

8. Castelli, *Martyrdom and Memory*, 4, 5, 30; for cultural memory and the invention of tradition, see Elsner, "Cultural Memory, Religious Practice," 101; Assmann, *Cultural Memory and Early Civilization*; Kloppenborg, "Memory," 102.

9. Misztal, *Theories of Social Remembering*, 13. See the words of Smith, *To Take Place*, 25.

10. Kirk, "Social and Cultural Memory," 10.

11. Kloppenborg, "Memory," 101–2, 115.

12. Kartzow, *Destabilizing the Margins*, 11; Olick, "Products," 7; Misztal, *Theories of Social Remembering*, 15.

13. Flexsenhar, "Recovering Paul's Hypothetical Slaves."

14. De Wet, *Unbound God*, 19.

15. I have adapted de Wet's concept of "kyriarchal eclipse," the idea that earthly masters are replicas or types of god in early Christian thought (*Unbound God*, 19).

16. "At times, the rules and dynamics of vertical slavery are inconsistent and paradoxical when compared with the dynamic of horizontal slavery." This "incoherency and paradoxicality of ancient slavery is in itself

a power strategy that enables the institution to absorb and utilize discourses, initially appearing to be in opposition to slavery, to the benefit of the system" (De Wet, *Unbound God*, 20).

17. Anthony, Introduction, xx.

18. Mendels, *Memory*, 103–13.

19. Galinsky, Introduction, 1.

20. See Pliny's correspondence with the emperor Trajan (*Ep.* 10.96–97).

21. On ethnicity in early Christianity, see Buell, *Why This New Race*; Concannon, "Early Christian Connectivity"; Hodge, *If Sons, Then Heirs.*

22. Jones, *Archaeology*, 13–14; Morgan, "Ethnic Expression."

23. Hall, *Hellenicity*, 16–17. While ethnicity and culture are not synonymous, the two overlapped in ways that effectively blurred the distinctions (Buell, *Why This New Race*, 45). For that reason, throughout this book the term "cultural," as in "cultural history," is used to mean an expression of the ethnic group.

24. Buell, *Why This New Race*, 36–58; Jones, *Archaeology*; Roymans, *Ethnic Identity.*

Appendix 1

1. Lampe, *From Paul to Valentinus*, 184, 206.

2. See Lindemann, *Die Clemensbriefe*, 13.

3. Louth, *Early Christian Writings*, 19.

4. For example, see Head, "'Witnesses'"; Caragounis, "Development of the Roman Church," 277.

5. Lampe *From Paul to Valentinus*, 185–86, 351 and n1.

6. Lampe, *From Paul to Valentinus*, 184–85; Lampe, "Urchristliche Missionswege," 123–27.

7. Mouritsen, "Freedmen and Freeborn," 283–86. See also Madsen, *Eager to Be Roman*, 99–100.

8. Just a few of the Tiberii Claudii from Rome: *AE* 1925, 14; 1931, 89; 1969/70, 32; 1975, 48; 1976, 90; 1981, 145; 1998, 1613; 1999, 390.

9. Lindemann, *Clemensbriefe*, 180.

10. Thompson, "Bauer's Early Christian Rome," 226 and n27; Hill, *Lost Teachings of Polycarp*, 21; Lampe, *From Paul to Valentinus*, 117, 351.

11. Hill, *Lost Teachings of Polycarp*, 22; Behr, *Irenaeus of Lyons*, 52, 67.

12. Clarke, "Irenaeus," 96.

13. Compare Herodian, *Hist.* 1.5.8 and 1.6.1, 1.7.6; 3.11.17.

14. Epiphanius, *Haer.* 64.3. See also Eusebius, *Hist. eccl.* 6.23.1.

15. For this official vocabulary, see *AE* 1988, 1021; 1975, 792; *CIL* 3.6075; *AE* 1998, 1305; Hill, *Lost Teachings of Polycarp*, 20.

16. See Purcell, "*Apparitores*," 128, 132, 137; Millar, *Emperor in the Roman World*, 66–67. See also *AE* 1980, 98.

17. *CIL* 6.1959; 6.1957; 6.1884.

18. Horster, "Living on Religion," 335. See also *IvE* 5.1544; 3.646.

19. The Armenian translation of the Greek of *Against the Heresies* (5th–8th c. CE) has in fact the plural "royal courts" (Hill, *Lost Teachings of Polycarp*, 18).

20. *Haer.* 4.30. Latin text from Migne, PG 7a, col. 1065. Translation adapted from Schaff, *ANF*, vol. 1 (1885).

21. It is even possible to make a rough estimate of their salaries from the *apparitores* at Urso. The scribes who worked for the magistrates (*duoviri*) there earned an annual salary of 1,200 sesterces, attendants earned 600, messengers 400, clerks 300. At 700–1,200 HS per year, the *apparitores*—in the city of Urso, at least—were not well-off (Horster, "Living on Religion," 335).

22. Smith, *Guilt by Association*, 133. Some have argued that Irenaeus's multivolume project was not completed at once but in a few instantiations (Chiapparini, "Irenaeus and the Gnostic Valentinus," 97; Kalvesmaki, "Original Sequence of Irenaeus," 417). Others have proposed that Irenaeus wrote to Florinus ("On the Sole Sovereignty") prior to book 4 of the *Adversus haereses*, and thus the passage concerning the faithful ones in the royal court would have been a jibe at Florinus himself (Behr, *Irenaeus of Lyons*, 67; Hill, *Lost Teachings of Polycarp*, 22, 76–77).

23. Behr, *Irenaeus of Lyons*, 95–97.

24. The use of *utensilia* is here synonymous with *vasa*. See Pliny, *NH* 13.11.22. The Vulgate thus renders the phrase with σκεύη as "vasa argentea et aurea" (Clarke, "Irenaeus," 96).

25. Behr, *Irenaeus of Lyons*, 75; Payton, *Irenaeus on the Christian Faith*, 50; Hill, *Lost Teachings of Polycarp*, 18; Lampe, *From Paul to Valentinus*, 117.

26. Irenaeus, *Haer.* 1.10.2; Secord, "Cultural Geography," 26, 29. See also Grant, *Irenaeus of Lyons*, 6–7.

27. Smith, *Guilt by Association*, 77–78, 81.

28. Brent, "Irenaeus," 36; Secord, "Cultural Geography," 26.

Appendix 2

1. Visconti, "Dissertazione," 42, 49–50.

2. An exception is De Spirito, "Paedagogium," 8. The text is usually dated to the early third century (Carletti, *Epigrafia dei cristiani*, 137–38), but compare Dal Covolo, *I Severi*, 46.

3. My emphasis. See Green, *Christianity in Ancient Rome*, 201; Mazzoleni, *Epigrafi*, 46.

4. McKechnie, "Christian Grave-Inscriptions," 432; Noviello, "Un paggio imperiale," 516; Clarke, "Two Christians," 122.

5. Carletti, *Epigrafia dei cristiani*, 137 (my emphasis).

6. McKechnie, "Christian Grave-Inscriptions," 432–33. See also Noviello, "Un paggio imperiale," 517.

7. Ilardi, "Epitaffio," 223 and fig. 3.2.5; Vatican Museum, GL 25,14, Inv. 7523. Ilardi says that in this inscription Alexander has inscribed a monogrammatic cross representing the name of Christ (*CIL* 6.9028). But both the identification of the person and the cross are doubtful. It is implausible that these Alexanders are the same person. The inscription was found on the opposite side of Rome, and the man here is an imperial freedman not a slave; the inscription includes an occupational description, mentions a wife, does not mention a son, and there are other known imperial personnel with the name Septimius Alexander (e.g., *CIL* 14.1595).

8. Clarke, "Two Christians," 122–23.

9. Harland, "Familial Dimensions." See *NSA* 1939, 86; *CIL* 6.3713; 6.9004; 6.30983.

10. Mohler, "Slave Education," 273.

11. The epitaph uses "qui in unu(m) deu(m) and includes a Christogram" (*CIL* 6.18080 = *ICUR* 3.8808).

12. *CIL* 6.8972, 7767, 8982–8986; *NSA* 1939, 86; *CIL* 6.1052.

13. Mohler, "Slave Education," 264.

14. *Pace* McKechnie, "Christian Grave-Inscriptions," 438.

15. "Caesar's boys" (*puerorum Caesaris*) on the Palatine (*CIL* 6.8977).

16. *CIL* 5.1039; 6.8977. See Seneca, *Vit. beat.* 17.2; *Tranq.* 1.8; *Ep.* 123.7 and 95.24; Martial 3.58.30.

17. Keegan, "Reading the 'Pages.'" And rather than the conventional interpretation of the Alexamenos graffito as a barb at a Christian, Larry Yarbrough suggests a broader interpretation that is not exclusively Christian (Yarbrough, "Shadow of an Ass").

18. Lampe, *From Paul to Valentinus*, 335; McKechnie, "Christian Grave-Inscriptions," 427; Gülzow, "Kallist von Rom," 105.

19. *CIL* 6.975; 6.3504; 6.9915; 6.14416; 6.10660; *AvP* 8,3.107.

20. Lampe, *From Paul to Valentinus*, 335n1.

21. Lampe, *From Paul to Valentinus*, 335, 13; Güzlow, "Kallist von Rom," 105 and n15.

22. Borg, *Crisis and Ambition*, 77–78.

23. McKechnie, "Christian Grave-Inscriptions," 432.

24. *CIL* 6.11951; 6.13073; 6.16472; 6.17430; 6.17790; 6.18378; 6.18850; 6.21617; 6.29273a. For Aelius Felix, see *CIL* 6.10707a: [D(is)] M(anibus) / [so]mno (a)eternali / [A]elius Aug(usti) lib(ertus) Felix / [et] Aelia Egloge co(n)iux / [vi]bos se fecerun(t) et / [fil]i(i)s naturalibus / [Ael]io Stefano Aeliae / [Eut]ychiae. The fragmentary text (56 × 81.5 cm) dates to the 2nd century CE, originally from Via Tiburtina, Cimitero del Verano.

25. *AE* 1987, 130; *CIL* 6.19966.

26. *CIL* 6.20446; 6.21934; 6.27923; *AE* 2004, 225.

27. *CIL* 6. 20446; 6.21934; 6.27923; *AE* 2004, 225; *CIL* 6.18378; *Malta* 2, 147.

28. Weaver's terminology (*Familia Caesaris*, 240).

BIBLIOGRAPHY

Alexander, Jeffrey C. "Toward a Theory of Cultural Trauma." In *Cultural Trauma and Collective Identity*, edited by Jeffrey C. Alexander, Ron Eyerman, Bernhard Giesen, Neil J. Smelser, and Piotr Sztompka, 1–30. Berkeley: University of California Press, 2004.

Alföldy, Géza. *The Social History of Rome.* Translated by David Braund and Frank Pollock. Baltimore: Johns Hopkins University Press, 1988.

Amati, Giorlamo. "Iscrizioni de' Volusii." *Giornale Arcadico di Scienze, Lettere ed Arti* 50 (1831): 255–57.

Anderson, Kay, Mona Domash, Steve Pile, and Nigel Thrift, eds. *Handbook of Cultural Geography.* London: Sage, 2003.

Ando, Clifford. *Imperial Ideology and Provincial Loyalty in the Roman Empire.* Berkeley: University of California Press, 2000.

Andreau, Jean. *Banking and Business in the Roman World.* New York: Cambridge University Press, 1999.

Anthony, Sean W. Introduction to *The Expeditions: An Early Biography of Muhammad*, by Ma'mar ibn Rashid, xv–xxxiv. Translated by Sean W. Anthony. New York: New York University Press, 2015.

Appadurai, Arjun. *Modernity at Large: Cultural Dimensions of Globalization.* Minneapolis: University of Minnesota Press, 1998.

Apter, Andrew. "Herskovits's Heritage: Rethinking Syncretism in the African Diaspora." *Diaspora* 1, no. 3 (1991): 235–60.

Asad, Talal. *Genealogies of Religion: Discipline and Reasons of Power in Christianity and Islam.* Baltimore: Johns Hopkins University Press, 1993.

Ascough, Richard S. *Paul's Macedonian Associations: The Social Context of Philippians and 1 Thessalonians.* Tübingen: Mohr Siebeck, 2003.

Assmann, Jan. *Cultural Memory and Early Civilization: Writing, Remembrance, and Political Imagination.* New York: Cambridge University Press, 2011.

———. *Religion and Cultural Memory: Ten Studies.* Translated by Rodney Livingstone. Stanford: Stanford University Press, 2006.

Baldwin, Matthew C. *Whose Acts of Peter? Text and Historical Context of the Actus Vercellenses.* Tübingen: Mohr Siebeck, 2005.

Barnes, Timothy. "Pre-Decian 'Acta Martyrum.'" *Journal of Theological Studies* 19, no. 2 (1968): 509–31.

———. "Proconsuls of Asia Under Caracalla." *Phoenix* 40 (1986): 202–5.

———. *Tertullian: A Historical and Literary Study.* Oxford: Clarendon Press, 1971.

Barton, I. M. "Caesar's Household at Carthage." *Museum Africum* 1 (1972): 18–27.

Batson, David. *The Treasure Chest of the Early Christians: Faith, Care, and Community from the Apostolic Age to Constantine the Great.* Grand Rapids, Mich.: Eerdmans, 2001.

Beard, Mary, John North, and Simon Price. *Religions of Rome.* Vol. 2. Cambridge: Cambridge University Press, 1998.

Beare, Francis Wright. *A Commentary on the Epistle to the Philippians.* 3rd ed. Black's New Testament Commentaries. London: A&C Black, 1973.

Behr, John. *Irenaeus of Lyons: Identifying Christianity.* Oxford: Oxford University Press, 2013.

Beltrán Lloris, Francisco. "The 'Epigraphic Habit' in the Roman World." In *The*

Oxford Handbook of Roman Epigraphy, edited by Christer Bruun and Jonathan Edmondson, 131–48. Oxford: Oxford University Press, 2015.

Benda-Weber, Isabella. "Textile Production Centres, Products, and Merchants in the Roman Province of Asia." In *Making Textiles in Pre-Roman and Roman Times: People, Places, and Identities*, edited by Margarita Gleba and Judit Pásztókai-Szeöke, 171–91. Oxford: Oxbow Books, 2013.

Birley, Anthony. "Attitudes to the State in the Latin Apologists." In *L'apologétique chrétienne gréco-latine à l'époque prénicénienn: Sept exposés suivis de discussions; Vandœuvres Genève, 13–17 septembre 2004*, edited by Antonie Wlosok and François Paschoud, 249–77. Geneva: Fondation Hardt, 2005.

———. "Persecutors and Martyrs in Tertullian's North Africa." *University of London Institute of Archaeology Bulletin* 29 (1992): 37–68.

———. *Septimius Severus: The African Emperor*. London: Eyre and Spottiswoode, 1971.

Bisbee, Gary. "The Acts of Justin Martyr: A Form-Critical Study." *Second Century* 3 (1983): 129–57.

———. *Pre-Decian Acts of Martyrs and Commentarii*. Philadelphia: Fortress Press, 1988.

Bockmuehl, Markus N. A. *A Commentary on the Epistle to the Philippians*. London: A&C Black, 1998.

———. *The Remembered Peter: In Ancient Reception and Modern Debate*. Tübingen: Mohr Siebeck, 2010.

Bodel, John. "Cicero's Minerva, *Penates*, and the Mother of the *Lares*: An Outline of Roman Domestic Religion." In *Household and Family Religion in Antiquity*, edited by John Bodel and Saul M. Olyan, 248–75. Malden, Mass.: Wiley-Blackwell, 2008.

———. "Epigraphy and the Ancient Historian." In *Epigraphic Evidence: Ancient History from Inscriptions*, edited by John Bodel, 1–56. London: Routledge, 2001.

———. "From *Columbaria* to Catacombs: Collective Burial in Pagan and Christian Rome." In *Commemorating the Dead: Texts and Artifacts in Context; Studies of Roman, Jewish, and Christian Burials*, edited by Laurie Brink and Deborah A. Green, 177–242. Berlin: Walter de Gruyter, 2008.

———. "Slave Labor and Roman Society." In *The Cambridge World History of Slavery*, vol. 1, *The Ancient Mediterranean World*, edited by Keith Bradley and Paul Cartledge, 311–36. Cambridge: Cambridge University Press, 2011.

Bodel, John, and Walter Scheidel. Introduction to *On Human Bondage: After Slavery and Social Death*, edited by John Bodel and Walter Scheidel, 1–14. Malden, Mass.: Wiley-Blackwell, 2017.

Boin, Douglas. *Coming Out Christian in the Roman World: How the Followers of Jesus Made a Place in Caesar's Empire*. New York: Bloomsbury Press, 2015.

———. *Ostia in Late Antiquity*. Cambridge: Cambridge University Press, 2013.

Borg, Barbara. *Crisis and Ambition: Tombs and Burial Customs in Third-Century CE Rome*. Oxford: Oxford University Press, 2013.

Bormann, Lukas. *Philippi: Stadt und Christengemeinde zur Zeit des Paulus*. Leiden: Brill, 1995.

Boulvert, Gérard. *Domestique et fonctionnaire sous le Haut-Empire romain: La condition de l'affranchi et de l'esclave du prince*. Paris: Belles Lettres, 1974.

———. *Esclaves et affranchis impériaux sous le Haut-Empire romain: Rôle politique et administratif*. Naples: Jovene, 1970.

Bowes, Kim. "Early Christian Archaeology: A State of the Field." *Religion Compass* 2, no. 4 (2008): 575–619.

Boyarin, Daniel. *Dying for God: Martyrdom and the Making of Christianity and Judaism*. Stanford: Stanford University Press, 1999.

Bradley, Keith R. *Apuleius and Antonine Rome: Historical Essays*. Toronto: University of Toronto Press, 2012.

———. *Slavery and Society at Rome*. Cambridge: Cambridge University Press, 1994.

———. *Slaves and Masters in the Roman World: A Study in Social Control*. New York: Oxford University Press, 1987.

Brandenburg, Hugo. "Überlegungen zu Ursprung und Entstehung der Katakomben Roms." In *Vivarium: Festschrift Theodor Klauser zum 90. Geburtstag*, edited by Ernst Dassmann,

Theodor Klauser, and Klaus Thraede, 11–45. Münster, Westfalen: Aschendorff, 1984.

Brandon, George. *Santería from Africa to the New World: The Dead Sell Memories.* Bloomington: Indiana University Press, 1993.

Brélaz, Cédric. "Philippi: A Roman Colony Within Its Regional Context." In *L'hégémonie romaine sur les communautés du Nord Égéen (IIe s. av. J.-C.–IIe s. ap. J.-C.): Entre ruptures et continuités,* edited by J. Fournier and M.-G. G. Parissaki. Athens: National Hellenic Research Foundation, forthcoming.

Bremmer, Jan A. *The Rise of Christianity Through the Eyes of Gibbon, Harnack, and Rodney Stark: A Valedictory Lecture on the Occasion of His Retirement from the Chair of Religious Studies, in the Faculty of Theology and Religious Studies.* Groningen: Barkhuis, 2010.

Brent, Allen. *Cyprian and Roman Carthage.* Cambridge: Cambridge University Press, 2010.

———. *Hippolytus and the Roman Church in the Third Century: Communities in Tension Before the Emergence of a Monarch-Bishop.* Leiden: Brill, 1995.

———. "How Irenaeus Has Misled the Archaeologists." In *Irenaeus: Life, Scripture, Legacy,* edited by Sara Parvis and Paul Foster, 35–52. Minneapolis: Fortress Press, 2012.

———. *The Imperial Cult and the Development of Church Order: Concepts and Images of Authority in Paganism and Early Christianity Before the Age of Cyprian.* Boston: Brill, 1999.

———. *A Political History of Early Christianity.* London: T&T Clark, 2009.

———. "Tertullian on the Role of the Bishop." In *Tertullian and Paul,* edited by Todd D. Still and David Wilhite, 165–85. New York: Bloomsbury, 2013.

Brickell, Katherine, and Ayona Datta, eds. *Translocal Geographies: Spaces, Places, Connections.* Burlington, Vt.: Ashgate, 2011.

Brodd, Jeffrey, and Jonathan L. Reed, eds. *Rome and Religion: A Cross-Disciplinary Dialogue on the Imperial Cult.* Atlanta: Society of Biblical Literature, 2011.

Bruce, F. F. *Philippians.* 2nd ed. Peabody, Mass.: Hendrickson Publishers, 1989.

Bruun, Christer. "Slaves and Freed Slaves." In *The Oxford Handbook of Roman Epigraphy,* edited by Christer Bruun and Jonathan Edmondson, 605–26. Oxford: Oxford University Press, 2015.

Buell, Denise Kimber. *Why This New Race: Ethnic Reasoning in Early Christianity.* New York: Columbia University Press, 2005.

Bulhart, V., ed. *Tertullianus, Ad martyras, Ad Scapulam, De fuga in persecutione, De monogamia, De virginibus velandis, De pallio.* Berlin: De Gruyter, 1957.

Burkert, Walter. *Ancient Mystery Cults.* Cambridge, Mass.: Harvard University Press, 1987.

Burkitt, F. Crawford. "The Oldest Manuscript of St. Justin's Martyrdom." *Journal of Theological Studies* 11 (1909): 61–66.

Burton, Graham. "Slaves, Freedmen, and Monarchy." *Journal of Roman Studies* 67 (1977): 162–66.

Cadoux, John Cecil. *The Early Church and the World: A History of the Christian Attitude to Pagan Society and the State down to the Time of Constantinus.* Edinburgh: Clark, 1925.

Callahan, Allen Dwight. "Dead Paul: The Apostle as Martyr in Philippi." In *Philippi at the Time of Paul and His Death,* edited by Charalambos Bakirtzis and Helmut Koester, 67–84. Eugene, Ore.: Wipf & Stock, 1998.

Caragounis, Chrys. "From Obscurity to Prominence: The Development of the Roman Church between Romans and 1 Clement." In *Judaism and Christianity in First-Century Rome,* edited by Karl P. Donfried and Peter Richardson, 254–79. Grand Rapids, Mich.: Eerdmans, 1998.

Carbaugh, Donal. "Cultural Discourse Analysis: Communication Practices and Intercultural Encounters." *Journal of Intercultural Communication Research* 36, no. 3 (2007): 167–82.

Carcopino, Jérôme. *De Pythagore aux apôtres: Études sur la conversion du monde romain.* Paris: Flammarion, 1956.

Carletti, Carlo. "'Epigrafia cristiana,' 'epgrafia dei cristiani': Alle origini della terza età dell'epigrafia." In *La terza età dell'epigrafia: Colloquio AIEGL Borghesi 86 (Bologna, Ottobre 1986),* edited by

Angela Donati, 115–35. Faenza: Fratelli Lega, 1988.

———. *Epigrafia dei cristiani in Occidente dal III al VII secolo: Ideologia e prassi.* Bari: Edipuglia, 2008.

———. *Iscrizioni cristiane di Roma: Testimonianze di vita cristiana (secoli III– VII).* Florence: Nardini, 1986.

———. "Nascita e sviluppo dei formulario epigrafico cristian: Prassi e ideologia." In *Le iscrizioni dei cristiani in Vaticano: Materiali e contributi scientifici per una mostra epigrafica,* edited by Ivan di Stefano Manzella, 143–64. Vatican City: Quasar, 1997.

———. "Pagani e cristiani nel sepolcreto della 'piazzola' sotto la Basilica Apostolorum a Roma." *Vetera Christianorum* 18 (1981): 287–307.

Carroll, Maureen. *Spirits of the Dead: Roman Funerary Commemoration in Western Europe.* Oxford: Oxford University Press, 2006.

Casagrande-Kim, Roberta. "The Journey to the Underworld: Topography, Landscape, and Divine Inhabitants of the Roman Hades." PhD diss., Columbia University, 2012.

Case, Shirley Jackson. *The Social Origins of Christianity.* Chicago: University of Chicago Press, 1923.

Castelli, Elizabeth A. *Martyrdom and Memory: Early Christian Culture Making.* New York: Columbia University Press, 2004.

Cavalieri, P. de' Franchi. "Gli Atti di Giustino." *Studi e Testi* 8 (1902): 33–36.

———. "Gli Atti di Giustino." *Studi e Testi* 9 (1902): 73–75.

Cerrato, J. A. *Hippolytus Between East and West: The Commentaries and the Provenance of the Corpus.* Oxford: Oxford University Press, 2002.

Chamberlain, Mary, and Selma Leydesdorf. "Transnational Families: Memories and Narratives." *Global Networks* 4, no. 3 (2004): 227–41.

Chiapparini, Giuliano. "Irenaeus and the Gnostic Valentinus: Orthodoxy and Heresy in the Church of Rome Around the Middle of the Second Century." *Zeitschrift für Antikes Christentum* 18, no. 1 (2014): 95–119.

Chiricat, Édouard. "The 'Crypto-Christian' Inscriptions of Phrygia." In *Roman Phrygia,* edited by Peter Thonemann, 198–214. Cambridge: Cambridge University Press, 2013.

Christol, Michael, and Thomas Drew-Bear. "Documents latins de Phrygie." *Tyche: Beiträge zur Alten Geschichte, Papyrologie und Epigraphik* 1 (1986): 41–87.

Clark, Gillian. *Christianity and Roman Society.* Cambridge: Cambridge University Press, 2004.

Clarke, Graeme W. "Irenaeus *Adv. Haer.* 4. 30. 1." *Harvard Theological Review* 59, no. 1 (1966): 95–97.

———. "Third-Century Christianity." In *The Cambridge Ancient History,* vol. 12, *The Crisis of Empire, AD 193–337,* edited by Alan Bowman, Peter Garnsey, and Averil Cameron, 589–671. Cambridge: Cambridge University, 2005.

———. "Two Christians in the *Familia Caesaris.*" *Harvard Theological Review* 64, no. 1 (1971): 121–24.

Claytor, W. Graham. "A Decian Libellus at Luther College (Iowa)." *Tyche* 30 (2015): 13–18.

Coarelli, Filippo. *Rome and Environs: An Archaeological Guide.* Translated by James J. Clauss and Daniel P. Harmon. Updated ed. Berkeley: University of California Press, 2014.

Collar, Anna. *Religious Networks in the Roman Empire: The Spread of New Ideas.* New York: Cambridge University Press, 2013.

Concannon, Cavan. "Early Christian Connectivity and Ecclesial Assemblages in Ignatius of Antioch." In *Across the Corrupting Sea: Post-Braudelian Approaches to the Ancient Eastern Mediterranean,* edited by Cavan Concannon and Lindsey A. Mazurek, 65–90. New York: Routledge, 2016.

Cooley, Alison. *The Cambridge Manual of Latin Epigraphy.* Cambridge: Cambridge University Press, 2012.

Corcoran, Simon. "Emperors and *Caesariani* Inside and Outside the Code." In *Société, économie, administration dans le Code Théodosien,* edited by Sylvie Crogiez-Pétrequin and Pierre Jaillette, 265–84. Villeneuve-d'Ascq: Universitaires du Septentrion, 2012.

Cottier, M., M. H. Crawford, C. V. Crowther, J.-L. Ferrary, B. M. Levick, O. Salomies, and M. Wörrle, eds. *The*

Customs Law of Asia. New York: Oxford University Press, 2008.

Crook, Zeba. *Reconceptualising Conversion: Patronage, Loyalty, and Conversion in the Religions of the Ancient Mediterranean.* Berlin: Walter de Gruyter, 2004.

Cumont, Franz. *The Oriental Religions in Roman Paganism.* 2nd ed. New York: Dover, 1956. Originally published in English in 1911.

Dal Covolo, Enrico. *I Severi e il cristianesimo: Ricerche sull'ambiente storico-istituzionale delle origini cristiane tra il secondo e il terzo secolo.* Rome: Las, 1989.

D'Arms, John. "Familia Caesaris: A Social Study of the Emperor's Freedmen and Slaves by P. R. C. Weaver." *American Journal of Archaeology* 96, no. 3 (1975): 335–39.

Davies, Penelope J. E. *Death and the Emperor: Roman Imperial Funerary Monuments, from Augustus to Marcus Aurelius.* Cambridge: Cambridge University Press, 2000.

Davis, David Brion. *Inhuman Bondage: The Rise of Fall and Slavery in the New World.* Oxford: Oxford University Press, 2006.

Davis, Lisa Fagan. "The Epitome of Pauline Iconography: BnF Français 50, the *Miroir Historial* of Jean de Vignay." In *A Companion to St. Paul in the Middle Ages,* edited by Steven Cartwright, 395–424. Leiden: Brill, 2013.

Deichmann, Friedrich Wilhelm, Giuseppe Bovini, and Hugo Brandenburg, eds. *Repertorium der christlich-antiken Sarkophage,* vol. 1, *Rom und Ostia.* Wiesbaden: Franz Steiner, 1967.

Deissmann, Adolf. *Light from the Ancient East: The New Testament by Recently Discovered Texts of the Greco-Roman World.* Translated by Lionel Strachan. Rev. ed. New York: George H. Doran, 1927.

Dekkers, Eligius, J. G. P. Borleffs, R. Willems, R. F. Refoulé, G. F. Diercks, and A. Kroymann. *Tertullianus, Opera I.* Corpus Christianorum Series Latina 1. Turnhout: Brelops, 1954.

Dello Russo, Jessica. "The Monteverde Jewish Catacombs on the via Portuense." *Roma Subterranea Judaica* 4 (2010): 1–37.

Demacopoulos, George E. *The Invention of Peter: Apostolic Discourse and Papal Authority in Late Antiquity.* Philadelphia: University of Pennsylvania Press, 2013.

Denecker, E., and K. Vandorpe. "Sealed Amphora Stoppers and Tradesmen in Greco-Roman Egypt: Archaeological, Papyrological, and Inscriptional Evidence." *BABesch: Annual Papers on Mediterranean Archaeology* 82 (2007): 115–28.

De Rossi, Giovanni Battista. "Del Cimitero S. Ermete." *Bullettino di Archeologia Cristiana* 5 (1894): 14–21.

———. "Della casa d'Aquila e Prisca sull'Aventino." *Bullettino di Archeologia Cristiana* 3 (1867): 44–47.

———. "Epigrafi rinvenute nell'arenaria tra i cimiteri di Trasone e dei Giordani nella Via Salaria Nova." *Bullettino di Archeologia Cristiana* 2 (1873): 5–80.

De Spirito, G. "Paedagogium a Capite Africae." *Lexicon Topographicum Urbis Romae* 4 (1999): 8.

de Wet, Chris L. *Preaching Bondage: John Chrysostom and the Discourse of Slavery in Early Christianity.* Berkeley: University of California Press, 2016.

———. *The Unbound God: Slavery and the Formation of Early Christian Thought.* New York: Routledge, 2018.

———. *The Unbound God: Slavery and the Formation of Early Christian Thought.* New York: Routledge, 2018.

Di Stefano Manzella, Ivan. "3.9. Stile, formulario, espressioni di fede." In *Le iscrizioni dei cristiani in Vaticano: Materiali e contributi scientifici per una mostra epigrafica,* edited by Ivan Di Stefano Manzella, 307. Vatican City: Quasar, 1997.

———. "La raccolta lapidaria." In *San Paolo fuori le mura a Roma,* edited by Carlo Pietrangeli, 266–81. Florence: Nardini, 1988.

Dölger, Franz Joseph. *Ichthys: Die Fisch-Denkmäler in der Frühchristlichen Plastik Malerei und Kleinkunst.* Vol. 5. Münster: Aschendorffsche Verlagsbuchhandlung, 1943.

Döllinger, Johann Joseph Ignaz von. *Hippolytus and Callistus; or, The Church of Rome in the First Half of the Third Century, with Special Reference to the Writings of Bunsen, Wordsworth, Baur, and Gieseler.* Edinburgh: T&T Clark, 1876.

Duncan-Jones, Richard. *The Economy of the Roman Empire: Quantitative Studies*. 2nd ed. Cambridge: Cambridge University Press, 1982.

Dunn, Geoffrey D. "Rhetorical Structure in Tertullian's *Ad Scapulam*." *Vigiliae Christianae* 56, no. 1 (2002): 47–55.

———. *Tertullian*. New York: Routledge, 2004.

Eastman, David L. *The Ancient Martyrdom Accounts of Peter and Paul*. Atlanta: Society of Biblical Literature, 2015.

———. "Jealousy, Internal Strife, and the Deaths of Peter and Paul: A Reassessment of 1 Clement." *Zeitschrift für Antikes Christentum* 18, no. 1 (2013): 34–53.

———. *Paul the Martyr: The Cult of the Apostle in the Latin West*. Atlanta: Society of Biblical Literature, 2011.

Eckardt, H., C. Chenery, S. Leach, M. Lewis, G. Müldner, and E. Nimmo. "A Long Way from Home: Diaspora Communities in Roman Britain." In *Roman Diasporas: Archaeological Approaches to Mobility and Diversity in the Roman Empire*, edited by Hella Eckardt, 99–130. Portsmouth, R.I.: Journal of Roman Archaeology, 2010.

Edwards, Mark. "Satire and Verisimilitude: Christianity in Lucian's 'Peregrinus.'" *Historia* 38, no. 1 (1989): 89–98.

———. "Severan Christianity." In *Severan Culture*, edited by Simon Swain, Stephen Harrison, and Jaś Elsner, 401–18. Cambridge: Cambridge University Press, 2007.

Ehrman, Bart D. *The Apostolic Fathers*. Vol. 1. Loeb Classical Library 24. Cambridge, Mass.: Harvard University Press, 2003.

———. *The Triumph of Christianity: How a Forbidden Religion Swept the World*. New York: Simon and Schuster, 2018.

Elliott, J. K. *The Apocryphal New Testament: A Collection of Apocryphal Christian Literature in an English Translation*. Oxford: Oxford University Press, 1993.

Elsner, Jaś. "Archaeologies and Agendas: Reflections on Late Ancient Jewish Art and Early Christian Art." *Journal of Roman Studies* 93 (2003): 114–28.

———. "Cultural Memory, Religious Practice, and the Invention of Tradition: Some Thoughts on Philostratus's Account of the Cult of Palaemon." In *Cultural Memories in the Roman Empire*, edited by Karl Galinsky, 101–15. Los Angeles: Getty Museum, 2015.

———. "Inventing Christian Rome: The Role of Early Christian Art." In *Rome the Cosmopolis*, edited by Catharine Edwards and Greg Woolf, 71–99. Cambridge: Cambridge University Press, 2003.

Eshleman, Kendra. *The Social World of Intellectuals in the Roman Empire: Sophists, Philosophers, and Christians*. Cambridge: Cambridge University Press, 2012.

Ewald, Björn Christian. "Funerary Monuments." In *The Oxford Handbook of Roman Sculpture*, edited by Elise A. Friedland, Melanie Grunow Sobocinski, and Elaine K. Gazda, 390–406. New York: Oxford University Press, 2015.

Fabre, Georges. "Mobilité et stratification: Le cas des serviteurs impériaux." In *La mobilité sociale dans le monde romain: Actes du colloque organize à Strasbourg (novembre 1988) par l'Institut et le Groupe de Recherche d'Histoire Romaine*, edited by Edmond Frézouls, 123–59. Strasbourg: AECR, 1992.

Faßbender, Andreas. "Untersuchungen zur Topographie von Grabstätten in Rom von der Späten Republik bis in die Spätantike." PhD diss., Cologne University, 2005.

Fea, Carlo. "Scavi romani." *Bullettino dell'Instituto di Corrispondenza Archeologica* 5b (1830): 121–24.

Fee, Gordon D. *Paul's Letter to the Philippians*. Grand Rapids, Mich.: Eerdmans, 1995.

Fennell, Christopher. *Crossroads and Cosmologies: Diasporas and Ethnogenesis in the New World*. Gainesville: University of Florida Press, 2007.

Ferrua, Antonio, ed. *La basilica e la catacomba di S. Sebastiano*. Vatican City: Pontificia Commissione di Archeologia Sacra, 1990.

———. *Inscriptiones christianae urbis Romae septimo saeculo antiquiores, Nova series*. Vol. 5, *Coemeteria reliqua Viae Appiae*. Vatican City: Pontifico Istituto di Archeologia Cristiana, 1971.

———. "Le iscrizioni pagane della Catacomba di Pretestato." *Rendiconti della Classe di Scienze Morali, Storiche e Filologiche* dell'Accademia dei Lincei, ser. 8, vol. 28 (1973): 63–99.

Fiensy, David A. *Christian Origins and the Ancient Economy.* Eugene, Ore.: Cascade, 2014.

Finley, Moses I. *Ancient Slavery and Modern Ideology.* New York: Penguin, 1980.

Finn, Thomas M. "Social Mobility, Imperial Civil Service, and the Spread of Early Christianity." *Studia Patristica* 17, no. 1 (1982): 31–37.

———. "Mission and Expansion." In *Early Christian World,* edited by Philip Esler, 1: 295–315. New York: Routledge, 2000.

Finney, Paul Corby. *The Invisible God: The Earliest Christians on Art.* New York: Oxford University Press, 1994.

Fiocchi Nicolai, Vincenzo. "The Origin and Development of Roman Catacombs." In *The Christian Catacombs of Rome: History, Decoration, Inscriptions,* edited by Vincenzo Fiocchi Nicolai, Fabrizio Bisconti, and Danilo Mazzoleni, 9–69. 2nd ed. Regensburg: Schnell & Steiner, 2002.

———. "Strutture funerarie ed edifici di culto paleocristiani di Roma dal III al VI secolo." In *Le iscrizioni dei cristiani in Vaticano: Materiali e contributi scientifici per una mostra epigrafica,* edited by Ivan Di Stefano Manzella, 121–41. Vatican City: Quasar. 1997.

Fishwick, Duncan. "A Votive Aedicula at Narbo." *Zeitschrift für Papyrologie und Epigraphik* 98 (1993): 238–42.

Fitzgerald, John T. "Philippians in the Light of Some Ancient Discussions of Friendship." In *Friendship, Flattery, and Frankness of Speech: Studies on Friendship in the New Testament World,* edited by John T. Fitzgerald, 141–69. Leiden: Brill, 1996.

Flexsenhar, Michael, III. "Marcia, Commodus' 'Christian' Concubine, and *CIL* X 5918." *Tyche: Beiträge zur Alten Geschichte, Papyrologie und Epigraphik* 31 (2016): 135–48.

———. "The Provenance of Philippians and Why It Matters: Old Questions, New Approaches." *Journal for the Study of the New Testament.* (forthcoming).

———. "Recovering Paul's Hypothetical Slaves: Rhetoric and Reality in 1 Corinthians 7:21." *Journal for the Study*

of Paul and His Letters 5, no. 1 (2015): 71–88.

Frend, W. H. C. *The Archaeology of Early Christianity: A History.* London: Geoffrey Chapman, 1996.

———. *Martyrdom and Persecution in the Early Church: A Study of Conflict from the Maccabees to Donatus.* 2nd ed. Eugene, Ore.: Wipf & Stock, 2014.

———. "Persecutions: Genesis and Legacy." In *The Cambridge History of Christianity,* vol. 1, *Origins to Constantine,* edited by Margaret M. Mitchell and Frances M. Young, 503–23. Cambridge: Cambridge University Press, 2006.

———. *The Rise of Christianity.* Philadelphia: Fortress Press, 1984.

Friesen, Steven J. *Imperial Cults and the Apocalypse of John: Reading Revelation in the Ruins.* Oxford: Oxford University Press, 2001.

———. "Poverty in Pauline Studies: Beyond the So-Called New Consensus." *Journal for the Study of the New Testament* 23, no. 3 (2004): 323–61.

———. *Twice Neokoros: Ephesus, Asia, and the Cult of the Flavian Imperial Family.* Leiden: Brill, 1993.

———. "The Wrong Erastus: Ideology, Archaeology, and Exegesis." In *Corinth in Context: Comparative Studies on Religion and Society,* edited by Steven J. Friesen, Daniel N. Schowalter, and James C. Walters, 231–56. Leiden: Brill, 2010.

Galinsky, Karl. Introduction to *Memory in Ancient Rome and Early Christianity,* edited by Karl Galinsky, 1–39. Oxford: Oxford University Press, 2016.

Garnsey, Peter. *Ideas of Slavery from Aristotle to Augustine.* New York: Cambridge University Press, 1996.

George, Michele. "Cupid Punished: Reflections on a Roman Genre Scene." In *Roman Slavery and Roman Material Culture,* edited by Michele George, 158–79. Toronto: University of Toronto Press, 2013.

Georges, Tobias. "Justin's School in Rome: Reflections on Early Christian 'Schools.'" *Zeitschrift für Antikes Christentum* 16, no. 1 (2012): 75–87.

Glancy, Jennifer A. "Christian Slavery in Late Antiquity." In *Human Bondage in the Cultural Contact Zone: Transdisciplinary*

Perspectives on Slavery and Its Discourses, edited by Raphael Hörman and Gesa Mackenthun, 63–79. New York: Waxmann, 2010.

———. *Slavery in Early Christianity*. Oxford: Oxford University Press, 2002.

Glover, T. R. *Tertullian: Apology, De spectaculis.* Loeb Classical Library 250. Cambridge, Mass.: Harvard University Press, 1931.

Gomez, Michael. *Exchanging Our Country Marks: The Transformation of African Identities in the Colonial and Antebellum South.* Chapel Hill: University of North Carolina Press, 1998.

Gradel, Ittai. *Emperor Worship and Roman Religion.* Oxford: Oxford University Press, 2002.

Granino Cecere, M. Grazia. "M. Aurelii Prosenetis Praedium." *Lexicon Topographicum Urbis Romae Suburbium* 1 (2001): 192.

Grant, Michael. *The Severans: The Changed Roman Empire.* London: Routledge, 1996.

Grant, Robert M. *Augustus to Constantine: The Rise and Triumph of Christianity in the Roman World.* 2nd ed. Louisville: Westminster John Knox Press, 2004.

———. *Irenaeus of Lyons.* New York: Routledge, 1997.

Green, Bernard. *Christianity in Ancient Rome: The First Three Centuries.* London: T&T Clark, 2010.

Gregory, Andrew. "*1 Clement:* An Introduction." *Expository Times* 117, no. 6 (2006): 223–30.

Groh, Dennis E. "Upper-Class Christians in Tertullian's Africa." *Studia Patristica* 14 (1976): 41–47.

Gülzow, Henneke. "Kallist von Rom: Ein Beitrag zur Soziologie der römischen Gemeinde." *Zeitschrift für die Neutestamentliche Wissenschaft* 58 (1967): 102–21.

Haensch, Rudolf. "Von den *Augusti liberti* zu den *Caesariani.*" In *Herrschaftsstrukturen und Herrschaftspraxis: Konzepte, Prinzipien und Strategien der Administration im römischen Kaiserreich*, edited by Anne Kolb, 153–64. Berlin: Akademie Verlag, 2006.

Halbwachs, Maurice. *On Collective Memory.* Edited by Lewis A. Coser. Chicago: University of Chicago Press, 1992.

Hall, Jonathan M. *Hellenicity: Between Ethnicity and Culture.* Chicago: University of Chicago Press, 2002.

Harders, Ann-Cathrin. "Beyond *Oikos* and *Domus:* Modern Kinship Studies and the Ancient Family." In *Families in the Greco-Roman World*, edited by Ray Laurence and Agneta Stromberg, 10–26. New York: Continuum Books, 2012.

Harland, Philip A. *Associations, Synagogues, and Congregations: Claiming a Place in Ancient Mediterranean Society.* Minneapolis: Fortress Press, 2003.

———. "Connections with Elites in the World of the Early Christians." In *Handbook of Early Christianity: Social Science Approaches*, edited by Anthony J. Blasi, Paul-André Turcotte, and Jean Duhaime, 385–408. Oxford: Altamira, 2002.

———. *Dynamics of Identity in the World of the Early Christians: Associations, Judeans, and Cultural Minorities.* New York: T&T Clark, 2009.

———. "Familial Dimensions of Group Identity: 'Brothers' (ΑΔΕΛΦΟΙ) in Associations of the Greek East." *Journal of Biblical Literature* 124, no. 3 (2005): 491–513.

Harnack, Adolf von. *The Mission and Expansion of Christianity in the First Three Centuries.* Translated by James Moffatt. 2 vols. New York: G. P. Putnam's, 1908.

Harrill, James Albert. "The Domestic Enemy: A Moral Polarity of Household Slaves in Early Christian Apologies and Martyrdoms." In *Early Christian Families in Context: An Interdisciplinary Dialogue*, edited by David L. Balch and Carolyn Osiek, 231–54. Grand Rapids, Mich.: Eerdmans, 2003.

———. *Slaves in the New Testament: Literary, Social, and Moral Dimensions.* Minneapolis: Fortress Press, 2006.

Harrison, James R. *Paul and the Imperial Authorities at Thessalonica and Rome: A Study in the Conflict of Ideology.* Tübingen: Mohr Siebeck, 2011.

Hawthorne, Gerald F. *Philippians.* Rev. ed. Nashville: Thomas Nelson, 2004.

Head, Peter M. "'Witnesses between You and Us': The Role of the Letter Carriers in 1 Clement." In *Studies on the Text of the New Testament and Early*

Christianity: Essays in Honour of Michael W. Holmes, edited by Daniel Gurtner, Juan Hernández Jr., and Paul Foster, 477–93. Leiden: Brill, 2015.

Hengel, Martin. *The Pre-Christian Paul.* Philadelphia: Trinity International Press, 1991.

———. *Property and Riches in the Early Church: Aspects of a Social History of Early Christianity.* Philadelphia: Fortress Press, 1974.

Hernández Guerra, Liborio. *Los libertos de la Hispania romana: Situación jurídica, promoción social y modos de vida.* Salamanca: Ediciones Universidad de Salamanca, 2013.

Herrmann-Otto, Elisabeth. *Ex ancilla natus: Untersuchungen zu den "hausgeborenen" Sklaven und Sklavinnen im Westen des Römischen Kaiserreiches.* Stuttgart: Steiner, 1994.

———. *Sklaverei und Freilassung in der griechisch-römischen Welt.* Hildesheim: Georg Olms, 2009.

Hilhorst, A. "The Text of the *Actus Vercellenses.*" In *The Apocryphal Acts of Peter: Magic, Miracles, and Gnosticism*, edited by Jan Bremmer, 148–60. Leuven: Peeters, 1998.

Hill, Charles E. *From the Lost Teachings of Polycarp: Identifying Irenaeus' Apostolic Presbyter and the Author of "Ad Diognetum."* Tübingen: Mohr Siebeck, 2006.

Hirschfeld, Amy K. "An Overview of the Intellectual History of Catacomb Archaeology." In *Commemorating the Dead: Texts and Artifacts in Context; Studies of Roman, Jewish, and Christian Burials*, edited by Laurie Brink and Deborah A. Green, 11–38. Berlin: Walter de Gruyter, 2008.

Hodge, Caroline Johnson. *If Sons, Then Heirs: A Study of Kinship and Ethnicity in the Letters of Paul.* Oxford: Oxford University Press, 2007.

Holleran, Claire. *Shopping in Ancient Rome: The Retail Trade in the Late Republic and the Principate.* Oxford: Oxford University Press, 2012.

Holloway, Paul A. *Philippians: A Commentary.* Hermeneia. Minneapolis: Fortress Press, 2017.

Hopkins, Keith. "Élite Mobility in the Roman Empire." *Past and Present* 32 (1965): 12–26.

———. *A World Full of Gods: The Strange Triumph of Christianity.* New York: Plume, 2001.

Horrell, David G. *Social Scientific Approaches to New Testament Interpretation.* Edinburgh: T&T Clark, 1999.

Horsley, G. H. R., ed. *New Documents Illustrating Early Christianity: A Review of the Greek Inscriptions and Papyri Published in 1977.* Vol. 2. North Ryde: Ancient History Documentary Research Centre, 1982.

Horster, Marietta. "Living on Religion: Professionals and Personnel." In *A Companion to Roman Religion*, edited by Jörg Rüpke, 331–42. Malden, Mass.: Wiley-Blackwell, 2011.

Hunt, Peter. *Ancient Greek and Roman Slavery.* Malden, Mass.: Wiley-Blackwell, 2018.

Ilardi, Karen. "3.2.5. Epitaffio di Fulvia Aphrodite posto dal marito, il liberto imperiale Septimius Alexander." In *Le iscrizioni dei cristiani in Vaticano: Materiali e contributi scientifici per una mostra epigrafica*, edited by Ivan Di Stefano Manzella, 322–23. Vatican City: Quasar, 1997.

Instinsky, Hans Ulrich. *Die alte Kirche und das Heil des Staates.* Munich: Kösel-Verlag, 1963.

———. "Marcus Aurelius Prosenes, Freigelassener und Christ am Kaiserhof." *Abhandlungen der Geistes und Sozialwissenschaftlichen Klasse* 3 (1964): 113–29.

Jastrzębowska, Elżbieta. "Paul Styger (1887–1939)—Archaeologist at Rome and Professor at Warsaw." *Archaeologia Polona* 47 (2009): 1–14.

———. *Untersuchungen zum christlichen Totenmahl aufgrund der Monumente des 3. und 4. Jahrhunderts unter der Basilika des Hl. Sebastian in Rom.* Frankfurt am Main: P. D. Lang, 1981.

Jeffers, James S. *Conflict at Rome: Social Order and Hierarchy in Early Christianity.* Minneapolis: Fortress Press, 1991.

Jensen, Robin Margaret. "Dining with the Dead: From the *Mensa* to the Altar in Christian Late Antiquity." In *Commemorating the Dead: Texts and Artifacts in Context; Studies of Roman,*

Jewish, and Christian Burials, edited by Laurie Brink and Deborah A. Green, 107–43. Berlin: Walter de Gruyter, 2008.

———. *Understanding Early Christian Art.* New York: Routledge, 2000.

Johnson, Aaron P. *Ethnicity and Argument in Eusebius' "Praeparatio Evangelica."* Oxford: Oxford University Press, 2006.

Johnson, Mark. "Pagan-Christian Burial Practices of the Fourth Century: Shared Tombs?" *Journal of Early Christian Studies* 5, no. 1 (1997): 37–59.

Johnson, Paul C. *Diaspora Conversions: Black Carib Religion and the Recovery of Africa.* Berkeley: University of California Press 2007.

———. *Secrets, Gossip, and Gods: The Transformation of Brazilian Candomblé.* New York: Oxford University Press, 2002.

Jones, F. Stanley. "The Pseudo-Clementines: A History of Research, Part I." *Second Century* 2, no. 1 (1982): 1–33.

———. "The Pseudo-Clementines: A History of Research, Part II." *Second Century* 2, no. 1 (1982): 63–96.

Jones, Siân. *The Archaeology of Ethnicity: Constructing Identities in the Past and Present.* New York: Routledge, 1997.

Joshel, Sandra R. *Slavery in the Roman World.* Cambridge: Cambridge University Press, 2010.

Joshel, Sandra R., and Lauren Hackworth Petersen. *The Material Life of Roman Slaves.* Cambridge: Cambridge University Press, 2015.

Judge, E. A. "The Social Pattern of the Christian Groups in the First Century." In *Social Distinctives of the Christians in the First Century: Pivotal Essays by E. A. Judge*, edited by David M. Scholer, 1–56. Peabody, Mass.: Hendrickson Publishers, 2008.

Kadushin, Charles. *Understanding Social Networks: Theories, Concepts, and Findings.* Oxford: Oxford University Press, 2012.

Kahlos, Maijastina. "The Emperor's New Images—How to Honour the Emperor in the Christian Empire?" In *Emperors and the Divine—Rome and Its Influence*, edited by Maijastina Kahlos, 119–38.

Helsinki: Helsinki Collegium for Advanced Studies, 2016.

Kalvesmaki, Joel. "The Original Sequence of Irenaeus, *Against Heresies* 1: Another Suggestion." *Journal of Early Christian Studies* 15, no. 3 (2007): 407–17.

Kartzow, Marianne Bjelland. *Destablizing the Margins: An Intersectional Approach to Early Christian Memory.* Eugene, Ore.: Pickwick, 2012.

Kaufmann, Carl Maria. *Handbuch der altchristlichen Epigraphik.* Freiburg im Breisgau: Herder, 1917.

Kautsky, Karl. *Foundations of Christianity: A Study in Christian Origins.* Reprint. New York: Routledge, 2014. Originally published in German in 1908.

Keegan, Peter. "Reading the 'Pages' of the *Domus Caesaris: Pueri Delicati*, Slave Education, and the Graffiti on the Palatine Paedagogium." In *Roman Slavery and Roman Material Culture*, edited by Michele George, 69–98. Toronto: University of Toronto Press, 2013.

Kelley, Nicole. *Knowledge and Religious Authority in the Pseudo-Clementines: Situating the Recognitions in Fourth-Century Syria.* Tübingen: Mohr Siebeck, 2006.

Keresztes, Paul. "From the Great Persecution to the Peace of Galerius." *Vigiliae Christianae* 37, no. 4 (1983): 379–99.

———. "Marcus Aurelius: A Persecutor?" *Harvard Theological Review* 61, no. 3 (1968): 321–41.

Kessler, Herbert L. "The Meeting of Peter and Paul in Rome: An Emblematic Narrative of Spiritual Brotherhood." *Dumbarton Oaks Papers* 41 (1987): 265–75.

Kirk, Alan. "Social and Cultural Memory." In *Memory, Tradition, and Text: Uses of the Past in Early Christianity*, edited by Alan Kirk and Tom Thatcher, 1–24. Leiden: Brill, 2005.

Klauck, Hans-Josef. *Ancient Letters and the New Testament: A Guide to Context and Exegesis.* Waco: Baylor University Press, 2006.

———. *The Apocryphal Acts of the Apostles: An Introduction.* Waco: Baylor University Press, 2008.

Kloppenborg, John S. "Memory, Performance, and the Sayings of Jesus." *Journal for the Study of the Historical Jesus* 10 (2012): 97–132.

Knipfing, John R. "The Libelli of the Decian Persecution." *Harvard Theological Review* 16, no. 4 (1923): 345–90.

Koester, Helmut. *Introduction to the New Testament.* Vol. 2, *History and Literature of Early Christianity.* 2nd ed. New York: Walter de Gruyter, 2000.

———. "Paul and Philippi: The Evidence from Early Christian Literature." In *Philippi at the Time of Paul and After His Death*, edited by Charalambos Bakirtzis and Helmut Koester, 49–66. Eugene, Ore.: Wipf & Stock, 1998.

Kolb, Anne, and Anne Joachim Fugmann. *Tod in Rom: Grabinschriften als Spiegel römischen Lebens.* Mainz am Rhein: Von Zabern, 2008.

Kotrosits, Maia. *Rethinking Early Christian Identity: Affect, Violence, and Belonging.* Minneapolis: Fortress Press, 2015.

Kraemer, Ross. "Jewish Tuna and Christian Fish: Identifying Religious Affiliation in Epigraphic Sources." *Harvard Theological Review* 84, no. 2 (1991): 141–62.

Kyrtatas, Demetris J. "Christians Against Christians: The Anti-heretical Activities of the Roman Church in the Second Century." *Historein* 6 (2006): 20–34.

———. *The Social Structure of the Early Christian Communities.* London: Verso, 1987.

Labarre, G., and M.-T. Le Dinahet. "Les métiers du textile en Asie Mineure de l'époque hellénistique à l'époque imperial." In *Aspects de l'artisanat du textile dans le monde méditerranéen (Egypte, Grèce, monde romain)*, 49–116. Lyon: Université Lumière-Lyon, 1996.

Lampe, Peter. *From Paul to Valentinus: Christians at Rome in the First Two Centuries.* Translated by Michael Steinhauser. Edited by Marshall D. Johnson. Minneapolis: Fortress Press, 2003.

———. "Urchristliche Missionswege nach Rom: Haushalte paganer Herrschaft als jüdisch-christliche Keimzellen." *Zeitschrift für die Neutestamentliche Wissenschaft* 92, nos. 1–2 (2001): 123–27.

Lane Fox, Robin. *Pagans and Christians.* New York: Knopf, 1987.

La Piana, George. "Foreign Groups in Rome During the First Centuries of the Empire." *Harvard Theological Review* 20, no. 4 (1927): 183–403.

Laurence, Ray. *Roman Archaeology for Historians.* London: Routledge, 2012.

Lavan, Luke, and Michael Mulryan. *The Archaeology of Late Antique "Paganism."* Leiden: Brill, 2011.

Lavan, Myles. *Slaves to Rome: Paradigms of Empire in Roman Culture.* Cambridge: Cambridge University Press, 2013.

Lazzati, Giuseppe. "Gli Atti di S. Giustino Martire."*Aevum* 27, no. 6 (1953): 473–97.

———. *Gli sviluppi della letteratura sui martiri nei primi quattro secoli: Con appendice di testi.* Turin: Società editrice internazionale, 1956.

Lee, A. D. *Pagans and Christians in Late Antiquity: A Sourcebook.* 2nd ed. New York: Routledge, 2015.

Leppin, Hartmut. "Old Religions Transformed: Religions and Religious Policy from Decius to Constantine." In *A Companion to Roman Religion*, edited by Jörg Rüpke, 96–108. Malden, Mass.: Wiley-Blackwell, 2007.

Levick, Barbara. *Julia Domna, Syrian Empress.* New York: Routledge, 2007.

Lewis, Nicola Denzey, "The Crafting of Memory in Late Roman Mortuary Spaces." In *Memory in Ancient Rome and Early Christianity*, edited by Karl Galinsky, 263–85. Oxford: Oxford University Press, 2016.

———. "Reinterpreting 'Pagans' and 'Christians' from Rome's Late Antique Mortuary Evidence." In *Pagans and Christians in Late Antique Rome: Conflict, Competition, and Coexistence in the Fourth Century*, edited by Michele Renee Salzman, Marianne Sághy, and Rita Lizzi Testa, 273–90. New York: Oxford University Press, 2016.

Lietzmann, Hans. *Petrus und Paulus in Rom: Liturgische und archäologische Studien.* Berlin: Walter de Gruyter, 1927.

Lieu, Judith. *Christian Identity in the Jewish and Graeco-Roman World.* Oxford: Oxford University Press, 2004.

———. *Image and Reality: The Jews in the World of the Christians in the Second Century.* Edinburgh: T&T Clark, 1996.

———. *Neither Jew nor Greek? Constructing Early Christianity.* New York: T&T Clark, 2002.

Lightfoot, J. B. *The Apostolic Fathers*. Pt. 1, S. *Clement of Rome*. Vol. 1. London: Macmillan, 1890.

———. *Saint Paul's Epistle to the Philippians*. 8th ed. London: Macmillan, 1888. Originally published in 1868.

Lindemann, Andreas. *Die Clemensbriefe*. Tübingen: Mohr Siebeck, 1992.

———. "The First Epistle of Clement." In *The Apostolic Fathers: An Introduction*, edited by Wilhelm Pratscher, 47–70. Waco: Baylor University Press, 2010.

Lipsett, B. Diane. *Desiring Conversion: Hermas, Thecla, Aseneth*. Oxford: Oxford University Press, 2011.

Lipsius, R., and M. Bonnet. *Acta apostolorum apocrypha*. Vol 1. Darmstadt: Wissenschaftliche Buchgesellschaft, 1959.

Litwa, David M, trans. *Hippolytus, Refutation of All Heresies*. Atlanta: Society of Biblical Literature, 2016.

Louth, Andrew. *Early Christian Writings: The Apostolic Fathers*. New York: Penguin Books, 1987.

Luijendijk, AnneMarie. *Greetings in the Lord: Early Christians and the Oxyrhynchus Papyri*. Cambridge, Mass.: Harvard University Press, 2008.

MacCulloch, Diarmaid. *A History of Christianity: The First Three Thousand Years*. New York: Penguin Books, 2010.

MacMullen, Ramsay. *Christianizing the Roman Empire (A.D. 100–400)*. New Haven: Yale University Press, 1984.

———. "The Epigraphic Habit in the Roman Empire." *American Journal of Philology* 103, no. 3 (1982): 233–46.

———. *Paganism in the Roman Empire*. New Haven: Yale University Press, 1981.

———. *Roman Social Relations, 50 B.C. to A.D. 284*. New Haven: Yale University Press, 1974.

———. "Two Types of Conversion to Early Christianity." *Vigiliae Christianae* 37, no. 2 (1983): 174–92.

Madsen, Jesper Majbom. *Eager to Be Roman: Greek Response to Roman Rule in Pontus and Bithynia*. London: Duckworth, 2009.

Magnuson, Eric. "Cultural Discourse in Action: Interactional Dynamics and Symbolic Meaning." *Qualitative Sociology* 28, no. 4 (2005): 371–98.

Malherbe, Abraham J. *Social Aspects of Early Christianity*. Eugene, Ore.: Wipf & Stock, 1983.

Malina, Bruce J. *The Social Gospel of Jesus: The Kingdom of God in Mediterranean Perspective*. Minneapolis: Fortress Press, 2001.

Mancini, Gioacchino. "Scavi sotto la Basilica di S. Sebastiano sull'Appia Antica." *Notizie degli Scavi di Antichità* 20 (1923): 3–79.

Manders, Erika. *Coining Images of Power: Patterns in the Representation of Roman Emperors on Imperial Coinage, A.D. 193–284*. Leiden: Brill, 2012.

Marcovich, Miroslav, ed. *Hippolytus, Refutatio omnium haeresium*. Berlin: Walter de Gruyter, 1986.

Markschies, Christoph. *Das antike Christentum: Frömmigkeit, Lebensformen, Institutionen*. 2nd ed. Munich: C. H. Beck, 2012.

Marshall, Howard I. *The Epistle to the Philippians*. London: Epworth, 1991.

Martin, Dale B. *Slavery as Salvation: The Metaphor of Slavery in Pauline Christianity*. New Haven: Yale University Press, 1990.

Marucchi, Orazio. *Le catacombe romane: Opera postuma*. Rome: La Libreria dello stato, 1932.

———. *Christian Epigraphy: An Elementary Treatise, with a Collection of Ancient Christian Inscriptions Mainly of Roman Origin*. Translated by J. Armine Willis. Chicago: Ares, 1912.

———. "Nota sulle memorie cristiane esplorate nello scavo di S. Sebastiano dalla Commissione di Archaeologia Sacra." *Notizie degli Scavi di Antichità* 20 (1923): 80–103.

———. "Notizie." *Nuovo Bullettino di Archeologia Cristiana* 14 (1908): 253–66.

———. "Nuovi scavi e nuovi studi nel Cimitero di Priscilla." *Nuovo Bullettino di Archeologia Cristiana* 8 (1902): 217–32.

Massey, Doreen B. *For Space*. London: Sage, 2005.

Mattingly, David J. *Imperialism, Power, and Identity: Experiencing the Roman Empire*. Princeton: Princeton University Press, 2010.

Mazza, Mario. "Struttura sociale e organizzazione economica della comunità cristiana di Roma tra II e III secolo." In *Origine delle catacombe romane: Atti della Giornata Tematica dei Seminari di Archeologia Cristiana (Roma, 21 Marzo 2005)*, edited by Vincenzo Fiocchi Nicolai and Jean Guyon, 15–28. Vatican City: Pontificio Istituto di Archeologia Cristiana, 2006.

Mazzoleni, Danilo. *Epigrafi del mondo cristiano antico*. Rome: Lateran University Press, 2002.

———. "Inscriptions in Roman Catacombs." In *The Christian Catacombs of Rome: History, Decoration, Inscriptions*, edited by Vincenzo Fiocchi Nicolai, Fabrizio Bisconti, and Danilo Mazzoleni, 147–85. 3rd ed. Regensburg: Schnell & Steiner, 2009.

———. "The Rise of Christianity." In *The Oxford Handbook of Roman Epigraphy*, edited by Christer Bruun and Jonathan Edmondson, 445–68. Oxford: Oxford University Press, 2015.

McCutcheon, Russell T. *Manufacturing Religion: The Discourse on Sui Generis Religion and the Politics of Nostalgia*. New York: Oxford University Press, 1997

McKechnie, Paul. "Christian Grave-Inscriptions from the *Familia Caesaris*." *Journal of Ecclesiastical History* 50 (1999): 427–41.

———. *The First Christian Centuries: Perspectives on the Early Church*. Downers Grove, Ill.: InterVarsity Press, 2001.

McKeown, Adam. *Chinese Migrant Networks and Cultural Change: Peru, Chicago, Hawaii, 1900–1936*. Chicago: University of Chicago Press, 2001.

McKeown, Niall. *The Invention of Ancient Slavery?* London: Duckworth, 2007.

Meeks, Wayne A. *The First Urban Christians: The Social World of the Apostle Paul*. 2nd ed. New Haven: Yale University Press, 2003.

Meggitt, Justin J. *Paul, Poverty, and Survival*. Edinburgh: T&T Clark, 1998.

———. "The Social Status of Erastus (Rom. 16:23)." *Novum Testamentum* 38, no. 3 (1996): 218–23.

Meiggs, Russell. *Roman Ostia*. 2nd ed. Oxford: Clarendon Press, 1973.

Mendels, Doron. *Memory in Jewish, Pagan, and Christian Societies of the Graeco-Roman World*. London: T&T Clark International, 2004.

Menjívar, Celilia. *Fragmented Ties: Salvadoran Immigrant Networks in America*.

Berkeley: University of California Press, 2000.

Meyer, Elizabeth A. "Epigraphy and Communication." In *The Oxford Handbook of Social Relations in the Roman World*, edited by Michael Peachin, 191–226. Oxford: Oxford University Press, 2011.

———. "Explaining the Epigraphic Habit in the Roman Empire: The Evidence of Epitaphs." *Journal of Roman Studies* 80 (1990): 74–96.

———. "New Histories of Slaves and Freed." *Classical Journal* 108, no. 2 (2012/13): 238–45.

Michaelis, Wilhelm. *Der Brief des Paulus an die Philipper*. Leipzig: A. Deichertsche Verlagsbuchhandlung, 1935.

Millar, Fergus. *The Emperor in the Roman World (31 BC–AD 337)*. Ithaca: Cornell University Press, 1977.

Misztal, Barbara. *Theories of Social Remembering*. Philadelphia: Open University Press, 2003.

Mitchell, Margaret. Foreword to *Augustus to Constantine: The Rise and Triumph of Christianity in the Roman World*, by Robert M. Grant, xiii–xxxvii. 2nd ed. Louisville: Westminster John Knox Press, 2004.

———. *The Heavenly Trumpet: John Chrysostom and the Art of Pauline Interpretation*. Louisville: Westminster John Knox Press, 2002.

———. "Looking for Abercius: Reimagining Contexts of Interpretation of the 'Earliest Christian Inscription.'" In *Commemorating the Dead: Texts and Artifacts in Context; Studies of Roman, Jewish, and Christian Burials*, edited by Laurie Brink and Deborah A. Green, 303–35. Berlin: Walter de Gruyter, 2008.

Mitchell, Stephen. "Requisitioned Transport in the Roman Empire: A New Inscription from Pisidia." *Journal of Roman Studies* 66 (1976): 106–31.

Mohler, S. L. "Slave Education in the Roman Empire." *Transactions of the American Philological Association* 71 (1940): 262–80.

Mommsen, Theodor. "Der Religionsfrevel nach römischem Recht." *Historische Zeitschrift* 64, no. 3 (1890): 389–429.

Moreland, Milton. "Moving Peter to Rome: Social Memory and Ritualized Space After 70 CE." In *Memory in Ancient Rome and Early Christianity*, edited by Karl Galinsky, 344–66. Oxford: Oxford University Press, 2016.

Moreschini, Claudio, and Enrico Norelli. *Early Christian Greek and Latin Literature: A Literary History*. Vol 1. Peabody, Mass.: Hendrickson Publishers, 2005.

Morgan, Catherine. "Ethnic Expression in the Early Iron Age and Early Archaic Greek Mainland." In *Ethnic Constructs in Antiquity: The Role of Power and Traditions*, edited by Tom Derks and Nico Roymans, 11–36. Amsterdam: Amsterdam University Press, 2009.

Morley, Neville. "Slavery Under the Principate." In *The Cambridge World History of Slavery*, vol. 1, *The Ancient Mediterranean World*, edited by Keith Bradley and Paul Cartledge, 265–86. New York: Cambridge University Press, 2011.

Moss, Candida R. *Ancient Christian Martyrdom: Diverse Practices, Theologies, and Traditions*. New Haven: Yale University Press, 2012.

———. *The Myth of Persecution: How Early Christians Invented a Story of Martyrdom*. New York: HarperOne, 2013.

Mouritsen, Henrik. *The Freedman in the Roman World*. Cambridge: Cambridge University Press, 2011.

———. "Freedmen and Decurions: Epitaphs and Social History in Imperial Italy." *Journal of Roman Studies* 95 (2005): 38–63.

———. "Freedmen and Freeborn in the Necropolis of Imperial Ostia." *Zeitschrift für Papyrologie und Epigraphik* 150 (2004): 281–304.

———. "Slavery and Manumission in the Roman Elite: A Study of the *Columbaria* of the Volusii and the Statilii." In *Roman Slavery and Roman Material Culture*, edited by Michele George, 43–68. Toronto: University of Toronto Press, 2013.

Müller, Ulrich B. *Der Brief des Paulus an die Philipper*. Leipzig: Evangelische Verlagsanstalt, 1993.

Musurillo, Herbert. *The Acts of the Christian Martyrs*. Oxford: Clarendon Press, 1972.

Nasrallah, Laura Salah. *Christian Responses to Roman Art and Architecture: The Second-Century Church amid the Spaces of Empire*. Cambridge: Cambridge University Press, 2010.

Nathan, Geoffrey S. *The Family in Late Antiquity: The Rise of Christianity and the Endurance of Tradition*. New York: Routledge, 2000.

Nieddu, Anna Maria. *La Basilica Apostolorum sulla Via Appia e l'area cimiteriale circostante*. Vatican City: Pontificio Istituto di Archeologia Cristiana, 2009.

Nock, A. D. *Conversion: The Old and the New in Religion from Alexander the Great to Augustine of Hippo*. Reprint. New York: Oxford University Press, 1998.

Nongbri, Brent. *Before Religion: A History of a Modern Concept*. New Haven: Yale University Press, 2013.

———. "Dislodging 'Embedded' Religion: A Brief Note on a Scholarly Trope." *Numen* 55, no. 4 (2008): 440–60.

North, John. "The Development of Religious Pluralism." In *The Jews Among Pagans and Christians: In the Roman Empire*, edited by Judith Lieu, John North, and Tessa Rajak, 147–73. New York: Routledge, 1992.

Novak, Ralph Martin. *Christianity and the Roman Empire: Background Texts*. Harrisburg, Pa.: Trinity Press International, 2001.

Noviello, Claudio. "VIII, 30: Un paggio imperiale." In *Terme di Diocleziano: La collezione epigrafica*, edited by Rosanna Friggeri, Maria Grazia Granino Cecere, and Gian Luca Gregori, 516–17. Milan: Electa, 2012.

———. "IX, 24: Stele con simboli cristiani." In *Terme di Diocleziano: La collezione epigrafica*, edited by Rosanna Friggeri, Maria Grazia Granino Cecere, and Gian Luca Gregori, 568–69. Milan: Electa, 2012.

Noy, David. *Foreigners at Rome: Citizens and Strangers*. London: Duckworth, 2000.

Nuffelen, Peter van. "Pagan Monotheism as a Religious Phenomenon." In *One God: Pagan Monotheism in the Roman Empire*, edited by Stephen Mitchell and Peter van Nuffelen, 16–33. Cambridge: Cambridge University Press, 2010.

Oden, Thomas C. *Early Libyan Christianity: Uncovering a North African Tradition.* Downers Grove, Ill.: IVP Academic, 2011.

Olick, Jeffrey K. "Products, Processes, and Practices: A Non-Reificatory Approach to Collective Memory." *Biblical Theology Bulletin* 36, no. 1 (2006): 5–14.

Pals, Daniel L. "Is Religion a *Sui Generis* Phenomenon?" *Journal of the American Academy of Religion* 55, no. 2 (1987): 259–82.

Panciera, Silvio. *La collezione epigrafica dei Musei Capitolini, inediti-revisioni-contributi al riordino.* Rome: Edizioni di Storia e Letteratura, 1987.

———. *Epigrafi, epigrafia, epigrafisti: Scritti vari editi e inediti (1956–2005) con note complementari e indici.* Rome: Quasar, 2006.

———. "Servire a palazzo: Nuove testimonianze di *officiales Augustorum* da Roma." In *Herrschen und Verwalten: Der Alltag der römischen Administration in der Hohen Kaiserzeit,* edited by Rudolf Haensch and Johannes Heinrichs, 60–79. Cologne: Böhlau, 2007.

Parker, Robert. "Public and Private." In *A Companion to the Archaeology of Religion in the Ancient World,* edited by Rubina Raja and Jörg Rüpke, 71–80. Malden, Mass.: Wiley-Blackwell, 2015.

Parrish, David, and Halûk Abbasoğlu, eds. *Urbanism in Western Asia Minor: New Studies on Aphrodisias, Ephesos, Hierapolis, Pergamon, Perge, and Xanthos.* Portsmouth, R.I.: Journal of Roman Archaeology, 2001.

Patterson, Orlando. "Revisiting Slavery, Property, and Social Death." In *On Human Bondage: After Slavery and Social Death,* edited by John Bodel and Walter Scheidel, 265–96. Malden, Mass.: Wiley-Blackwell, 2017.

———. *Slavery and Social Death: A Comparative Study.* Cambridge, Mass.: Harvard University Press, 1982.

Pavis D'Escurac, Henriette. "La *Familia Caesaris* et les affaires publiques: Discretam domum et rem publican (Tacite, *Annales,* XIII, 4)." In *Le système palatial en Orient, en Grèce et à Rome: Actes du Colloque de Strasbourg 19–22*

juin 1985, edited by Edmond Lévy, 393–410. Leiden: Brill, 1987.

Payton, James R. *Irenaeus on the Christian Faith: A Condensation of "Against Heresies."* Eugene, Ore.: Pickwick, 2011.

Peachin, Michael. Introduction to *The Oxford Handbook of Social Relations in the Roman World,* edited by Michael Peachin, 3–36. Oxford: Oxford University Press, 2011.

Pergola, Philippe. *Le catacombe romane: Storia e topografia.* Argomenti 8. Rome: Carocci, 1998.

Perkins, Judith. *Roman Imperial Identities in the Early Christian Era.* New York: Routledge, 2009.

———. "Social Geography in the *Apocryphal Acts of the Apostles.*" In *Space in the Ancient Novel,* edited by Michael Paschalis and Stavros A. Frangoulidis, 118–31. Groningen: Barkhus, 2002.

Perry, Jonathan Scott. *The Roman Collegia: The Modern Evolution of an Ancient Concept.* Leiden: Brill, 2006.

Pervo, Richard I. *The Acts of Paul: A New Translation with Introduction and Commentary.* Eugene, Ore.: Cascade Books, 2014.

———. "The Ancient Novel Becomes Christian." In *The Novel in the Ancient World,* edited by G. Schmeling, 685–712. Leiden: Brill, 1996.

———. *The Making of Paul: Constructions of the Apostle in Early Christianity.* Minneapolis: Fortress Press, 2010.

Peterlin, Davorin. *Paul's Letter to the Philippians in the Light of Disunity in the Church.* Leiden: Brill, 1995.

Pleket, H. W. "The Roman State and the Economy: The Case of Ephesos." In *Economie antique: Les échanges dans l'antiquité; Le rôle de l'état,* 115–26. Saint Bertrand-de-Comminges: Musée archéologique départemental de Saint-Bertrand-de-Comminges, 1994.

Poupon, Gérard. "Les 'Actes de Pierre' et leur remaniement." *Aufstieg und Niedergang der römischen Welt* 2.25.6 (1988): 4363–4483.

Prell, Christina. *Social Network Analysis: History, Theory, and Methodology.* London: Sage Publications, 2012.

Price, Simon R. "From Noble Funerals to Divine Cult: The Consecration of Roman Emperors." In *Rituals of Royalty: Power and Ceremonial in Traditional Societies*, edited by David Cannadine and Simon Price, 56–105. Cambridge: Cambridge University Press, 1987.

———. *Rituals and Power: The Roman Imperial Cult in Asia Minor*. Cambridge: Cambridge University Press, 1984.

Purcell, Nicholas. "The *Apparitores*: A Study in Social Mobility." *Papers of the British School at Rome* 51 (1983): 125–73.

———. "Romans in the Roman World." In *The Cambridge Companion to the Age of Augustus*, edited by Karl Galinsky, 85–106. Cambridge: Cambridge University Press, 2005.

Quacquarelli, Antonio. *Q.S.F. Tertulliani Ad scapulam*. Rome: Desclee, 1957.

Quilici, L. *Collatia*. Forma Italiae 1.10. Rome: De Luca, 1974.

Raja, Rubina. *Urban Development and Regional Identity in the Eastern Roman Provinces, 50 BC–AD 250: Aphrodisias, Ephesos, Athens, Gerasa*. Copenhagen: University of Copenhagen Press, 2012.

Ramsay, William M. *The Church in the Roman Empire Before A.D. 170*. London: Hodder and Stoughton, 1893.

Rankin, David. *From Clement to Origen: The Social and Historical Context of the Church Fathers*. Burlington, Vt.: Ashgate, 2006.

———. *Tertullian and the Church*. New York: Cambridge University Press, 1995.

Rebillard, Éric. *The Care of the Dead in Late Antiquity*. Ithaca: Cornell University Press, 2009.

———. *Christians and Their Many Identities in Late Antiquity, North Africa, 200–450 CE*. Ithaca: Cornell University Press, 2012.

———. "Koimétérion et Coemeterium: Tombe, Tombe Sainte, Nécropole." *Mélanges de l'École Française de Rome: Antiquité* 105 (1993): 975–1001.

———. "Late Antique Limits of Christianness: North Africa in the Age of Augustine." In *Group Identity and Religious Individuality in Late Antiquity*, edited by Éric Rebillard and Jörg Rüpke, 293–317. Washington, D.C.: Catholic University of America, 2015.

Reed, Annette Y. "Heresiology and the (Jewish-) Christian Novel: Narrativized Polemics in the Pseudo-Clementine Homilies." In *Heresy and Identity in Late Antiquity*, edited by Eduard Iricinschi and Holger M. Zellentin, 273–98. Tübingen: Mohr Siebeck, 2008.

Reicke, Bo. "Caesarea, Rome, and the Captivity Epistles." In *Apostolic History and the Gospel: Biblical and Historical Essays Presented to F. F. Bruce*, edited by W. Ward Gasque and Ralph P. Martin, 277–86. Exeter: Paternoster, 1970.

Reumann, John Henry Paul. *Philippians: A New Translation with Introduction and Commentary*. New Haven: Yale University Press, 2008.

———. "Philippians, Especially Chapter 4 as a 'Letter of Friendship': Observations on a Checkered History of Scholarship." In *Friendship, Flattery, and Frankness of Speech: Studies on Friendship in the New Testament World*, edited by John T. Fitzgerald, 83–106. Leiden: Brill, 1996.

Revell, Louise. *Roman Imperialism and Local Identities*. New York: Cambridge University Press, 2009.

Rives, James B. "Christian Expansion and Christian Ideology." In *The Spread of Christianity in the First Four Centuries: Essays in Explanation*, edited by William V. Harris, 15–42. Boston: Brill, 2005.

———. "The Decree of Decius and the Religion of Empire." *Journal of Roman Studies* 89 (1999): 135–54.

———. "The Piety of a Persecutor." *Journal of Early Christian Studies* 4, no. 1 (1996): 1–25.

———. *Religion and Authority in Roman Carthage: From Augustus to Constantine*. New York: Oxford University Press, 1995.

Rodgers, R. H. *Frontinus: De aquaeductu urbis Romae*. Cambridge: Cambridge University Press, 2004.

Rowan, Clare. *Under Divine Auspices: Divine Ideology and the Visualisation of Imperial Power in the Severan Period*. Cambridge: Cambridge University Press, 2012.

Roymans, Nico. *Ethnic Identity and Imperial Power: The Batavians in the Early Roman Empire*. Amsterdam: Amsterdam University Press, 2004.

Rutgers, Leonard. *Subterranean Rome: In Search of the Roots of Christianity in the Catacombs of the Eternal City*. Leuven: Peeters, 2000.

Saller, Richard. "The Family and Society." In *Epigraphic Evidence*, edited by John Bodel, 95–117. New York: Routledge, 2001.

———. Introduction to *Commemorating the Dead: Texts and Artifacts in Context; Studies of Roman, Jewish, and Christian Burials*, edited by Laurie Brink and Deborah A. Green, 1–10. Berlin: Walter de Gruyter, 2008.

Scheid, John. "Sacrifices for Gods and Ancestors." In *A Companion to Roman Religion*, edited by Jörg Rüpke, 263–72 Malden, Mass.: Wiley-Blackwell, 2008.

Schenk, Wolfgang. *Die Philipperbriefe des Paulus: Kommentar.* Stuttgart: W. Kohlhammer, 1984.

Schmidt, Carl. "Zur Datierung der alten Petrusakten." *Zeitschrift für die Neutestamentliche Wissenschaft* 29, no. 1 (1930): 150–55.

Schmidt, Carl, and Wilhelm Schubart. ΠΡΑΞΙΣ ΠΑΥΛΟΥ: *Acta Pauli nach dem Papyrus der Hamburger Staats- und Universitäts-Bibliothek.* Glückstadt: Augustin, 1936.

Schneemelcher, Wilhelm. *New Testament Apocrypha.* Vol. 2, *Writings Relating to the Apostles, Apocalypses, and Related Subjects.* Translated by R. McL. Wilson. Rev. ed. Louisville: Westminster John Knox Press, 2003.

Schöllgen, Georg. *Ecclesia sordida? Zur Frage der sozialen Schichtung frühchristlicher Gemeinden am Beispiel Karthagos zur Zeit Tertullians.* Münster: Aschendorff, 1984.

Schumacher, Leonhard. "Hausgesinde–Hofgesinde: Terminologische Überlegungen zur Funktion der *familia Caesaris* im 1. Jh. n. Chr." In *Fünfzig Jahre Forschungen zur antiken Sklaverei an der Mainzer Akademie, 1950–2000: Miscellanea zum Jubiläum*, edited by Heinz Bellen and Heinz Heinen, 331–52. Stuttgart: Franz Steiner, 2001.

———. "Slaves in Roman Society." In *The Oxford Handbook of Social Relations in the Roman World*, edited by Michael Peachin, 589–608. Oxford: Oxford University Press, 2011.

Secord, Jared. "The Cultural Geography of a Greek Christian: Irenaeus from Smyrna to Lyons." In *Irenaeus: Life, Scripture, Legacy*, edited by Sara Parvis and Paul Foster, 25–34. Minneapolis: Fortress Press, 2012.

Selinger, Reinhard. *The Mid-Third-Century Persecutions of Decius and Valerian.* Frankfurt am Main: P. Lang, 2004.

Sensbach, Jon F. *A Separate Canaan: The Making of an Afro-Moravian World in North Carolina, 1763–1840.* Chapel Hill: University of North Carolina Press, 1998.

Smit, Peter-Ben. *Paradigms of Being in Christ: A Study of the Epistle to the Philippians.* London: T&T Clark, 2013.

Smith, Anthony D. "Chosen Peoples: Why Ethnic Groups Survive." *Ethnic and Racial Studies* 15, no. 3 (1992): 436–56.

Smith, Geoffrey S. *Guilt by Association: Heresy Catalogues in Early Christianity.* Oxford: Oxford University Press, 2015.

Smith, Jonathan Z. *Drudgery Divine: On the Comparison of Early Christianities and the Religions of Late Antiquity.* Chicago: University of Chicago Press, 1990.

———. *Imagining Religion: From Babylon to Jonestown.* Chicago: University of Chicago Press, 1982.

———. "The Social Description of Early Christianity." *Religious Studies Review* 1, no. 1 (1975): 19–25.

———. *To Take Place: Toward Theory in Ritual.* Chicago: University of Chicago Press, 1987.

Snyder, Glenn E. *Acts of Paul: The Formation of a Pauline Corpus.* Tübingen: Mohr Siebeck, 2013.

Snyder, Graydon. *Ante Pacem: Archaeological Evidence of Church Life Before Constantine.* Macon: Mercer University Press, 1985.

Solin, Heikki. "Pagano e cristiano." In *Epigrafia di confine, confine dell'epigrafia: Atti del Colloquio AIEGL, Borghesi, 2003*, edited by Angeli Bertinelli, Angela Donati, and Maria Gabriella, 197–221. Florence: Fratelli Lega, 2004.

Sorti, Marta. *I cristiani e l'impero romano.* 2nd ed. Milan: Jaca Book, 2004.

Spera, Lucrezia. "The Christianization of Space Along the Via Appia: Changing Landscape in the Suburbs of Rome," *American Journal of Archaeology* 107, no. 1 (2003): 23–43.

———. *Il complesso di Pretestato sulla Via Appia: Storia topografica e monumentale di un insediamento funerario paleocristiano nel suburbio di Roma.* Vatican City:

Pontificio Istituto di Archeologia Cristiana, 2004.

———. *Il paesaggio suburbano di Roma dall'antichità al Medioevo: Il comprensorio tra le vie Latina e Ardeatina dalle Mura Aureliane al III miglio.* Rome: L'Erma di Bretschneider, 1999.

Standhartinger, Angela. "Letter from Prison as Hidden Transcript: What It Tells Us About the People at Philippi." In *The People Beside Paul: The Philippian Assembly and History from Below*, edited by Joseph A. Marchal, 107–40. Atlanta: Society of Biblical Literature, 2015.

Stark, Rodney. *The Rise of Christianity: A Sociologist Reconsiders History.* Princeton: Princeton University Press, 1996.

Stegemann, Ekkehard, and Wolfgang Stegemann. *The Jesus Movement: A Social History of Its First Century.* Minneapolis: Fortress Press, 1999.

Steinbock, Bernd. *Social Memory in Athenian Public Discourse: Uses and Meanings of the Past.* Ann Arbor: University of Michigan Press, 2013.

Strong, Anise K. "A Christian Concubine in Commodus' Court?" *Eugesta* 4 (2014): 238–59.

Styger, Paul. *Römische Märtyrergrüfte.* Berlin: Verlag für Kunstwissenschaft, 1935.

———. *Die römischen Katakomben: Archäologische Forschungen über den Ursprung und die Bedeutung der altchristlichen Grabstätten.* Berlin: Verlag für Kunstwissenschaft, 1933.

Tabbernee, William. "Epigraphy." In *The Oxford Handbook of Early Christian Studies*, edited by Susan Ashbrook Harvey and David G. Hunter, 120–40. Oxford: Oxford University Press, 2008.

Tajra, Harry W. *The Martyrdom of St. Paul: Historical and Judicial Context, Traditions, and Legends.* Tübingen: Mohr Siebeck, 1994.

Talloen, Peter. "From Pagan to Christian: Religious Iconography in Material Culture from Sagalassos." In *The Archaeology of Late Antique "Paganism,"* edited by Luke Lavan and Michael Mulryan, 575–608. Leiden: Brill, 2011.

Tartara, P. "Località S. Maria (Torre Maura) (circ. VIII)." *Bullettino della Commissione Archeologica Comunale di Roma* 92 (1987/88): 408–14.

Taylor, Claire. "Migration and the Demes of Attica." In *Demography and the Graeco-Roman World: New Insights and Approaches*, edited by Claire Holleran and April Pudsey, 117–34. Cambridge: Cambridge University Press, 2011.

Taylor, Walter F. *Paul, Apostle to the Nations: An Introduction.* Minneapolis: Fortress Press, 2012.

Telbe, Mikael. *Paul Between Synagogue and State: Christians, Jews, and Civic Authorities in 1 Thessalonians, Romans, and Philippians.* Stockholm: Almqvist & Wiksell International, 2001.

Terpstra, Taco T. *Trading Communities in the Roman World: A Micro-economic and Institutional Perspective.* Leiden: Brill, 2013.

Testini, Pasquale. *Archeologia cristiana: Nozioni generali dalle origini alla fine del sec. VI. propedeutica, topografia cimiteriale, epigrafia, edifici di culto.* 2nd ed. Bari: Edipuglia, 1980.

———. *Le catacombe e gli antiche cimiteri cristiani in Roma.* Bologna: Cappelli, 1966.

Theissen, Gerd. "The Social Structure of Pauline Communities: Some Critical Remarks on J. J. Meggitt, *Paul, Poverty, and Survival.*" *Journal for the Study of the New Testament* 84 (2001): 65–84.

Thomas, Christine M. *The Acts of Peter, Gospel Literature, and the Ancient Novel: Rewriting the Past.* Oxford: Oxford University Press, 2003.

Thomas, Christine M., and Cengiz İçten. "The *Ostothekai* of Ephesos and the Rise of Sarcophagus Inhumation: Death, Conspicuous Consumption, and Roman Freedmen." In *Akten des Symposiums des Sarkophag-Corpus 2001. Marburg, 2–7 July 2001*, edited by Guntram Koch, 335–44. Mainz: Verlag Philipp von Zabren, 2007.

Thomas, Edmund. "'Nero's Tomb' and the Crisis of the Third Century: Roman Sarcophagi as Private and Public Monuments." *Res* 61/62 (2012): 132–51.

Thompson, Glen L. "Bauer's Early Christian Rome and the Development of 'Orthodoxy.'" In *Orthodoxy and Heresy in Early Christian Contexts: Reconsidering*

the Bauer Thesis, edited by Paul Hartog,
213–34. Eugene, Ore.: Pickwick, 2015.

Thurston, Bonnie Bowman, and Judith Ryan.
Philippians and Philemon. Sacra Pagina.
Collegeville, Minn.: Liturgical Press,
2005.

Tilley, Christopher. *Metaphor and Material
Culture.* Malden, Mass.: Wiley-
Blackwell, 1999.

Tolotti, Francesco. *Il cimitero di Priscilla: Studio
di topografia e architettura.* Vatican City:
Società Amici delle Catacombe presso
Pontificio Istituto di Archeologia
Cristiana, 1970.

——. *Memorie degli apostoli in Catacumbas:
Rilievo critico della memoria e della
Basilica Apostolorum al III miglio della
Via Appia.* Rome: Società "Amici delle
Catacombe," Pontificio Istituto di
Archeologia cristiana, 1953.

——. "Sguardo d'insieme al monumento
sotto S. Sebastiano e nuovo tentativo
di interpretarlo." *Rivista di Archeologia
Cristiana della Pontificia Commissione
di Archeologia Sacra, Roma* 60 (1984):
123–61.

Toner, Jerry P. *The Day Commodus Killed a
Rhino: Understanding the Roman Games.*
Baltimore: Johns Hopkins University
Press, 2014.

Tortorella, Stefano. "Il sepolcreto della
'piazzola' sotto S. Sebastiano sulla
Via Appia e il loculo di *Atimetus.*" In
*Marmoribus vestita: Miscellanea in onore
di Federico Guidobaldi*, vol. 2, edited
by Olof Brandt, Federico Guidobaldi,
and Philippe Pergola, 1359–73. Vatican
City: Pontificio Istituto di Archeologia
Cristiana, 2011.

Toynbee, J. M. C., and J. B. Ward-Perkins.
*The Shrine of St. Peter and the Vatican
Excavations.* London: Longmans, 1956.

Treggiari, Susan. *Roman Social History.*
London: Routledge, 2002.

——. "Social History: Recent
Interpretations." *Social History /
Histoire Scoiale* 8 (1975): 149–64.

Tripolitis, Antonia. *Religions of the Hellenistic-
Roman Age.* Grand Rapids, Mich.:
Eerdmans, 2002.

Turcan, Robert. *The Cults of the Roman Empire.*
Translated by Antonia Nevill. Malden,
Mass.: Wiley-Blackwell, 1996.

Tweed, Thomas A. *Our Lady of the Exile:
Diasporic Religion at a Cuban Catholic
Shrine in Miami.* New York: Oxford
University Press, 2007.

Ulrich, Jörg. "What Do We Know About
Justin's 'School' in Rome?" *Zeitschrift
für Antikes Christentum* 16, no. 1 (2012):
62–74.

Van den Hoek, Annewies. "'The Saga of
Peter and Paul: Emblems of Catholic
Identity in Christian Literature and
Art." In *Pottery, Pavements, and Paradise:
Iconographic and Textual Studies on Late
Antiquity*, edited by Annewies van den
Hoek and John Joseph Herrmann,
310–26. Leiden: Brill, 2013.

Vander Stichele, Caroline, and Todd Penner.
*Contextualizing Gender in Early Christian
Discourse: Thinking Beyond Thecla.* New
York: T&T Clark, 2009.

Visconti, Pietro Ercole. "Dissertazione sopra
una antica iscrizione cristiana."
*Dissertazioni della Pontificia Accademia
Romana di Archeologia* 6 (1835): 41–52.

Voeks, Robert A. *Sacred Leaves of Candomblé:
African Magic, Medicine, and Religion
in Brazil.* Austin: University of Texas
Press, 1997.

Vössing, Konrad. *Schule und Bildung im
Nordafrika der römischen Kaiserzeit.*
Brussels: Latomus, 1997.

Wallace-Hadrill, Andrew. "The Imperial
Court." In *The Cambridge Ancient
History*, vol. 10, *The Augustan Empire,
43 BC–AD 69*, edited by Alan K.
Bowman, Edward Champlin, and
Andrew Lintott, 283–308. Cambridge:
Cambridge University Press, 1996.

Waszink, J. H. "Some Observations on
Tertullian '*Ad Scapulam.*'" *Vigiliae
Christianae* 13, no. 1 (1959): 46–57.

Weaver, P. R. C. *Familia Caesaris: A Social Study
of the Emperor's Freedmen and Slaves.*
Cambridge: Cambridge University
Press, 1972.

——. "Phaon: Freedman of Nero." *Zeitschrift
für Papyrologie und Epigraphik* 151
(2005): 243–52.

——. "'P.Oxy.' 3312 and Joining the
Household of Caesar." *Zeitschrift für
Papyrologie und Epigraphik* 149 (2004):
196–204.

——. "Social Mobility in the Early Roman
Empire: The Evidence of the Imperial
Freedmen and Slaves." *Past and Present*
37 (1967): 3–20.

Webster, Jane. "Routes to Slavery in the Roman World: A Comparative Perspective on the Archaeology of Forced Migration." In *Roman Diasporas: Archaeological Approaches to Mobility and Diversity in the Roman Empire*, edited by Hella Eckardt, 45–66. Portsmouth, R.I.: Journal of Roman Archaeology, 2010.

Welborn, Laurence L. "On the Date of First Clement." *Biblical Research* 29 (1984): 35–54.

Wheatley, Alan Brent. *Patronage in Early Christianity: Its Use and Transformation from Jesus to Paul of Samosata*. Eugene, Ore.: Pickwick, 2011.

White, L. Michael. "Adolf von Harnack and the 'Expansion' of Early Christianity: A Re-Appraisal of Social History." *Second Century* 5, no. 2 (1985/86): 97–127.

———, ed. *Social Networks in the Early Christian Environment: Issues and Methods for Social History*. Atlanta: Society of Biblical Literature, 1992.

Wilhite, David E. *Tertullian the African: An Anthropological Reading of Tertullian's Context and Identities*. New York: De Gruyter, 2007.

Winterling, Aloys. *Aula Caesaris: Studien zur Institutionalisierung des römischen Kaiserhofes in der Zeit von Augustus bis Commodus (31 v. Chr.-192 n. Chr.)*. Munich: R. Oldenbourg, 1999.

Witherington, Ben, III. *Friendship and Finances in Philippi: The Letter of Paul to the Philippians*. Valley Forge: Trinity Press International, 1994.

———. *Paul's Letter to the Philippians: A Socio-Rhetorical Commentary*. Grand Rapids, Mich.: Eerdmans, 2011.

Woolf, Greg. "Monumental Writing and the Expansion of Roman Society in the Early Empire." *Journal of Roman Studies* 86 (1996): 22–39.

Yarbrough, Oliver Larry. "The Shadow of an Ass: On Reading the Alexamenos Graffito." In *Text, Image, and Christians in the Graeco-Roman World: A Festschrift in Honor of David Lee Balch*, edited by Aliou Cissé Niang and Carolyn Osiek, 239–54. Eugene, Ore.: Pickwick, 2012.

Zanker, Paul, and Björn Christian Ewald. *Living with Myths: The Imagery of Roman Sarcophagi*. Oxford: Oxford University Press, 2012.

Zuiderhoek, Arjan. *The Politics of Munificence in the Roman Empire: Citizens, Elites, and Benefactors in Asia Minor*. New York: Cambridge University Press, 2009.

INDEX

Lightning Source UK Ltd.
Milton Keynes UK
UKHW011336230421
382350UK00008B/243